PC Interfacing

To Cindy

PC Interfacing

using Centronic, RS232 and Game Ports

Pei An, BSc PhD

University of Manchester, UK

Newnes

OXFORD AMSTERDAM BOSTON LONDON NEW YORK PARIS
SAN DIEGO SAN FRANCISCO SINGAPORE SYDNEY TOKYO

Newnes
An imprint of Elsevier Science
Linacre House, Jordan Hill, Oxford OX2 8DP
225 Wildwood Avenue, Woburn, MA 01801-2041

First published 1998
Reprinted 1999, 2001, 2002

British Library Cataloguing in Publication Data
A catalogue record for this book is available from the British Library

Library of Congress Cataloguing in Publication Data
A catalogue record for this book is available from the Library of Congress

ISBN 0 7506 3637 8

For information on all Newnes publications
visit our website at www.newnespress.com

Transferred to digital print 2008
Printed and bound by CPI Antony Rowe, Eastbourne

Contents

Preface

This book is aimed at demonstrating how a personal computer can be used practically in interfacing applications by using its Centronic, RS232 and game ports. The book contains a collection of interfacing experiments and ideas using the most up-to-date electronic devices to show how a PC gathers information from the real world and how it exerts control over external devices. Having a quick look of the contents at this moment will give you some ideas of the variety of the experiments. There is a control software written in either Turbo Pascal or Visual Basic to accompany some experiments. The combination of hardware and software embodies the true meaning of computer interfacing.

The Centronic, RS232 and game ports are the most popular ports that almost every computer has, thus the circuits introduced in this book can be used universally for all types of computers: desktop, laptop and palmtop IBM-PCs and compatibles, Macintosh PCs, Amiga PCs and PSION palmtop computers.

The book is intended to address a wide range of people. It is for:

- people who use a computer to interact with the real world;
- programmers who write software for PCs which are interacting with the real world;
- electronic engineers who want to connect digital electronic devices to a computer;
- students who want to understand computer interfacing by conducting hands-on experiments;
- people who explore innovative PC applications.

The book has eight chapters, each covering a specific topic. Chapter 1 takes a tour of the Centronic, RS232 and game port. It gives their hardware details inside the PC and explains how to use software to control the ports. The software is written in various programming languages.

Chapter 2 shows how to construct some useful tools for PC interfacing experiments. In particular, it gives the details of three experimental boards for the Centronic, RS232 and game port. The boards provide a visual indication of the status of I/O lines in the ports. This allows users to visualize I/O operations through the port. The experimental boards will be used in all the experiments to be introduced in this book.

Chapter 3 presents the software drivers, resource libraries and windows DLLs for the three boards. Turbo Pascal 6 for DOS, Turbo Pascal for Windows and Visual Basic version 3 are the programming languages. The programming libraries and DLLs can be used in your own programs.

Chapter 4 explains some basic methods for expanding the Centronic, RS232 and game ports. Useful circuit diagrams and software listings are presented.

Chapter 5 shows various methods for driving external devices. The devices include relays, LEDs, DC motors, stepper motors, message display modules, mains operated devices and many more. Useful circuit diagrams and software listings are given.

Chapter 6 is concerned with catching data from the real world into the computer. The topics include analogue-to-digital converters, voltage-to-frequency converters and various sensors with digital outputs. Experimental circuits are provided to enable a computer to read in the information of temperature, flow rate of fluid, light intensity, magnetic field, etc.

Chapter 7 shows how a computer is connected to other devices such as digital-to-analogue converters, clocks, memories and signal generators.

Chapter 8 focuses on computer remote control and network applications. The topics include modem, radio transmitter and receiver modules, radio transceivers and mains modem.

Hands-on experiments

This book contains a number of PC interfacing experiments. Each experiment involves an electronic circuit and a software driver. Most of the components are available from RS Components. RS stock numbers of components are given in the text to assist readers to conduct experiments. The Web site of the RS Components is http://www.rs-components.com/rs/.

The programming languages used are Turbo Pascal 6 for DOS, Turbo Pascal for Windows and Visual Basic 3. A complete program list is given for each experiment. The software can be downloaded from the link which appears with this title on the Newnes web page, http://www.newnespress.com.

Caution!

This book introduces some devices that may use voltages which can be dangerous or lethal. Use proper electrical safety procedures at all times.

Please note

Although every care has been taken with the writing of this book to ensure that any experiments, designs and programs contained herein, operate in a correct and safe manner, the author does not accept responsibility in any way for the failure, including faults in hardware design and programs to work correctly or to cause damage to any other equipment that it may be connected to or used in conjunction with, or in respect of any other damage or injury that may be so caused.

Acknowledgements

First of all I would like to thank Mr Duncan Enright for his idea in initiating this book. My thanks also go to Dr Shuisheng He, Dr Jiankang Li, Dr Jing Zhao, Dr Feibiao Zhou, Dr Xiaohong Peng and Dr Cindy Qiu for reading the manuscript. I would like to thank the following companies who assisted me in writing the book by providing samples and relevant documentation: RS Components, UCC International, Three Five Systems and Speake and Co. Ltd.

Trade mark notice

Amiga is a trade mark of Commodore Business Machines Corporation

Analog Devices is a trade mark of Analog Devices Incorporated

Allegro MicroSystems is a trade mark of Allegro Microsystems Incorporated

Cystal Semiconductors is a trade mark of Cystal Semiconductors Incorporated

Dallas Semiconductor is a trade mark of Dallas Semiconductor Corporation

GEC Plessey Semiconductors is a trade mark of GEC Plessey Semiconductors Limited

Harris Semiconductors is a trade mark of Harris Corporation

Hewlett Packard is a trade mark of Hewlett Packard Corporation

Hitachi is a trade mark of Hitachi Ltd

Holtek is a trade mark of Holtek Microelectronics Incorporated

IBM is a trade mark of International Business Machines

Isocom is a trade mark of Isocom Ltd

Maplin is a trade mark of Maplin plc

Maxim is a trade mark of Maxim Integrated Products Incorporated

Microchip is a trade mark of Microchip Technology Incorporated

MS-DOS, Visual Basic, Windows are trade marks of Microsoft Corporation

National Semiconductors is a trade mark of National Semiconductors Incorporated

NEC is a trade mark of NEC Corporation

Newport Components is a trade mark of Newport Components Incorporated

Optek is a trade mark of Optek Technology, Inc.

Philips Semiconductors is a trade mark of Philips Semiconductors

PSION is a trade mark of PSION plc

Quality Technologies is a trade mark of Quality Technologies

Radio Solutions is a trade mark of Radio Solutions Ltd

Radiometrix is a trade mark of Radiometrix Ltd

RS is a trade mark of RS Components Ltd

SGS-Thomson is a trade mark of SGS-Thomson Microelectronics

Siemens is a trade mark of Siemens AG

Sharp is a trade mark of Sharp Corporation

Speake & Co. Ltd. is a trade mark of Speake & Co. Ltd.

Texas Instruments is a trade mark of Texas Instruments Incorporated

Three Five Systems is a trade mark of Three Five Systems Incorporated

Timely is a trade mark of Timely Technology Ltd

Toshiba is a trade mark of Toshiba Corporation

Turbo Pascal is a trade mark of Borland International Inc.

UCC is a trade mark of UCC International Ltd

Xicor is a trade mark of Xicor Semiconductor Incorporated

Centronic, RS232 and game ports

The Centronic, RS232 and game ports are the most common I/O ports that a modern computer has. Some notebook computers may not have a game port, but the Centronic and the RS232 ports are the universal features of all types of computers.

Originally, these ports were designed for specific applications. Centronic ports are used for connecting computers to printers; RS232 ports for connecting printers, modems and mice; and game ports for connecting joysticks. They can also be used for other interfacing applications. Peripheral devices designed for these ports not only provide the easiest way of connection to computers but also offer a universal hardware solution for all computers. Therefore, it would be very useful to understand how these ports work and how to make the best use of them.

1.1 The Centronic port

The *Centronic port*, also known as the *printer port* or the *parallel port*, is an industrial standard interface designed for connecting printers to a computer. A computer at least has one such a port installed. The port may come with the computer's mother-boards or with plug-in I/O cards. Adding more Centronic ports is easy and inexpensive. In total, four Centronic ports may be installed on a computer and they have logic names LPT1 to LPT4.

This book describes the Centronic port from the point of view that it is used as a general purpose I/O interface. Operations specific to printers are not discussed in detail.

1.1.1 Port connectors

The port connectors on a computer and on a printer are different. The one on the computer is a 25 pin D-type female connector (Figure 1.1(a)), and the latter is a 36-pin female Centronic-type connector (Figure 1.1(b)). The pin functions of the two connectors are shown in Figure 1.1. To connect a printer to a computer, a printer cable is used (Figure 1.2). The length of the cable must not exceed 5 metres. The Centronic interface is not for long distance operations.

1.1.2 Internal hardware organization

The circuit of a generic Centronic port inside a PC is shown in Figure 1.3. Eight-bit data is latched into IC1 by writing to a port having an address: base address+0. This operation pulls down

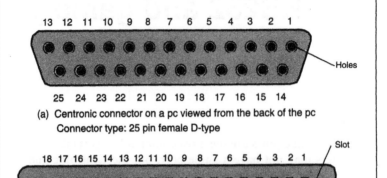

13 12 11 10 9 8 7 6 5 4 3 2 1

— Holes

25 24 23 22 21 20 19 18 17 16 15 14

(a) Centronic connector on a pc viewed from the back of the pc
     Connector type: 25 pin female D-type

Slot

18 17 16 15 14 13 12 11 10 9 8 7 6 5 4 3 2 1

36 35 34 33 32 31 30 29 28 27 26 25 24 23 22 21 20 19

(b) Centronic connector on a printer viewed from the back of the printer
    Connector type: 36 pin female Centronic-type

Pin functions of the Centronic port connectors

Connectors on		Direction	Name	Explanations
pcs	printers	(for pc)		
1	1	OUTPUT	$\overline{\text{STROBE}}$	low to strobe data into printer
2	2	OUTPUT	DB0	data bit 0
3	3	OUTPUT	DB1	data bit 1
4	4	OUTPUT	DB2	data bit 2
5	5	OUTPUT	DB3	data bit 3
6	6	OUTPUT	DB4	data bit 4
7	7	OUTPUT	DB5	data bit 5
8	8	OUTPUT	DB6	data bit 6
9	9	OUTPUT	DB7	data bit 7
10	10	INPUT	$\overline{\text{ACK}}$	low to indicate data received, printer ready
11	11	INPUT	BUSY	high to indicate printer busy
12	12	INPUT	PE	high to indicate printer paper empty
13	13	INPUT	$\overline{\text{SLCT}}$	high to indicate printer on line
14	14	OUTPUT	LF/CR	auto linefeed after carriage return
15	32	INPUT	$\overline{\text{ERROR}}$	low to indicating printer error
16	31	OUTPUT	$\overline{\text{INITIALIZE}}$	low to initialize printer
17	36	OUTPUT	$\overline{\text{SLIN}}$	low to select printer
18-25	19-30 and 33		GND	twisted-pair return Ground
	18,34		Unused	
	16		Logic GND	logic ground
	17		Chasis GND	chasis ground

Figure 1.1 **Pin-out of the Centronic port connectors on computers
and printers**

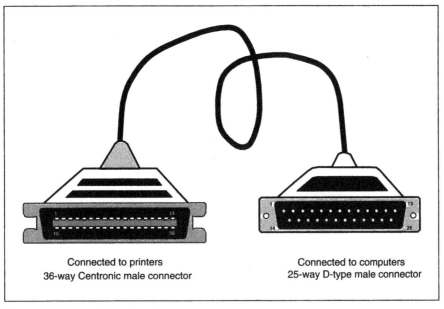

Figure 1.2 The printer lead

-WRITE_DATA. The output of the data forms the Data group. Data can be read into the computer from the same address via IC2 under the control of -READ_DATA. When reading data, the output from IC1 must be in high impedance state. This is achieved by making pin 1 (OUTPUT ENABLE) of IC1 high. A 6-bit control word is latched to IC3 by writing to base address+2 which pulls down -WRITE_CONTROL. Bit 0 to bit 3 are output to the port connector to form the Control group. Some of the lines are inverted by open-collector inverters (IC6 and IC7). All the output lines are pulled to +5V by 4k7 resistors. These bits can be read back into the computer at the same address via IC4a under the control of -READ_CONTROL. Bit 4 of the control byte enables the interrupt and bit 5 enables or disables the output of IC1. Five lines in the port connector (the Status group) can be read into the computer via IC4b under the control of -READ_STATUS. The address associated with this is base address+1. These inputs are pulled to +5V by 4k7 resistors and one of the lines is inverted.

In original IBM PCs, the output enable of IC1 is tied to ground to permanently enable the outputs. This is the uni-directional version of the Centronic port. From IBM PS/2, the output enable of IC1 is connected to bit 5 of the control register IC3 as shown in Figure 1.3 and the port becomes a bi-directional port. It should be pointed out that many Centronic ports that come with plug-in I/O cards are uni-directional Centronic ports. A simple program can be used to detect whether your Centronic port is a uni-directional or a bi-directional one.

Each output line in the Data group is capable of sourcing 2.6 mA current with the voltage varying between 2.6 to 5V. Each can sink 24 mA. The lines in the Control group have a much smaller capacity to source and to sink current. They can only source 100 µA and sink 8 mA current. For both ports, short circuiting of any two outputs and connecting any lines to the ground or +5V power

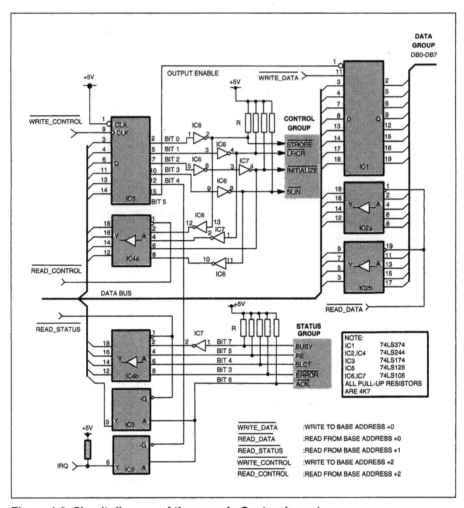

Figure 1.3 Circuit diagram of the generic Centronic port

supply rail are strictly avoided. As the lines in the data port could supply a small current, they can supply power to a circuit which is connected to the Centronic port. The rate of data transfer through the Centronic port is greater than 1 Mbyte/second.

In this chapter, the uni-directional Centronic port is discussed in detail. The I/O lines in the port are organized into three groups, namely, the Data group, the Control and the Status group. Figure 1.4 gives the logic structure of the Centronic port.

Data group

This sends data from PCs to external devices. It has eight latched output lines and the group is associated with an 8-bit CPU port. The address is: base address.

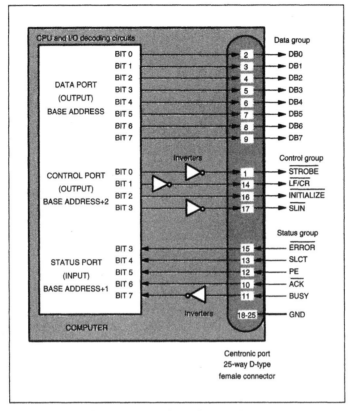

Figure 1.4 Logic structure of the Centronic port on computers

Control group

This controls the operation of external devices. It contains four latched output lines (-STROBE, -LF/CR, -SLIN and -INITIALIZE) which are from the computer to the devices. The group is controlled by a CPU port having an address: base address+2. -STROBE, -LF/CR and -SLIN lines are inverted. -INITIALIZE is not.

Status group

The group is used by the computer to obtain the current status of external devices. It contains five lines (-ERROR, SLCT, PE, -ACK and BUSY), which are directed from external devices to the computer. It is fed into a CPU port, the address of which is: base address+1. BUSY line is inverted and the other four lines are not.

The bit functions of each I/O port are summarized in Table 1.1.

Table 1.1

Data group
bits 0–7	bit 0 to bit 7

Control group
bit 0 (-STROBE)	0=normal; 1=output of data
bit 1 (-LF/CR)	0=normal; 1=auto line feed after carriage return
bit 2 (-INITIALIZE)	0=initialize printer; 1=normal
bit 3 (-SLIN)	0=deselect printer; 1=Select printer
bit 4 (-IRQ)	0=printer interrupt disabled; 1=enabled
bit 5 (-Data I/O)	0=output data; 1=input data from data port

Status group
bits 0–2 (UNUSED)	Unused
bit 3 (-ERROR)	0=printer error; 1=no error
bit 4 (SLCT)	0=printer not on-line; 1=printer on-line
bit 5 (PE)	0=printer has paper; 1=out of paper
bit 6 (-ACK)	0=printer acknowledges; 1=normal
bit 7 (BUSY)	0=printer busy; 1=not busy

The base addresses for LPT1 and LPT2 are shown below:

LPT1: 956D (3BCh) or 888D (378h)
LPT2: 632D (278h)

The base address for LPT1 varies. This depends on the hardware configuration of the computer. There are two ways to obtain the base address. One is to check the hardware configuration of your computer. The other is to find the addresses directly from the user's program by using the facilities provided by the computer's basic input output system (BIOS). When a computer is powered on or reset, the BIOS checks all the possible Centronic ports. If it finds one, it writes the addresses (a 2-byte word) of that port to two specific memory locations. For LPT1, the locations are 0000h:0408h and 0000h:0409h. The former stores the LSB byte and the latter stores the MSB byte of the base address. By reading the content of these memory locations, the base address of the LPT1 can be obtained. The memory locations for LPT1 to LPT4 are listed as follows:

LPT1: 0000:0408h – 0000:0409h
LPT2: 0000:040Ah – 0000:040Bh
LPT3: 0000:040Ch – 0000:040Dh
LPT4: 0000:040Eh – 0000:040Fh

There is another useful memory location, 0000:4011h. It stores the total number of Centronic ports installed. The information is contained in bit 6 and bit 7.

bit 7=0, bit 6=0: no Centronic port installed
bit 7=0, bit 6=1: one Centronic port installed
bit 7=1, bit 6=0: two Centronic ports installed
bit 7=1, bit 6=1: three Centronic ports installed

1.1.3 Software control

(a) How to obtain the base address of a Centronic port

The following program is written in QBASIC. It displays the total number of installed Centronic port and the base addresses of LPT1 to LPT3. Line 20 reads the byte stored in the memory location 0000:0411h using the 'PEEK()' command. Bit 7 and bit 6 of this byte are masked by 'AND (128 + 64)'. Then the result is shifted 6 bits towards the LSB using a division command '/ 64'. Line 30 reads two bytes from two memory locations holding the LSB and MSB part of the base address for LPT1. Lines 40 and 50 perform the same action for LPT2 and LPT3.

```
10    DEF SEG = 0
20    PRINT "Number of Centronic ports: ", (PEEK(&H411) AND (128 + 64)) / 64
30    PRINT "Address of LPT1: ", PEEK(&H408) + 256 * PEEK(&H409)
40    PRINT "Address of LPT1: ", PEEK(&H40A) + 256 * PEEK(&H40B)
50    PRINT "Address of LPT1: ", PEEK(&H40C) + 256 * PEEK(&H40D)
60    INPUT x
```

The following TP6 procedure finds the number of Centronic interfaces installed and assigns the number to a variable `Number_of_LPT`. Then it reads base addresses from memory locations holding the addresses of LPT1 to LPT4. Next the program asks the user to select an LPT to which an external circuit is to be connected. Finally it assigns the selected base address to `Centronic_address`. In Turbo Pascal 6, 'MEM[base:offset]' and 'MEMW[base:offset]' are used for reading memory locations. 'MEM[...]' reads a byte from a memory location. 'MEMW[...]' reads a 2-byte word from the memory location specified and the one above it.

```
(* ——Resource Library No. A1 (Detection of LPT base address)—— *)
Procedure Centronic_address;
(* $000:$0408 holds the printer base address for LPT1
   $000:$040A holds the printer base address for LPT2
   $000:$040C holds the printer base address for LPT3
   $000:$040e holds the printer base address for LPT4
   $000:$0411 number of parallel interfaces in binary format *)
var
    lpt:array[1..4] of integer;
    number_of_lpt,LPT_number,code:integer;
    kbchar:char;
begin
    clrscr;
    LPT_number:=1;                       (* to set default printer *)
    number_of_lpt:=mem[$0000:$0411];     (* to read number of installed Centronic ports *)
    number_of_lpt:=(number_of_lpt and (128+64)) shr 6;  (* Bit manipulation *)
    lpt[1]:=memw[$0000:$0408];           (* Memory read procedure *)
    lpt[2]:=memw[$0000:$040A];
    lpt[3]:=memw[$0000:$040C];
```

```
lpt[4]:=memw[$0000:$040E];

textbackground(blue); clrscr;

textcolor(yellow); textbackground(red); window(10,22,70,24); clrscr;

writeln('Number of LPT installed    :  ',number_of_lpt:2);

writeln('Addresses for LPT1 to LPT 4:  ',lpt[1]:3,'   ', lpt[2]:3,'   ', lpt[3]:3,'   ', lpt[4]:3);

write('Select LPT to be used (1,2,3,4)    :  ');

delay(1000);

if number_of_lpt>1 then begin    {select LPT1 through LPT4 if more than 1 LPT installed}

   repeat

        kbchar:=readkey;                      (* read input key *)

        val(kbchar, LPT_number, code);    (* change character to value *)

     until (LPT_number>=1) and (LPT_number<=4) and (lpt[LPT_number]<>0);

                              end;

clrscr;

P_address:=lpt[LPT_number];

writeln('Your selected printer interface:  LPT',LPT_number:1);

write('LPT  Address                 :  ',P_address:3);

delay(1000);

textbackground(black); window(1,1,80,25); clrscr;

end;
```

The following CENTRONIC(X) function is a Window Dynamic Link Library (DLL) function written in Turbo Pascal for Windows. It can be called by programs written by other Windows programming languages such as Visual Basic and Visual C. Centronic (0) returns the number of LPTs installed. Centronic (1) returns the base address of LPT1. Centronic (2) returns the base address of LPT2, etc.

```
Function Centronic(x:integer):integer; export;
(* $000:$0408 holds the printer base address for LPT1
   $000:$040A holds the printer base address for LPT2
   $000:$040C holds the printer base address for LPT3
   $000:$040e holds the printer base address for LPT4
   $000:$0411 number of parallel interfaces in binary format *)
var
     number_of_LPT, LPT1, LPT2, LPT3, LPT4 :integer;
begin
     number_of_LPT:=mem[$40:$11];                      (* read number of parallel ports *)
     number_of_LPT:=(number_of_lpt and (128+64)) shr 6;
     lpt1:=0; lpt2:=0; lpt3:=0; lpt4:=0;
     LPT1:=memw[$40:$08];                              (* Memory read procedure *)
     LPT2:=memw[$40:$0A];
     LPT3:=memw[$40:$0C];
     LPT4:=memw[$40:$0E];
     case x of
        0:   centronic:=number_of_LPT;
```

```
    1:      centronic:=lpt1;
    2:      centronic:=lpt2;
    3:      centronic:=lpt3;
    4:      centronic:=lpt4
  end;
end;
```

(b) How to output and input data via the Centronic port

Printer commands and BIOS interrupt routines

In QBASIC, the printer instruction is 'PRINT'. In TP6, it is 'WRITELN(LST)'. Another method for controlling printers uses the BIOS interrupt INT 17h. A typical sequence for outputting data via the Centronic port is shown in Figure 1.5. First the computer checks if the printer is ready to accept new data by checking the BUSY line. When it is low (not busy), the computer places the data on the data port. After 500 ns, the computer brings the -STROBE low. This will result in the printer changing to the busy state (BUSY=1). The printer receives the data and processes the data. Next the printer sets the -ACK low to indicate that the received data has been processed. In the same time the printer brings the BUSY line low. For most computers, only -STROBE and BUSY lines are used for handshaking. -ACK handshake is not used.

The advantage of using the method is that the standard printer instructions can be used and the instructions can be found in almost any programming languages. It has a disadvantage. Each port has a dedicated purpose and they operate together, therefore the method is not flexible for general

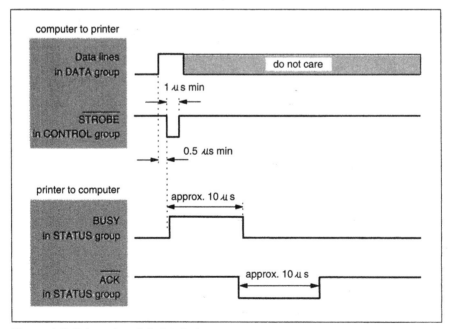

Figure 1.5 Printer handshake timing sequence

purpose I/O operations. If an external circuit is connected to the computer, a special logic circuit should be provided to generate signals of BUSY and -ACK. If a computer only uses the BUSY line for handshake there is an easy way of doing this. BUSY is connected permanently to the digital ground to indicate that the circuit is always ready to accept data. PE is connected to the ground to indicate that the 'printer' always has paper and -ERROR connected to the high state. If PE and -ERROR are not connected this way, error messages will appear when the computer issues a print command. A more flexible way of controlling the Centronic port is to use direct I/O access.

Direct I/O access

This method controls the data, control and status ports separately using direct I/O access. In this case, the Centronic port is treated as three separate I/O ports: two of which are output and one of which is input. Let us take an example of controlling the LPT1. Assuming that the addresses of the data, control and status ports are 888D, 890D and 889D, respectively, to send data to the data and the control ports, the following QBASIC commands are used:

```
OUT 888, X
OUT 890, X
```

X is the output value in decimal. Some lines in the control port are inverted. This has to be taken into account when outputting the data. To read data from the status port, the following command can be used:

```
Y=INP[889]
```

Y is the decimal value of the input data. The input data bits correspond to bit 3 to bit 7 of the status port and one line is inverted. This has to be taken into account.

The following TP6 procedures write data to the data and the control ports. Both procedures require the base address of the selected Centronic port and the value of the output data. Output data to the control port requires bit manipulation. There is no such a problem for the data port.

```
(* ——Resource Library No. A4 (Write data to DATA port of pc)—— *)
Procedure Write_data_port(P_address:integer; port_data:byte);
(* no lines in the Data port are not inverted *)
begin
     port[P_address]:=port_data;    (* output a byte to the data port *)
end;


(* ——Resource Library No. A5 (Write data to CONTROL port of pc)—— *)
Procedure Write_control_port(P_address:integer; port_data:byte);
(* Bit 0, Bit 1 and Bit 3 are inverted. Bit manipulation is required *)
begin
    if port_data and 1 =1 then port_data:=port_data and (255-1)
       else port_data:=port_data or 1;
    if port_data and 2 =2 then port_data:=port_data and (255-2)
       else port_data:=port_data or 2;
```

```
        if port_data and 8 =8 then port_data:=port_data and (255-8)
           else port_data:=port_data or 8;
        port[P_address+2]:=port_data;  (* output a byte to the control port *)
end;
```

The following TP6 function reads bit 3 to bit 6 from the status port. It requires the base address of the selected Centronic port. The function also performs bit manipulation and returns the value of the 4-bit input data.

```
(* ----Resource Library No. A3 (Read data into pc)---- *)
Function Read_status_port(P_address:integer):byte;
var
   byte1:byte;
begin
        byte1:=port[P_address+1];       (* read a byte from the status port *)
        byte1:=byte1 and 120;           (* 01111000 (MSB to LSB) and 0dddd... = 0dddd000 *)
        Read_status_port:=byte1 shr 3;(* shift 3 bit right, Read_status_port = 0000hhhh *)
end;
```

The following Windows DLLs are used for outputting and inputting data via the Centronic port. They are written in Turbo Pascal for Windows.

```
(* ----Resource Library No. A4 (Write data to DATA port of pc)---- *)
Function Write_data_port(P_address:integer; port_data:integer):integer; export;
(* no lines in the Data port are not inverted *)
begin
     port[P_address]:=port_data;    (* output a byte to the data port *)
end;


(* ----Resource Library No. A5 (Write data to CONTROL port of pc)---- *)
function Write_control_port(P_address:integer; port_data:integer):integer;export;
(* Bit 0, Bit 1 and Bit 3 are inverted. Bit manipulation is required *)
begin
        if port_data and 1 =1 then port_data:=port_data and (255-1)
           else port_data:=port_data or 1;
        if port_data and 2 =2 then port_data:=port_data and (255-2)
           else port_data:=port_data or 2;
        if port_data and 8 =8 then port_data:=port_data and (255-8)
           else port_data:=port_data or 8;
        port[P_address+2]:=port_data;  (* output a byte to the control port *)
end;


(* ----Windows Resource Library No. A3 (Read data into pc)---- *)
Function Read_status_port(P_address:integer):integer; export;
var
   byte1:byte;
```

```
begin
       byte1:=port[P_address+1];      (* read a byte from the status port *)
       byte1:=byte1 and 120;          (* 01111000 (MSB to LSB) and 0dddd... = 0dddd000 *)
       Read_status_port:=byte1 shr 3;  (* shift 3 bit right, Read_status_port = 0000hhhh *)
end;
```

(c) Bit manipulation

This section discusses some basic bit manipulation techniques. The topics include bit weight, making a particular bit of a byte high, making a bit of a byte low and shifting bits.

Bit weight

The relationship between a bit and its bit weight is given below:

bit 0	1 (decimal value)
bit 1	2
bit 2	4
bit 3	8
bit 4	16
bit 5	32
bit 6	64
bit 7	128

To make a bit high

The following example shows how to make bit 3 (bit weight = 8) of the data port to go high while keeping the status of others unchanged. If the original status of bit 3 is high, it will still be high. If the original status is low, it becomes high.

```
10     x= Original_data OR 8
20     OUT 888, x
```

Line 10 performs the 'OR' operation. The truth table of the OR operation is shown below:

```
0 OR 0 = 0
0 OR 1 = 1
1 OR 0 = 1
1 OR 1 = 1
```

Example of the bit-wise OR operation

```
Data-1: XXXXXXXX (bit 7 to bit 0)
Data-2: 00001000
Data-1 OR Data-2: XXXX1XXX
```

To make a bit low

The following a QBasic example shows how to make bit 4 (bit weight = 16) of the data port go low.

```
10     x= Original_data and (255 - 16)
20     OUT 888, x
```

Line 10 performs the AND operation. The truth table of the AND operation is shown below.

    0 AND 0 = 0
    0 AND 1 = 0
    1 AND 0 = 0
    1 AND 1 = 1

Example of the bit-wise AND operation

    Data-1: XXXXXXXX (bit 7 to bit 0)
    Data-2: 11101111
    Data-1 AND Data-2: XXX0XXXX

To shift bits left or right

As shown above, when inputting a four bit data bit 0, bit 1, bit 2 and bit 3 into the status port, the bits are connected internally to bit 3, bit 4, bit 5 and bit 6 of the I/O port. In order to reproduce the value of the input data, bit shift should be performed. In TP6, two shift instructions are available. SHL shifts bits left (towards MSB) and SHR shifts bits right (towards LSB). The following examples show these two operations.

    Data: 11111111 (bit 7 to bit 0)
    255 SHL 3: 11111000
    255 SHR 3: 00011111

1.2 RS232 serial interface

The RS232 serial interface is an industrial standard bi-directional asynchronous serial data communication interface. For computers, it is used for connecting printers, modems, mice, etc. The communication distance is 20 metres.

Unlike a parallel I/O port, which consists of a number of data lines and each time transmits a byte, the serial data transmission requires only one line. A byte is transmitted bit by bit. This reduces data lines between devices. It reduces the rate of data transfer too.

1.2.1 Serial data transmission

The serial data stream itself contains the information of synchronization and the actual data to be transferred. A serial data format includes four parts: a start bit (1 bit), serial data bits (5, 6, 7 or 8 bits), a parity check bit (1 bit) and stop bits (1 or 1.5 bit). Figure 1.6 shows a typical serial data format. When no data is sent, the data line is at logic high. This is called the waiting stage. The beginning of a data transmission is indicated by pulling the line to the logic low state for 1 bit time. This bit is the start bit. The data bits are then sent out one after another with the least significant bit (LSB) sent first. The number of the data bits can be 6, 7 or 8. Following the data bits comes the parity bit which is used to check transmission errors occurred during the data transmission. The last bits are the stop bits, which pull the data line to the high state for at least 1 bit time to indicate the end of the data transmission. The number of the stop bits can be 1, 1.5 and 2 bits. A specially designed electronic device which generates and

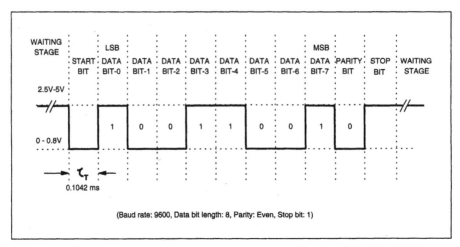

Figure 1.6 The format of a serial data transmission produced by the UARTs

receives the asynchronous serial data is called the Universal Asynchronous Receiver/Transmitter (UART). The serial data transmission format is generated by the transmitting UART. The receiver detects the leading edge of the start bit. It then waits for one and a half bit times before reading the data bit. The reading should come exactly in the middle of the first data bit. It waits for one bit time and reads the second bit. This time the reading comes exactly in the middle of the second data bit. After reading all the data bits, the receiver detects the parity of the received data for error checking and resets itself during the stop bit. It is then ready for receiving the next data transmission.

The rate at which the data bits are sent is measured by the baud rate. It is defined as 1 over the time period between the shortest signal transition (see Figure 1.6). The standard baud rates for an RS232 serial port are 110, 150, 300, 600, 1200, 2400, 4800, 9600 and 19200. Knowing the baud rate, the number of bytes to be transmitted per second can be calculated. For example, if a serial data has 8 data bits, no parity check and 1 stop bit, the total length of serial data bits is 10. The transfer rate for characters is the baud rate divided by 10. A baud rate of 9600 will transfer 960 characters per second.

The parity check can be ODD, EVEN or NONE. The odd and even parities indicate that the total number of ones ('1') in the transmitted serial data is an odd number or an even number. This is the simplest method for detecting transmission errors occurred during a data transmission. It is only reliable to detect single-bit errors. Errors occurred to several bits can not be detected. The parity bit is generated by the transmitting UART in such a way that the number of ones ('1') in the data bits plus the parity bit is an odd or an even number as declared. At the receiver end, the receiving device must also be configured to have the same parity check. The receiving UART counts the number of ones in the received data. If the data does not have a right parity, an error is generated to indicate that a transmission error has been detected. If the parity check is declared as NONE, the parity bit will not be generated and checked.

Most AT computers use 16450 UARTs. XT computers use 8250 UARTs. The UARTS have a TTL voltage level. In order to achieve a long distance communication, the TTL voltage level is converted to higher voltage level (logic 0 = −12 to −3V, logic 1 = +3V to +12V). This is achieved by using dedicated RS232 drivers/receivers. All drivers/receivers have an inverting action.

1.2.2 RS232 port connector and connections

A standard RS232 interface is a 25-pin interface housed in a 25-pin or a 9-pin D-type male connector. Figure 1.7 gives the pin-out and functions of connectors.

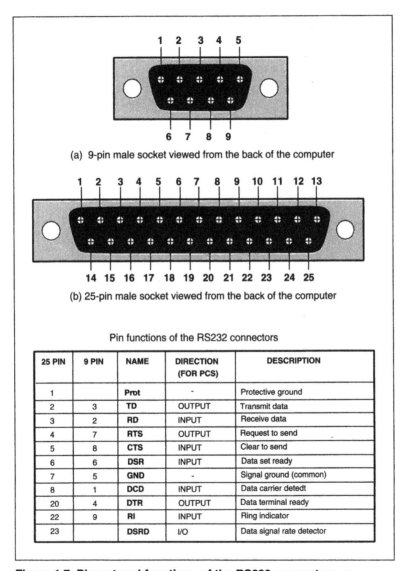

(a) 9-pin male socket viewed from the back of the computer

(b) 25-pin male socket viewed from the back of the computer

Pin functions of the RS232 connectors

25 PIN	9 PIN	NAME	DIRECTION (FOR PCS)	DESCRIPTION
1		Prot	-	Protective ground
2	3	TD	OUTPUT	Transmit data
3	2	RD	INPUT	Receive data
4	7	RTS	OUTPUT	Request to send
5	8	CTS	INPUT	Clear to send
6	6	DSR	INPUT	Data set ready
7	5	GND	-	Signal ground (common)
8	1	DCD	INPUT	Data carrier detedt
20	4	DTR	OUTPUT	Data terminal ready
22	9	RI	INPUT	Ring indicator
23		DSRD	I/O	Data signal rate detector

Figure 1.7 Pin-out and functions of the RS232 connectors on computers

Table 1.2

Prot	Protective ground. It is connected to the metal screening of the cable and the chassis of the equipment.
GND	Ground line. It provides a common voltage reference for all signals.
TD	Transmitting Data. Serial data is transmitted on this line. It is an output line from the computer.
RD	Receiving Data. Serial data is received from the line. It is an input line to the computer.
RTS	Request To Send. It is a handshake line and indicates that a transmitting device is ready to send data. It is an output from the computer. If handshake is not required, it can be used as an output.
CTS	Clear To Send. It is a handshake line from which a receiving device tells a transmitting device that it is ready to receive data. It is an input to the computer. If handshake is not used, it could be used as an input.
DTR	Data Terminal Ready. It is a handshake line and indicates that a transmitting device is ready. It is an output from the computer. If handshake is not used, it can be used as another output.
DSR	Data Set Ready. It is a handshake line from which a receiving device tells the transmitting device that the data set is ready. It is an input to the computer. If handshake is not used, it can be used as another input.

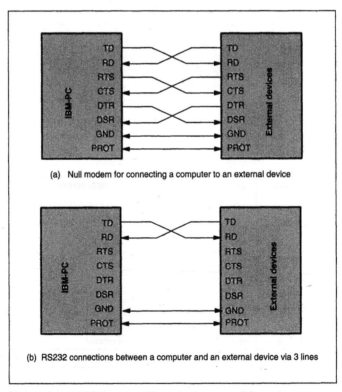

(a) Null modem for connecting a computer to an external device

(b) RS232 connections between a computer and an external device via 3 lines

Figure 1.8 RS232 connections between a PC and an external device

Two types of RS232 link between a computer and an external device are shown in Figure 1.8. The arrows show the direction of data flow. Figure 1.8(a) is known as the null modem. Figure 1.8(b) shows a connection using only three lines. One line is for transmitting data and the other for receiving data. The connection is arranged so that the transmitting line of the first device is connected to the receiving line of the second device.

1.2.3 Internal hardware organization

An IBM-PC computer can have up to four RS232 interfaces installed. They are labelled COM1 to COM4. Each COM port is associated with a 16450 UART inside the computer.

(a) 8250/16450 UART

Figure 1.9 shows the internal block diagram. There are eight 8-bit internal registers within the UART. The I/O addresses of these internal registers are calculated by adding the offset of the register to the base address of the COM port. The offsets and functions of the UART registers are summarized below.

00h Transmitter hold register/receiver buffer register: store received data and hold data to be transmitted
01h Interrupt enable register: set the mode of interrupt request

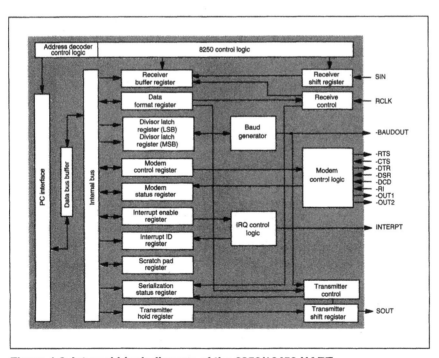

Figure 1.9 Internal block diagram of the 8250/16450 UART

02h   Interrupt identification register: check the mode of interrupt request
03h   Data format register: set the format of serial data transmission
04h   Modem control register: set modem controls (RTS, DTR, etc.)
05h   Serialization status register: contain information on status of the receiver and transmitter section
06h   Modem status register: contain the current status of DCD, RI, DSR and CTS
07h   Scratch-pad register: act as a memory byte

Offset 00h is the receiver buffer register and the transmitter hold register. The transmitter hold register can be accessed if the DLAB bit in the data format register (offset 03h) is zero. If a byte is written to this address, it is transferred to the transmitter shift register and it is output serially. After a serial data is successfully received and converted into the parallel format, the data is transferred into the receiver buffer register. After reading the data from the register, the buffer register is cleared and is ready for receiving the next data.

Offset 01h is the interrupt enable register by which you configure the interrupt generated by the UART. The bit functions of bit 7 to bit 0 are shown as follows:

0 0 0 0 SINP ERBK TBE RxRD

bit 7-4	always zero
SINP	1: interrupt on state-change of -CTS, -DSR, -DCD and -RI
	0: no interrupt
ERBK	1: interrupt on parity, overrun, framing errors or break
	0: no interrupt
TBE	1: interrupt on transmitter hold register empty
	0: no interrupt
RxRD	1: interrupt when one byte is ready in receiver buffer register
	0: no interrupt

Offset 02h is the interrupt identification register which indicates whether an interrupt is pending. A pending interrupt is indicated by bit 0 of the register. Bit 1 and bit 2 indicate the causes of this interrupt. The bit functions of bit 7 to bit 0 of the register are shown below:

0 0 0 0 0 ID1 ID0 -PND

-PND	1 = no interrupt pending; 0=interrupt pending,
ID1, ID0	00 = change of an RS-232 input signal (priority 3)
	01 = transmitter hold register empty (priority 2)
	10 = data ready in the receiver buffer register (priority 1)
	11 = data transfer error or break (priority 0, highest priority)

Once an interrupt is generated, it must be cleared before it is able to respond to the next interrupt. The action required to clear the interrupt is shown below:

ID1=0, ID0=0:	read the modem status register (offset 06h)
ID1=0, ID0=1:	write to the transmitter hold register (offset 00h) or read the interrupt identification register (offset 02h)
ID1=1, ID0=0:	read data byte from the receiver buffer register (offset 00h)
ID1=1, ID0=1:	read the serialization status register (offset 05h)

Offset 03h is the data format register which defines the serial data format such as the baud rate, number of data bits, number of stop bits and parity check. The bit functions for bit 7 to bit 0 are given below:

DLAB BRK PAR2 PAR1 PAR0 STOP DAB1 DAB0

DLAB	1=access to the divisor latches
	0=access to the receiver buffer/transmitter hold register (offset 00h) and the interrupt enable register (offset 01h)
BRK	1=break on, 0=break off
PAR2,1,0	000=none, 001=odd, 011=even, 101=mark, 111=space
STOP	1= 2 stop bits, 0= 1 stop bit
DAB1, 0	00=5 data bits, 01=6 data bits, 10=7 data bits, 11=8

When DLAB bit is 1, the receiver buffer/transmitter hold register (00h) and the interrupt enable register (01h) are used for loading the divisor. The first one holds the LSB byte and the second holds the MSB byte. They form a 16-bit divisor and the value is calculated using the following equation:

$$\text{Divisor} = \text{byte}_{\text{register 00h}} + 256 \times \text{byte}_{\text{register 01h}}$$

In a computer, the clock frequency to the UARTs is 1.8432 MHz. Inside the UART, the reference frequency is the clock frequency divided by 16, giving 115200 Hz. The relationship between the divisor and the baud rate is:

$$\text{Baud rate} = \frac{115200}{\text{Divisor}}$$

A baud rate of 9600 requires a divisor of 12. Therefore when loading the divisor bytes into the registers, '12' should be loaded into the receiver/transmitter buffer register (00h) and '0' loaded into the interrupt enable register (01h). If 1 is loaded into the divisor registers, it gives the highest baud rate, 115200.

Offset 04h is the modem control register. It is used to control the UART modem control logic. In general interfacing applications, the register can be used to control two outputs, RTS and DTR. The bit functions of bit 7 to bit 0 of the register are shown below:

0 0 0 LOOP -OUT2 -OUT1 -RTS -DTR

bits 7–5	always zero
Loop	1= enabled loop back, 0= disabled loop back
-OUT2	1=enabled, 0=disabled, used internally
-OUT1	1=enabled, 0=disabled, used internally
-RTS	1=enabled, 0=disabled, available from the RS232 connector
-DTR	1=enabled, 0=disabled, available from the RS232 connector

Offset 05h is the serialization status register which contains the information on the status of the receiver and transmitter of the UART. Together with the Interrupt identification register (offset 02h), a source of interrupt can be identified. The bit functions of bit 7 to bit 0 of the register are shown below:

0 TXE TBE BREK FRME PARE OVFE RxRD

TXE (transmitter empty)	1 = no byte in the transmitter hold register and the shift register
	0 = one byte in the transmitter hold and shift register
TBE (transmitter buffer empty)	1 = one byte in the transmitter hold register
	0 = one byte in the transmitter hold register
BREK (break)	1 = detected 0 = no break
FRME (frame error)	1 = error detected 0 = no error
PARE (parity error)	1 = error detected 0 = no error

OVRE (overrun error)	1 = error detected 0 = no error
RxRD (received data ready)	1 = received data in the receiver buffer register
	0 = no received data

Offset 06h is the modem status register. It can be used to determine the status of RS232 input signals such as DCD, DSR, CTS. For general purpose interfacing applications, this register can be used to read three digital input lines. The bit functions for bit 7 to bit 0 are shown below:

-DCD -RI -DSR -CTS DDCD DRI DDSR DCTS

-DCD (data carrier detect)	1=DCD active	0=DCD inactive
-RI (ring indicator)	1= RI active	0=RI inactive
-DSR (data set ready)	1=DSR active	0=DSR inactive
-CTS (clear to send)	1=CTS active	0=CTS inactive
DDCD (delta data carrier detect)	1=DCD change since last read	
	0=DCD not changed	
DRI (delta ring detect)	1=RI change since last read	
	0=RI not changed	
DDSR (delta data set ready)	1=DSR change since last read	
	0=DSR not changed	
DCTS (delta clear to send)	1=CTS change since last read	
	0=CTS not changed	

Offset 07h register is a scratch-pad memory which is a random access memory byte. Writing data into the register has no effect on the operation of the UART.

(b) RS232 driver/receivers

The RS232 output control signals (-RTS and -DTR) and input status signals (-CTS, -DSR, -DSR) are processed by the UART in an inverted form. The serial data signal SIN and SOUT are in a non-inverting form. The UART produces the TTL/CMOS voltage levels only. RS232 line drivers/receivers are connected between the UART and the RS232 connector. The drivers convert the TTL voltage to the RS232 voltage level and the receivers convert the RS232 level to the TTL level. All the drivers/receivers have inverting action. The logic structure of the RS232 port is shown in Figure 1.10.

(c) Base addresses of COM ports

The base addresses of COM1 to COM4 are summarized below.

COM1: 3F8h
COM2: 2F8h
COM3: 3E8h
COM4: 2E8h

When a computer is switched on or reset, the BIOS checks all possible RS232 addresses. If it finds an installed one, it writes the base address (a 2-byte word) into specific memory locations. For COM1, the locations are 0000:0400h and 000:0401h. By reading these locations, the base address can be obtained. The memory locations for COM1 to COM4 are listed below.

COM1: 0000:0400h – 0000:0401h
COM2: 0000:0402h – 0000:0403h
COM3: 0000:0404h – 0000:0405h

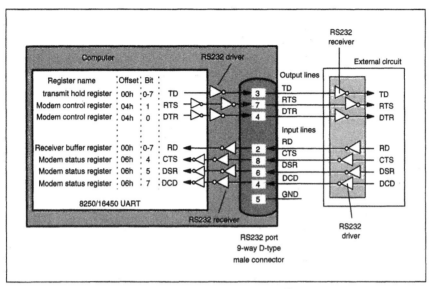

Figure 1.10 Logic structure of the RS232 port

COM4: 0000:0406h – 0000:0407h

Another useful one-byte memory location is 000:4011h. It stores the total number of COMs installed. The information is contained in bit 3, bit 2 and bit 1 of the byte.

bit 3=0, bit 2=0, bit 1=0   no COM port installed
bit 3=0, bit 2=0, bit 1=1   one COM port installed
bit 3=0, bit 2=1, bit 1=0   two COM ports installed
bit 3=0, bit 2=1, bit 1=1   three COM ports installed
bit 3=1, bit 2=0, bit 1=0   four COM ports installed

1.2.4 Software control

(a) How to obtain the base address of a COM port

The following program is written in QBASIC. It prints the number of COM ports installed and the base addresses of the installed ports. Line 20 reads the byte stored in the memory location 0000:0411h using the 'PEEK()' command. Bit 0, bit 1 and bit 2 of the byte contain the information about the number of COMs installed. These three bits are masked by 'AND (1+2+4)', giving the number of installed ports. Line 30 reads two bytes from two memory locations holding the base address for COM1. Lines 40, 50 and 60 perform the same action for COM2 to COM4.

```
10    DEF SEG = 0

20    PRINT "Number of RS232 ports: ", (PEEK(&H411) AND (1+2+4))

30    PRINT "Address of LPT1: ", PEEK(&H400) + 256 * PEEK(&H401)

40    PRINT "Address of LPT1: ", PEEK(&H402) + 256 * PEEK(&H403)
```

```
50   PRINT "Address of LPT1: ", PEEK(&H404) + 256 * PEEK(&H405)
60   PRINT "Address of LPT1: ", PEEK(&H406) + 256 * PEEK(&H407)
70   INPUT x
```

The following function written in TP6 detects the number of RS232 ports installed and assigns the number to a variable `Number_of_COM`. Then it reads base addresses from memory locations holding the addresses of COM1 to COM4. Next it allows the user to select a COM port to be used. Finally the procedure assigns the selected base address to a variable, `RS232_address`.

```
(* ——Resource Library No. A6 (detection of COM base address)—— *)
Procedure COM_address;
(* $0000:$0400 holds the printer base address for COM1
   $0000:$0402 holds the printer base address for COM2
   $0000:$0404 holds the printer base address for COM3
   $0000:$0406 holds the printer base address for COM4
   $0000:$0411 number of parallel interfaces in binary format *)
var
   COM:array[1..4] of integer;
   COM_number, number_of_com, code: integer;
   kbchar:char;
begin
     clrscr;
     COM_number:=1; (*defaut printer *)
     number_of_COM:=mem[$0000:$0411]; (* read number of parallel ports *)
     number_of_COM:=(number_of_COM and (8+4+2)) shr 1;
     COM[1]:=memw[$0000:$0400];         (* Memory read procedure *)
     COM[2]:=memw[$0000:$0402];
     COM[3]:=memw[$0000:$0404];
     COM[4]:=memw[$0000:$0406];
     textbackground(blue); clrscr;
     textcolor(yellow); textbackground(red); window(10,22,70,24); clrscr;
     writeln('Number of COM installed    :  ',number_of_COM:2);
     writeln('Addresses for COM1 to COM4: ',COM[1]:3,'   ', COM[2]:3,'   ', COM[3]:3,'   ', COM[4]:3);
     write('Select COM to be used (1,2,3,4)    :  ');
     delay(1000);
     if number_of_COM>1 then begin   (* select COM1 through COM4 if more than 1 LPT installed *)
       repeat
           kbchar:=readkey;                 (* read input key *)
           val(kbchar, COM_number, code);   (* change character to value *)
       until (COM_number>=1) and (COM_number<=4) and (COM[COM_number]<>0);
                         end;
     clrscr;
     RS232_address:=COM[COM_number];
     writeln('Your selected RS232 interface:  COM',COM_number:1);
     write('RS232   Address               :  ',RS232_address:4);
```

```
        delay(1000);
        textbackground(black); window(1,1,80,25); clrscr;
end;
```

The RS232(X) is a Windows DLL function written in Turbo Pascal for Windows. RS232 (0) returns the number of COMs installed. RS232 (1) returns the base address of COM1. RS232 (2) returns the base address of COM2, etc.

```
(* ——Resource Library No. A6 (detection of COM base address)—— *)
Function RS232(x:integer):integer; export;
{Universal auto detection of COM base address}
{ $0000:$0400 holds the printer base address for COM1
  $0000:$0402 holds the printer base address for COM2
  $0000:$0404 holds the printer base address for COM3
  $0000:$0406 holds the printer base address for COM4
  $0000:$0411 number of parallel interfaces in binary format}
var
      number_of_COM, COM1, COM2, COM3, COM4 :integer;
begin
      number_of_COM:=mem[$40:$11]; {read number of parallel ports}
      number_of_COM:=(number_of_COM and (8+4+2)) shr 1;
      COM1:=0; COM2:=0; COM3:=0; COM4:=0;
      COM1:=memw[$40:$00];          {Memory read procedure}
      COM2:=memw[$40:$02];
      COM3:=memw[$40:$04];
      COM4:=memw[$40:$06];
      case x of
          0:    RS232:=number_of_COM;
          1:    RS232:=COM1;
          2:    RS232:=COM2;
          3:    RS232:=COM3;
          4:    RS232:=COM4;
      end;
end;
```

(b) How to initialize a COM port

Before a COM can be used, it must be configured to have a specific serial data format. The configuration includes the settings of the baud rate, number of data bits, number of stop bits and the parity check bit. There are three methods of doing this.

The first method is to use the 'MODE' command under DOS prompt. The syntax of the command is:

MODE COMm: baud=b, parity=p, data=d, stop=s, retry=r
or MODE COMm: b, p, d, s, r

'MODE COM1: 96,n,8,1' configures COM1 port to have a baud rate of 9600, no parity check, 8-bit data length and 1-bit stop bit. The command can be included in the AUTOEXEC.BAT file. The disadvantage of this method is that it does not allow users to change the serial data format within a user's program.

The second method uses the BIOS interrupt, INT 14h, which allows the configuration to be made within a user's program. This requires that register AH is loaded with 0, DX is loaded with a number 0 to 3 representing COM1 to COM4. AL is loaded with an 8-bit initialization code. The bit functions of bit 7 to bit 0 of this code are shown below:

BD2 BD1 BD0 PAR1 PAR0 STOP DA1 DA0

BD2 to 0:	define baud rate bits
	111= 9600 011= 600 110= 4800 010= 300
	101= 2400 001= 150 100= 1200 000= 110
PAR1,0	Define parity check
	00= No parity 10= No parity 01= Odd 11= Even
STOP:	Define stop bit
	0= 1 1= 2
DA1, 0:	Define data length
	10= 7 bit 11= 8 bit

The following TP6 program shows how to achieve the same function as the DOS command 'MODE COM1: 96,n,8,1'.

```
Procedure initialize;

{COM1:  9600, no parity check, 8 bit data and 1 stop bit}

var    register:registers;

begin

      with register do begin

          ah:=0;                       {load interrupt function number}

          al:=128+64+32+0+0+0+2+1;     {load initialization code, 11100011B}

          dx:=0;                       {COM1 is to be initialized, DX=0 for COM1, DX=1 for COM2, DX=2 for COM3...}

          intr($14, register);         {Call the BIOS interrupt}

                      end;

end;
```

A limitation of this method is that the baud rate can be set only up to 9600. The 16450 UART can run at 115200 baud rate. This can only be achieved by direct register access as shown below.

The third method configures the COM port by writing the configuration data directly into the data format register (offset = 03h) of the UART. This is the most flexible way to configure the serial data format. The following program written in TP6 configures the data format register. The procedure requires the information of the base address of the selected COM port, the baud rate, parity checking mode, data bit length and the stop bit length. The procedure converts the input baud rate into a 16-bit divisor and loads the divisor into the corresponding registers.

```
(* ──Resource Library No. A9 (to write to the data serialization register)── *)

Procedure Write_data_format(RS232_address, Baud, Parity, Data_bit, Stop_bit:integer);

var

    byte1, byte2, output_byte: byte;

      divisor: integer;
```

```
begin
        divisor:=115200 div Baud;
        if divisor<=255 then begin byte1:=divisor; byte2:=0 end;
        if divisor>255 then begin byte2:=divisor div 256; byte1:=divisor mod 256; end;
        output_byte:=(data_bit-5) + 4*(stop_bit-1) + 8*(parity);
    port[RS232_address+3]:=128;{Loading serial data format, first bit of the register is 1}
        port[RS232_address+0]:=Byte1;        {LSB of the divisor is 1}
        port[RS232_address+1]:=Byte2;        {MSB of the divisor is 0}
        port[RS232_address+3]:=output_byte;  {Load divisor and other parameters}
end;
```

The following DLL function written in Turbo Pascal for Windows has the same function.

```
(* ——Resource Library No. A9 (write to the data serialization register)—— *)
Function Write_data_format(RS232_address, Baud, Parity, Data_bit, Stop_bit:integer):integer; Export;
var
    byte1, byte2, output_byte: byte;
        divisor: integer;
begin
        divisor:=115200 div Baud;
        if divisor<=255 then begin byte1:=divisor; byte2:=0 end;
        if divisor>255 then begin byte2:=divisor div 256; byte1:=divisor mod 256; end;
        output_byte:=(data_bit-5) + 4*(stop_bit-1) + 8*(parity);
    port[RS232_address+3]:=128;{Loading serial data format, first bit of the register is 1}
        port[RS232_address+0]:=Byte1;        {LSB of the divisor is 1}
        port[RS232_address+1]:=Byte2;        {MSB of the divisor is 0}
        port[RS232_address+3]:=output_byte;  {Load divisor and other parameters}
end;
```

(c) How to transmit and receive serial data

There are several ways to read and send serial data via the RS232 interface. One way is to use printer command and BIOS interrupt calls. The other is to use the direct port access. The latter is more flexible for general purpose I/O operations. Let us take an example of COM1. To send data from the COM1, you can write data directly to the transmitter hold register, 3F8h. The following QBASIC instruction can be used:

```
OUT 3F8h, X
```

X is the data in decimal. To read data from the COM1 port, you may read data from the receiver buffer register, 3F8h, and the following command can be used (Y is the input byte in decimal):

```
Y=INP[3F8h]
```

The following two procedures having the same functions are written in TP6.

```
(* ——Resource Library No. A10 (to write to the transmit buffer register)—— *)
Procedure write_transmit_buffer(RS232_address, Output_byte: integer);
```

```
begin
     port[RS232_address]:=Output_byte;
end;


(* ——Resource Library No. A12 (to read data from receive buffer register)— *)
Function Read_receive_buffer(RS232_address:integer):integer;
begin
     Read_receive_buffer:=port[RS232_address];
end;
```

The following two functions are DLLs written in Turbo Pascal for Windows.

```
(* ——Resource Library No. A10 (to write to the transmit buffer register)— *)
Function write_transmit_buffer(RS232_address, Output_byte: integer):integer; Export;
begin
     port[RS232_address]:=Output_byte;
end;


(* ——Resource Library No. A12 (to read data from receive buffer register)— *)
Function Read_receive_buffer(RS232_address:integer):integer; Export;
begin
     Read_receive_buffer:=port[RS232_address];
end;
```

(d) How to read and write data via handshake lines

To output data from RTS and DTR lines, you should write to the particular bits of the modem control register (offset 04h). Bit 1 and bit 0 corresponds to RTS and DTR. The following TP6 procedure and Windows DLL function control the status of RTS and DTR. The procedures require the base address of the selected COM port and status of RTS and DTR which should be either 1 or 0. In these two procedures, RTS and DTR are inverted before they are output to the port. This is due to the use of the TTL/RS232 transceivers which have an inverting action. The transceivers are used externally for voltage level translation.

```
(* ——Resource Library No. A11 (to write to the modem status register)— *)
Procedure Write_modem_status(RS232_address, RTS, DTR:integer);
(* RTS and DTR = 0 or 1, RTS and DRT are inverted by MAX238 on the experimental board *)
(* RTS=bit 1, DTR=bit 0 of Modem control register, offset 04 *)
begin
     RTS:=1-RTS;
     DTR:=1-DTR;
     Port[RS232_address+4]:=RTS*2 + DTR   (* to output to the register 04 *)
end;


(* ——Resource Library No. A11 (to write to the modem status register)— *)
Function Write_modem_status(RS232_address, RTS, DTR:integer):integer; Export;
```

```
(* RTS and DTR = 0 or 1, RTS and DRT are inverted by MAX238 on the experimental board *)
(* RTS=bit 1, DTR=bit 0 of Modem control register, offset 04 *)
begin
    RTS:=1-RTS;
    DTR:=1-DTR;
    Port[RS232_address+4]:=RTS*2 + DTR   (* to output to the register 04 *)
end;
```

To read data from DSR, CTS and DCD lines, we should read the modem status register (offset 06h). The following TP6 procedure and Windows DLL functions are written for this purpose. The status of DCD, DSR and CTS can be read by putting different value of 'x'. These procedures require the base address of the selected COM port. The DCD DSR and CTS status are inverted. Again this is because of the use of the TTL/RS232 transceivers in the external circuit.

```
(* ----Resource Library No. A13 (to read modem status register)---- *)
Function Read_modem_status(RS232_address, x:integer):integer;
(* X=1 select DCD bit, x=2 select DSR bit, x=3 select CTS bit *)
(* DCD=bit 7, DSR=bit 5, CTS=bit 4 of Modem status register, offset 06h *)
(* All bits are inverted by the Max238 on the experimental board *)
var
    input_byte:byte;
begin
    input_byte:=port[RS232_address+6];
    case x of
    1:   Read_modem_status:=1-round((input_byte and 128)/128);
    2:   Read_modem_status:=1-round((input_byte and 32)/32);
    3:   Read_modem_status:=1-round((input_byte and 16)/16);
    end;
end;


(* ----Resource Library No. A13 (to read modem status register)---- *)
Function Read_modem_status(RS232_address, x:integer):integer; Export;
(* X=1 select DCD bit, x=2 select DSR bit, x=3 select CTS bit *)
(* DCD=bit 7, DSR=bit 5, CTS=bit 4 of Modem status register, offset 06h *)
(* All bits are inverted by the Max238 on the experimental board *)
var
    input_byte:byte;
begin
    input_byte:=port[RS232_address+6];
    case x of
    1:   Read_modem_status:=1-round((input_byte and 128)/128);
    2:   Read_modem_status:=1-round((input_byte and 32)/32);
    3:   Read_modem_status:=1-round((input_byte and 16)/16);
    end;
end;
```

1.3 Game ports

Most desktop computers also provide a game port from which one or two joysticks can be connected. Although it is primarily designed for joysticks, it can be used also for other interfacing applications. The port provides four digital input lines and four analogue input lines. The digital input lines read digital data and the analogue inputs measure resistance. The resistance value should be within the range from 0 to 100 kΩ.

A joystick has two 100 kΩ potentiometers arranged perpendicular to each other to indicate the X and Y positions of the joystick. It also has two normally-open buttons. The corresponding lines are pulled to logic high by internal circuitry of the joystick. When the buttons are pressed, the lines become low.

1.3.1 Port connector

The game port is housed in a 15-way female 'D' type connector. The pin-out, functions and the typical connection to joysticks are given in Figure 1.11.

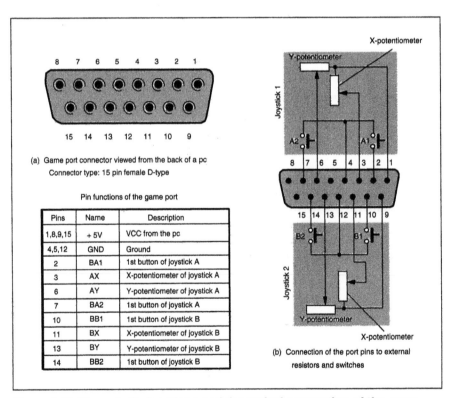

(a) Game port connector viewed from the back of a pc
Connector type: 15 pin female D-type

Pin functions of the game port

Pins	Name	Description
1,8,9,15	+ 5V	VCC from the pc
4,5,12	GND	Ground
2	BA1	1st button of joystick A
3	AX	X-potentiometer of joystick A
6	AY	Y-potentiometer of joystick A
7	BA2	1st button of joystick A
10	BB1	1st button of joystick B
11	BX	X-potentiometer of joystick B
13	BY	Y-potentiometer of joystick B
14	BB2	1st button of joystick B

(b) Connection of the port pins to external resistors and switches

Figure 1.11 Pin-out, pin functions and the typical connection of the game port

1.3.2 Internal hardware organization

The internal circuit diagram of the generic game port is given in Figure 1.12. The logic structure of the game port is given in Figure 1.13. We can see that the 8-bit data of the data bus consists of four bits from four NE555s via IC5a and four bits from the button inputs via IC5b. The four button status inputs are pulled to +5V by pull-up resistors. The port is connected to a CPU I/O port having an address of 201h. The bit functions from bit 7 to bit 0 of the port are shown below:

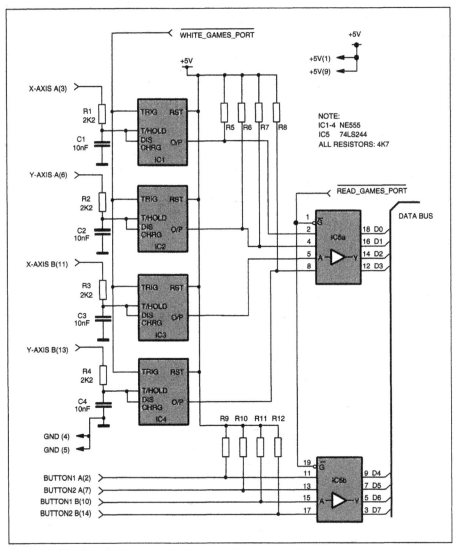

Figure 1.12 Circuit diagram of the generic game port

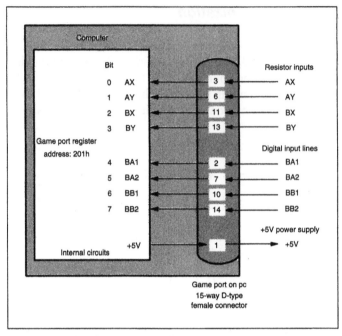

Figure 1.13 Logic structure of the game port on computers

BB2 BB1 BA2 BA1 BY BX AY AX

BB2, BB1, BA2 and BA1:   digital input lines
BY, BX, AY and AX: monostable output status

The status of BB2, BB1, BA2 and BA1 can be checked. The measurement of resistance has a different approach. Monostable circuits based on 555s are utilized. The outputs of the 555s are normally low. When writing a byte to the port 201h, -WRITE_GAME_ PORT goes low for a short period of time. The low going edge of the signal triggers the four monostables and BY, BX, AY and AX lines become 1. The monostable has a 10 nF capacitor, which is charged via a 2.2 kΩ resistor on the adapter board and the potentiometer inside the joystick. If the voltage across the capacitor increases above a threshold level, the monostable output becomes 0. The period in which the output is 1 is determined by the external resistance value, assuming that the values of the internal capacitor and resistance are fixed. The time interval and the external resistance are related by the following equation:

$$\text{Resistance } (\Omega) = \frac{\text{Time interval } (\mu s) - 24.2\mu s}{0.011}$$

The time interval may vary in the range 24.2 μs for a zero external resistance and 1124 μs for a 100 kΩ resistor. However, uncertainties in the internal capacitor and resistor make the equation invalid. In practice, a calibration should be carried out which involves measurements of the one-shot period when the input resistance is zero and when the input resistance is precisely 100 kΩ.

Some game port adaptors on computers only support joystick A. In this case, only two resistance channels and two digital input channels are available.

1.3.3 Software control

In the QBASIC programming language, there are two instructions which are specific to the game port. One is the 'STICK(x)' function and the other is the 'STRIG(x)' function. For the STICK function, x can be a value of 0, 1, 2 and 3 and is used to read X and Y potentiometers of joystick A and B.

x=0 read X coordinate of joystick A
x=1 read Y coordinate of joystick B
x=2 read X coordinate of joystick A
x=3 read Y coordinate of joystick B

When using this instruction, you must call STICK(0) first before you call STICK(1), STICK(2) or STICK(3). STICK function returns a coordinate value which varies from 6 for zero resistance to about 150 for 100 kΩ resistance.

STRIG(x) returns -1 if the condition is true. It returns 0 if the condition is not true. x can be a value of 0 to 7 and is used to select a specific joystick button status condition.

x=0 1st button of joystick A was pressed since last STRIG(0)
x=1 1st button of joystick A was currently pressed
x=2 1st button of joystick B was pressed since last STRIG(2)
x=3 1st button of joystick B was currently pressed
x=4 2nd button of joystick A was pressed since last STRIG(4)
x=5 2nd button of joystick A was currently pressed
x=6 2nd button of joystick B was pressed since last STRIG(6)
x=7 2nd button of joystick B was currently pressed

The following QBASIC program prints the X and Y coordinate values of joystick A on the screen and shows the status of the two buttons.

```
10 dummy=STICK(0)
20 print "Coordinate of X: ", STICK(0)
30 print "Coordinate of Y: ", STICK(1)
40 print "Current status of 1st button:  ", STRIG(1)
50 print "Current status of 2nd button: ", STRIG(5)
60 end
```

The following TP6 function returns the status of a particular bit specified by a variable Bitx. The content of the joystick register is read into the computer and assigned to `Input_byte`. Then the status of a particular bit is obtained by masking the selected bit.

```
(* ——Resource Library No. A14 (to read Game port register)—— *)
Function Read_Game_port(Bitx:integer):integer;
(* Game port address: 201H
   Bitx (1 to 8) selects status of AX, AY, BX, BY, BA1, BA2, BB1 and BB2 *)
```

```
var
    input_byte:byte;
begin
      input_byte:=port[$201];
      Read_game_port:=round((input_byte and bit_weight(bitx))/bit_weight(bitx));
end;
```

To determine the resistance value, firstly you output a byte to the 201h port to start the one-shot monostable. The corresponding bit in the joystick register rises to 1. Then, you continuously poll the corresponding bit to see if it falls to 0. The time period required is obtained. The most convenient way to find the time period is to use the third counter of the 8253/8254 timer chip inside the PC. The counter can be configured as a free running count-down timer. If the counters are loaded with a value of 255, the value of the counters reaches zero for every 55 millisecond. Only counter 3 of the 8253 can be used for the purpose. Counters 1 and 2 are already used by the computer's operating system.

The following TP6 function allows the period for a resistance channel to be measured. The channel is specified by x. The function issues a write operation to the game port using PORT [$201]:=0 to start the monostables. Immediately following this, the value in the 8253 counter is read and is assigned to Time 1. Next, a loop continuously checks if the associated register bit goes low. As soon as it does so, the 8253 counter is read again and the value is assigned to Time 2. The time interval is then calculated. This function uses two other function/procedures. One is the init_8253. It writes 255 to the low and high order counters of the counter 3 and configures it as a free running counter. 'Read_8253' is a function to read the high-order and low-order bytes of the counter 3.

```
(*—Resource Library No. A16 (to get time interval of the multivibrator after one shot)—— *)
Function Interval_Game_port(x:integer):integer;
(* x selects AX (x=1), AY (x=2), BX (x=3), BY (x=4) *)
var
    Time1, Time2, dummy: integer;


Procedure init_8253;
(* Initialize 8253 *)
begin
(*  Control word= b6H = 10110111b
     10  = select counter 2
     11  = read/write low count byte first then high byte
     011 = mode 3
     0   = binary counting with 16-bit *)
     Port[$43]:=$b6; (* load control word to the control register of 8253 *)
     Port[$42]:=255; (* load low count byte *)
     port[$42]:=255; (* load high count byte *)
     port[$61]:=port[$61] or 1; (* disable speaker *)
     port[$43]:=$80; (* 80H is the counter latch command for counter 3 *)
end;


Function read_8253:integer;
```

```
(* read low order and high order bytes of the counters *)
var
    low_byte, high_byte:byte;
begin
     low_byte:=port[$42];
     high_byte:=port[$42];
     read_8253:=low_byte + 256* high_byte;
end;


Var
    i:integer;
begin
     init_8253;
     for i:=1 to 100 do i:=i;
     i:=0;
     dummy:=bit_weight(x);
     port[$201]:=0;
     Time1:=read_8253;
     repeat i:=i+1 until (port[$201] and dummy=0) or (i>=5000);
     Time2:=read_8253;
     Interval_game_port:=time1-time2;
     if i>=5000 then Interval_game_port:=0;
end;
```

The Windows DLLs are written in Turbo Pascal for Windows.

```
(* ——Resource Library No. A14 (to read Game port register)—– *)
Function Read_Game_port(Bitx:integer):integer;Export;
(* Game port address: 201H
    Bitx selects status of AX, AY, BX, BY, BA1, BA2, BB1 and BB2 *)
var
    input_byte:byte;
begin
     input_byte:=port[$201];
     Read_game_port:=round((input_byte and bit_weight(bitx)/bit_weight(bitx)));
end;


(* ——Resource Library No. A15 (to write to Game port register)—– *)
Function Write_Game_port:integer;Export;
(* output byte 0 to the game port to start the multi-vibrators *)
begin
     port[$201]:=0;
end;
```

```
(* ——Resource Library No. A16 (to get time interval of the multivibrator after one shot)—— *)
Function Interval_Game_port(x:integer):integer;Export;
(* x selects AX (x=1), AY (x=2), BX (x=3), BY (x=4) *)
var
    Time1, Time2, dummy: integer;

Procedure init_8253;
(* Initialize 8253 *)
begin
(*  Control word= b6H = 10110111b
     10  = select counter 2
     11  = read/write low count byte first then high byte
     011 = mode 3
     0   = binary counting with 16-bit *)
    Port[$43]:=$b6; (* load control word to the control register of 8253 *)
    Port[$42]:=255; (* load low count byte *)
    port[$42]:=255; (* load high count byte *)
    port[$61]:=port[$61] or 1; (* disable speaker *)
    port[$43]:=$80; (* 80H is the counter latch command for counter 3 *)
end;

Function read_8253:integer;
(* read low order and high order bytes of the counters *)
var
    low_byte, high_byte:byte;
begin
    low_byte:=port[$42];
    high_byte:=port[$42];
    read_8253:=low_byte + 256* high_byte;
end;

Var
    i:integer;
begin
    init_8253;
    for i:=1 to 10 do i:=i; (* a short delay *)
    i:=0;
    dummy:=bit_weight(x);
    port[$201]:=0;
    Time1:=read_8253;
    repeat i:=i+1 until (port[$201] and dummy=0) or (i>=10000);
    Time2:=read_8253;
    Interval_game_port:=time1-time2;
    if i>=10000 then Interval_game_port:=0;
end;
```

Tools for experimenters

The voltage required by TTL and CMOS logic chips is +5V. +12V, –5V and –12V are used by some A/D converters and operational amplifiers. Some circuit ideas of power supplies are given in Section 2.2 of this chapter. Measurement tools are used for measuring voltage, current, resistance and other physical properties or showing the waveform of a signal. Multimeters and oscilloscopes are essential tools for these purposes. For digital experiments in particular, logic probes are used for checking logic status and detecting digital pulses. Some logic probe circuits are given in Section 2.3. Analogue and digital signal generators are used for generating signals. Section 2.4 shows some circuit ideas. All interfacing experiments described in this book are carried out using three experimental boards, namely the Centronic experimental board, the RS232 experimental board and the game port experimental board. Section 2.5 gives the hardware details of the boards. The circuit-making tools are used to construct experimental circuits. They include breadboards, stripe boards and printed circuit boards.

2.1 Power supplies

2.1.1 DC power supply

An 8–15V 1A DC power supply is required by the three interfacing boards. Any DC power supplies having a suitable output voltage range and a current rating can be used. Batteries can be used too.

Figure 2.1 shows a circuit of a dual DC power supply system. It provides +16V and –16V DC power supply rails with each rated at 1.8 A. The mains side of the power supply consists of a primary mains switch, a 110V/230V voltage selector, a primary fuse and a transformer. The transformer is of 50VA capacity with two independent primary windings that can be connected in series for 240V operation or in parallel for 110V operations. The fuse for the primary winding is a standard quick-action 3A fuse. The fuses for the secondary windings are the resettable fuses (RS183-9629). When the fuses are subject to a current overload, they rapidly switch from a low resistance state to a very high resistance state. Once the fault condition has been removed, they automatically reset themselves within a short period of time, returning to the low resistance state.

2.1.2 +5V, –5V, +12V, –12V and other voltage supplies

The simplest way of generating a fixed voltage is to use Zener diodes. The regulated voltage can vary from 2.4V to 75V using the BZX79 series diodes. The diodes in this series are rated at 500 mW and

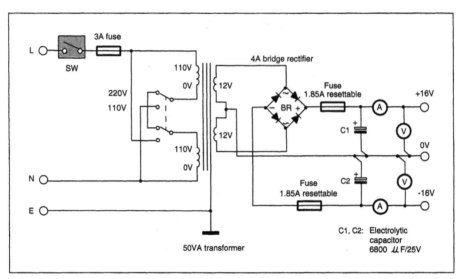

Figure 2.1 +16V and −16V power supply system

the tolerance of the stabilizing voltage is 5%. Figure 2.2 shows a circuit which converts a 16V DC voltage into 5.1V with a supply current of 20 mA.

The most common way of generating a fixed voltage is to use the 78 and 79 series voltage regulators. The former generates positive voltages and the latter generates negative voltages. They offer different stabilizing voltages (5, 9, 12, 15, 24, −5, −12, −15, −24V, etc.) with a typical tolerance of 5%. 78L and 79L series are rated at 100 mA; 78 and 79 series at 1A and 78S and 79S series at 2A. All the regulators are equipped with an automatic over-temperature shutdown facility. Figure 2.3 shows a circuit supplying +5V, −5V, +12V and −12V voltages. The input DC supply may be provided by the circuit shown in Figure 2.1. The 78 and 79 series regulators are used. Heat sinks with a capacity of several °C per Watt should be used for all regulators. 1A resettable fuses are used for each power supply rail.

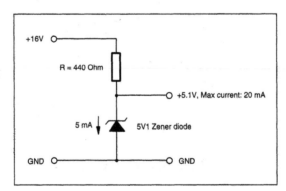

Figure 2.2 +5V power supply using a Zener diode

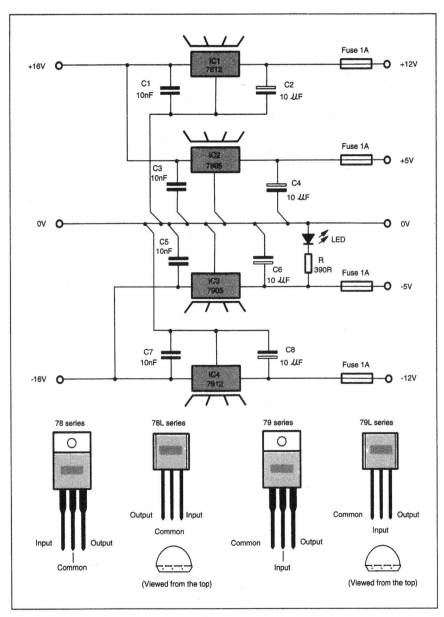

Figure 2.3 +5V, −5V, +12V and −12V power supply system

These voltage regulators have a high voltage drop. This means that the incoming supply voltage should be at least 2 to 3 volts higher than the output voltage. They also exhibit a high quiescent current, typically, 1 to 8 mA. There are other types of regulators which feature a lower voltage drop. The LM2930A (SGS-Thomson) is a 5V regulator and has a 0.4 V voltage drop when the supply current is 400 mA. When the supply current drops to 150 mA, the voltage drop could be as low as 0.2V. It also includes protection features such as ±40V input overvoltage protection, polarity protection, thermal shutdown and current limiting. The quiescent current is 22 mA for a 150 mA supply current. The LM2940CT (National Semiconductor) is a 1A +5V low voltage drop regulator. The voltage drop is between 0.5 to 1.0V. It has a quiescent current of typically 3 mA for an input and output voltage difference above 3V. If the difference becomes less than 3V, the quiescent current increases to 10 mA. It also features thermal overload and short-circuit protection. Figure 2.4 shows the pin-out of the two regulators and typical application circuits.

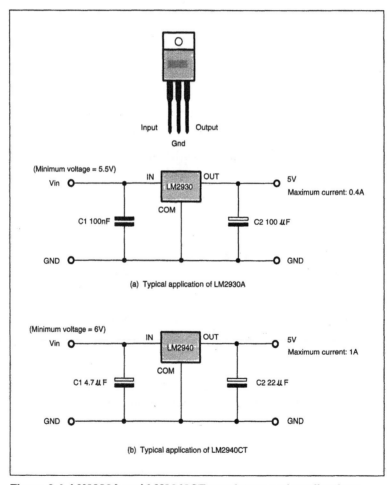

Figure 2.4 LM2930A and LM2940CT regulators and applications

The HT-7230, -7233, -7250 and -7290 (Holtek) give fixed voltages of 3.0V, 3.3V, 5.0V and 9.0V, respectively, with a typical tolerance of 5%. The maximum output current is 100 mA. The voltage drop is typically 100 mV and the quiescent current is 500 μA. The HT-1030 and HT-1050 exhibit a quiescent current of 3.5 μA and supply a fixed voltage of 3V and 5V. Their current rating is 30 mA. Figure 2.5 shows an application circuit using these regulators.

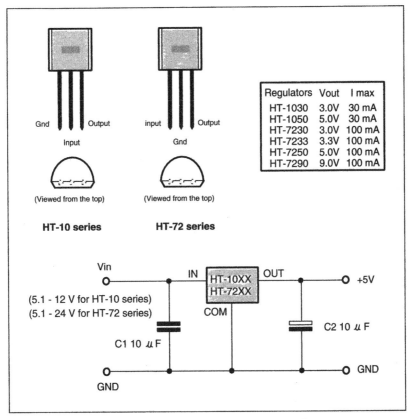

Regulators	Vout	I max
HT-1030	3.0V	30 mA
HT-1050	5.0V	30 mA
HT-7230	3.0V	100 mA
HT-7233	3.3V	100 mA
HT-7250	5.0V	100 mA
HT-7290	9.0V	100 mA

Figure 2.5 HT-72XX and HT-10XX series voltage regulators

Variable voltage regulators are also very useful. Figure 2.6 shows a circuit using an L200C (SGS-Thomson) adjustable voltage regulator. It can supply a regulated voltage from 2.85 to 36V with an output current up to 2 A. It features current limiting, thermal shutdown and input over voltage protection up to 60V. The quiescent current is typically 4.2 mA. A heat sink with a capacity of several °C per watt should be used.

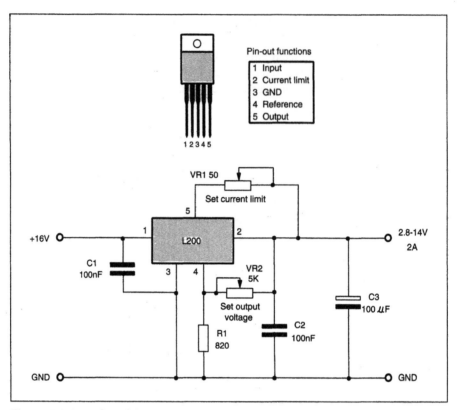

Figure 2.6 L200C variable voltage regulator and its typical application

2.1.3 Voltage references

In A/D and D/A applications, precision voltage references are required. The REF-03CNB, REF-02CP and REF-01CP (Analog Devices) give 2.50V, 5.00V and 10.0V voltage with a typical ±1% tolerance. The maximum output current is 21 mA. The input voltage should be at least 2V higher than the output voltage and the quiescent current is about 1 mA. They all feature short circuit protection. Figure 2.7 shows the pin-out of the devices.

The LM4040-XX (National Semiconductor) series are micropower shunt voltage references, which are available in several voltages: 2.500V, 4.096V, 5.000V, 8.192V and 10.000V and have several precision grades: grade A: 0.1%, grade B: 0.2% and grade C: 0.5%, grade D: 1% and grade E: 2%. The quiescent current of the devices varies from 60 µA for the 2.5V reference to 100 µA for the 10V reference. All versions have a maximum supply current of 15 mA. The pin-out and a typical application are given in Figure 2.8.

The TLE2425CLP (Texas Instruments) is another voltage reference which outputs a voltage of 2.50V with a tolerance of ±0.8%. It sinks or sources 20 mA current. The quiescent current is

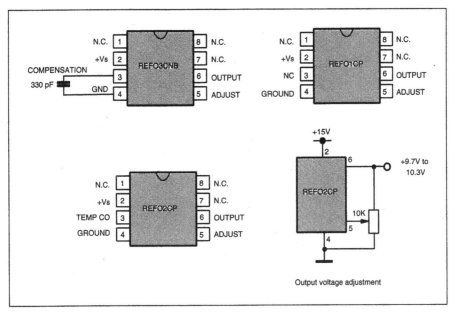

Figure 2.7 REF-XX series voltage reference ICs

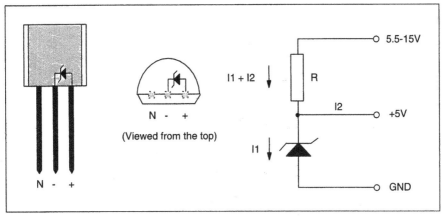

Figure 2.8 Pin-out of LM4040 and a typical application

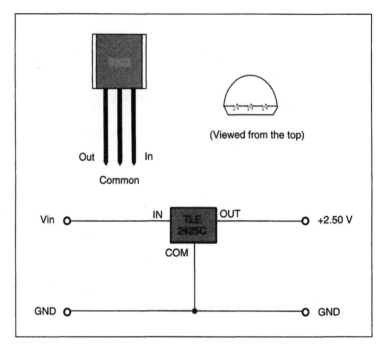

Figure 2.9 Pin-out a typical application of TLE2425

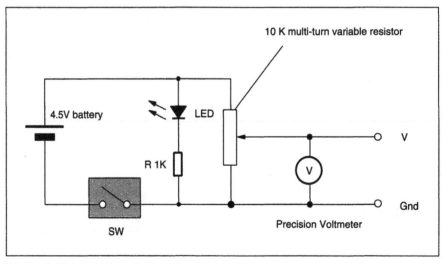

Figure 2.10 Variable voltage generator

170 µA. The input voltage is in the range 4V to 40V. The pin-out and a typical application are given in Figure 2.9.

A variable reference voltage generator is shown in Figure 2.10. It is built around a multi-turn potentiometer and is a very useful device in testing A/D and D/A converters. The output voltage could vary from several millivolts to several volts. A precision digital voltmeter should be used to monitor the voltage.

2.1.4 Voltage converters

The circuit shown in Figure 2.11(a) is a voltage inverter which converts +5V voltage to –5V using an SI7660CJ voltage converter (Siliconix). The chip is able to generate a negative voltage output which is

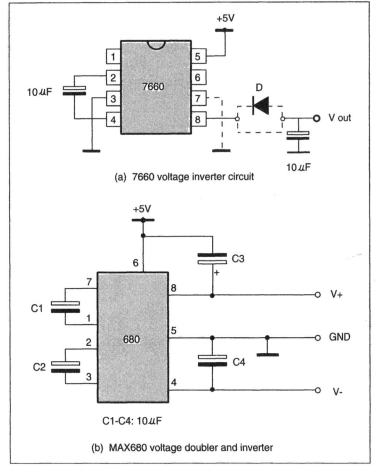

(a) 7660 voltage inverter circuit

(b) MAX680 voltage doubler and inverter

Figure 2.11 Voltage converter circuits

equal to the positive voltage input in the range 1.5V to 10V. Pin 7 should be tied to ground for a supply voltage below 3.5V. For supply voltages above 6.5V, a diode should be connected in series of the output. The output has an internal resistance of 70 Ω. If a 10 mA current is drawn from the output, the voltage will be 4.3V. The quiescent current is 170 μA and the maximum output current is 40 mA.

The circuit shown in Figure 2.11(b) converts a +5V voltage to +10V and –10V using a MAX680CPA voltage doubler and inverter (Maxim). The input voltage ranges from 2V to 6V. The internal resistances for the positive and negative output are 150 Ω and 90 Ω respectively. If a 10 mA current is drawn from both outputs, the positive voltage falls to 7V and the negative voltage becomes –6.1V. The quiescent current of the device is typically 1 mA for a 5V power supply.

2.1.5 Isolated voltage supply circuits

This circuit is used when a complete isolation between two circuits is required. NME and NMA series DC-to-DC converters (Newport Components) are high efficiency voltage converters, the outputs of which are isolated up to 1000V relative to the input. The NME series operate from a 5V or 12V DC input and provide an isolated +5V, 12V or 15V output, depending on types. Up to 200 mA supply current is available from the 5V type, 84 mA from the 12V type and 67 mA from the 15V type. The NMA series provide dual ±5V, ±12V and ±15V DC supplies from a single 5V or 12V DC input. Up to 100 mA is available from the 5V type and 42 mA from the 15V type. The pin-out of the devices is shown in Figure 2.12.

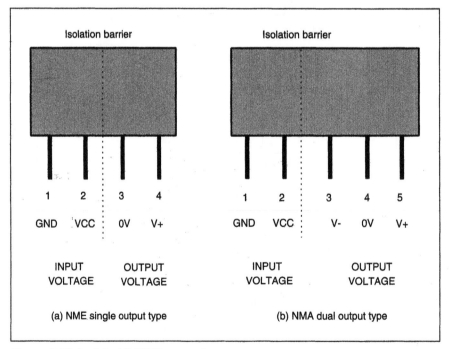

Figure 2.12 Isolated DC/DC converters

2.2 Logic level detectors

A simple TTL logic probe can be constructed using a buffer IC such as the 74LS241 or 74LS245. Such a circuit is shown in Figure 2.13(a). Current limiting resistors are used for LEDs. When the input of the buffer is high, the output will go high. This switches on the corresponding LED. This digital probe provides multi-channel test inputs. It is unable to detect transition status and high frequency pulse trains.

Figure 2.13(b) shows a circuit of an advanced logic probe. It is built around an LM339 voltage comparator. It has three LEDs, red, green and yellow. When the probe detects a logic high state, the red LED illuminates. When it detects a logic low, the green LED illuminates. When a transitional status is detected, the green and red LEDs are both off but the yellow LED illuminates. If it detects a train of pulses, the red and green LEDs both illuminate. The circuit, however, is still not able to detect pulses with a very short duration. A pulse stretching circuit should be used. A 555 configured as a monostable can be adopted for this purpose.

2.3 Digital and analogue signal generators

2.3.1 Digital signal generators

Figure 2.14(a) shows an eight-channel logic status generator circuit. It consists of eight single pole double throw (SPDT) switches and eight 1k metal film resistors. When a switch is off, the status of the corresponding channel is high. When it is switched on, a logic low is generated. At logic high, each channel can drive up to 25 LSTTL chips. This logic generator suffers that the output signal is not 'clean' when it changes the status. When the switch changes position, the output signal does not change from one state to the other instantly. It consists of a number of oscillations within a very short period of time. To solve this problem, a de-bouncing circuit is used. Figure 2.14(b) shows such a circuit using a Schmitt trigger inverter, 74LS14. When the switch is closed, the output gives logic 1. When the switch is open, the output gives logic 0.

Another logic generator is the toggle action switch. When a switch is pressed momentarily, the output changes status. The status is maintained until the switch is pressed again. Figure 2.14(c) gives such a circuit.

Figure 2.15 shows two square wave generator circuits. The first one is based on a 555 timer. It gives a 1 kHz signal with a 67% duty cycle. Figure 2.15(b) is an oscillator producing square wave signals having various frequencies. It uses a CD4060 16-stage ripple counter. The original frequency is determined by Rt and Ct.

To achieve a higher accuracy in frequency, crystal oscillators are used. Figure 2.16 shows three circuits. The first signal generator uses a 10 MHz crystal oscillator and a 74LS04 inverter. It generates a digital signal precisely at 10 MHz. Lower frequencies can be obtained using dividers. Figure 2.16(b) shows a crystal oscillator circuit using a 2.4576 crystal oscillator and a 16 stage ripple counter CD4060. It outputs square wave signals of various frequencies at different pins. Figure 2.16(c) shows another circuit using an EX0-3 programmable crystal oscillator (Interface Quartz Devices). It has an on-board programmable frequency divider which provides $1/2$ to $1/2^n$ (n=1, 2 to 8) divisions of the

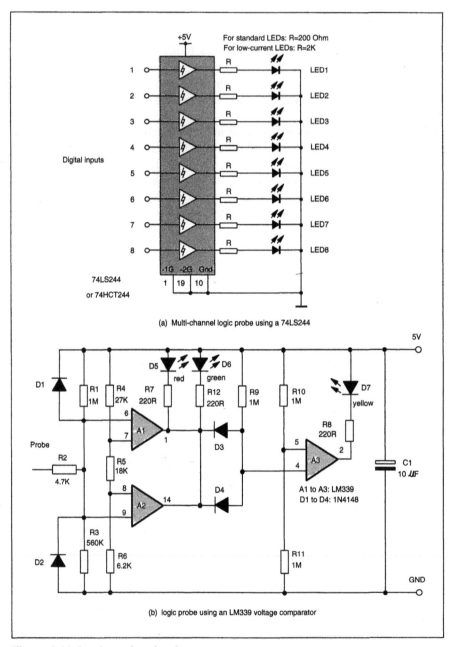

Figure 2.13 Logic probe circuits

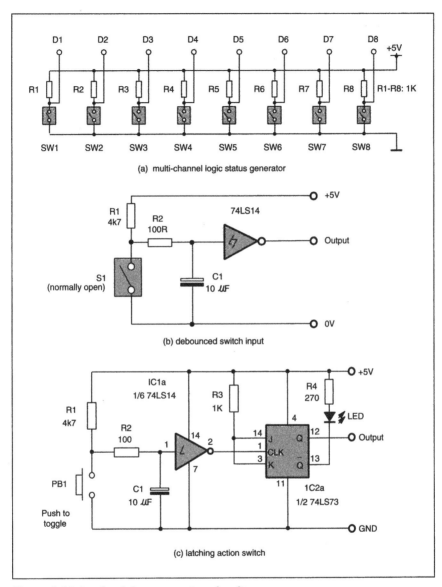

(a) multi-channel logic status generator

(b) debounced switch input

(c) latching action switch

Figure 2.14 Logic status generator circuits

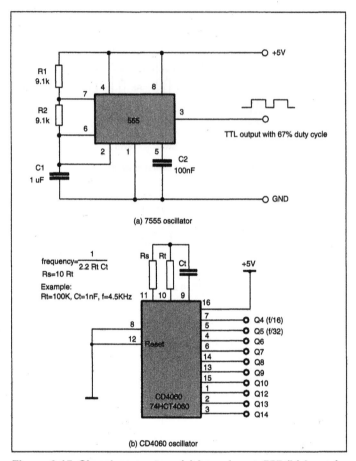

(a) 7555 oscillator

(b) CD4060 oscillator

Figure 2.15 Signal generators (a) based on a 555 (b) based on a CD4060

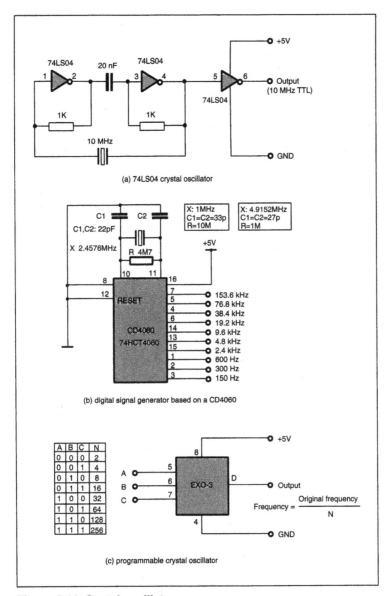

(a) 74LS04 crystal oscillator

(b) digital signal generator based on a CD4060

(c) programmable crystal oscillator

Figure 2.16 Cystal oscillators

original frequency. The original signal is generated by an on-board crystal oscillator. Divisions are selected by three pins (A, B and C). Available original frequencies are 12 MHz (RS296-879), 14.318 MHz (RS296-885), 18 MHz (RS296-891) and 19.661 MHz (RS296-908).

2.3.2 Analogue signal generators

Figure 2.17 shows an analogue signal generator circuit using a popular ICL8038BC function generator IC (Harris Semiconductor). It gives sine, square and triangular signals with frequencies adjustable from 20 Hz to 18 kHz. The outputs from the ICL8038 is buffered by three op-amps.

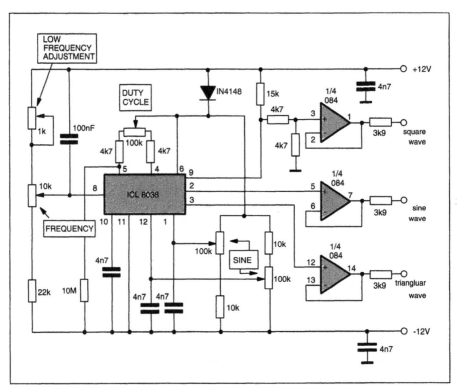

Figure 2.17 ICL8038 digital signal generator

2.4 Centronic port, RS232 and game port experimental boards

These boards serve as the interfaces between the computer and user's experimental circuits. On each board, LEDs are provided to indicate the logic status of each input and output line. This enables users to trace the effect of I/O operations. Each I/O line has a detachable screw terminal from which user's experimental circuits can be connected. All the digital lines fed into the computer are buffered by Schmitt trigger buffers. All the boards require a single rail 8–15V unregulated DC power supply. The on-board 7805 +5V 1A voltage regulator converts the input voltage to +5 V. The current of the regulated power supply is limited by a 1A on-board fuse. The boards use popular electronic components and are constructed on single sided PCB boards. The boards allow various interfacing experiments to be carried out using the Centronic port, RS232 port and the game port.

2.4.1 Centronic experimental board

Figure 2.18 shows the circuit diagram of the Centronic experimental board. DB0 to DB7 of the data port of the Centronic port are fed into the inputs of 74LS244 Schmitt trigger buffers (IC2) via eight 100 Ω resistors (RL2, eight-way resistor array). The outputs of the buffers are connected to an eight-way detachable screw terminal. Each line is also connected to a low current LED via a 3.3K resistor. When a line has a logic high state, the corresponding LED illuminates. The four output lines of the control port are connected in the same way as for the data port. Four inputs are connected to the inputs of four Schmitt trigger buffers of IC3. The outputs of the buffers are connected to the four input lines of the status port via four 100Ω resistors. The status port has five input lines, but only four of them are connected this way. The logic status of these lines is monitored by LEDs.

The fifth input line of the status port (the BUZY input) is connected permanently to the ground. This is a very useful feature if high level printer control commands are used to control the board. In this case, the BUZY line is used as a handshake line and it is always low, indicating that the Centronic experimental board is always ready to receive data.

The power supply incorporates a 1A +5V 7805 fixed voltage regulator (see Figure 2.19). Power is fed to the board via a power connector SK1. SW1 controls the on/off of the power. A 1A fuse is used on the board to limit the total current. The on/off status is indicated by an LED. The 7805 regulator requires a heat sink. The input unregulated power supply and the regulated +5V DC are both connected to a four-way screw terminal (J1). The components utilized on the board are listed in Table 2.1.

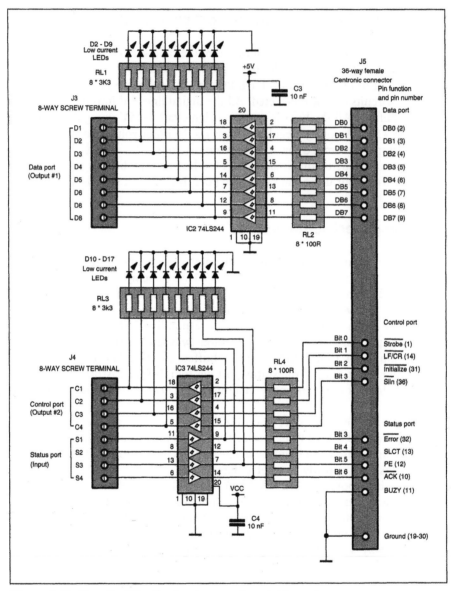

Figure 2.18 Circuit of the Centronic experimental board

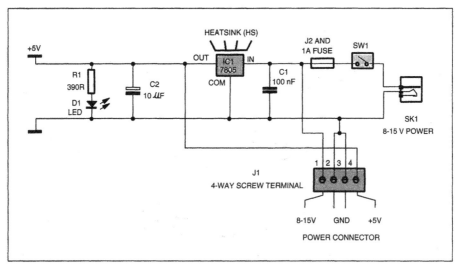

Figure 2.19 Power supply circuit for the three interfacing boards

Table 2.1

Resistors (all 1% 0.25W metal film resistors)
R1	390R
RL1, RL3	3.3K eight-way resistor array
RL2, RL4	100R eight-way resistor array

Capacitors
C1, C3, C4	100 nF
C2	10 µF

Semiconductors
IC1	7805 1A +5V voltage regulator
IC2, IC3	74LS244
D1	5mm green LED
D2–D17	Low power 3 mm red LEDs

Connectors
J1	Four-way detachable screw terminal block set
J2	Fuse holder
J3, J4	Eight-way detachable screw terminal block set
J5	36-way female Centronic type connector
SK1	2.5 mm male power connector

Others
SW1	PCB mounting miniature SPDT switch
Fuse	1A 25 mm length
Heat sink	(5 deg/watts)
PCB boards	
Holders for 3mm LEDs	
PCB pilar & screws	

2.4.2 RS232 experimental board

The circuit diagram of the RS232 experimental board is given in Figure 2.20. The three outputs of the RS232 port of a PC (TD, RTS and DTR) are fed into the MAX238 RS232-TTL driver/receiver (IC3, Maxim), where the RS232 voltage level is converted to TTL level. The outputs from the IC3 are fed into Schmitt trigger buffers 74LS244 (IC2), the outputs from which are connected to three screw terminals (J3). The logic status of each line is monitored by low current LEDs. The four input signals (RD, DSR, DCD and CTS) are fed into the 74LS244 buffers. The outputs from the buffer are fed into IC3 where the TTL voltage level is converted into the RS232 level. Their logic status is monitored by LEDs. The power supply system is the same as that for the Centronic experimental board.

The MAX238 is an RS232/TTL receiver/transmitter that meets all the EIA RS-232C specifications while requiring only a single +5V supply. The two on-chip charge pump voltage converters generate +10 V and –10 V power supplies from a single +5V supply. The IC contains eight voltage level converters, four of which convert the TTL/CMOS level into the RS232 level, and four of which convert the RS232 voltage level into the TTL/CMOS level. It requires five external 1.0 µF capacitors. All the voltage converters have an inverting action. The components utilized on the board are listed in Table 2.2.

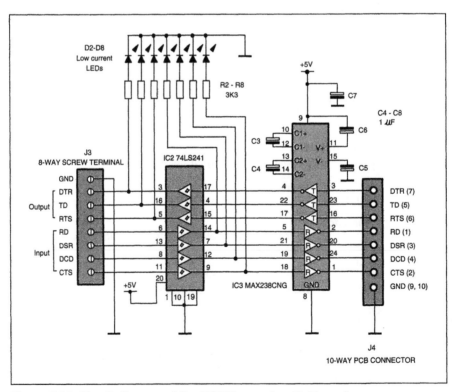

Figure 2.20 Circuit diagram of the RS232 experimental board

Table 2.2

Resistors (all 1% 0.25W metal film resistors)	
R1	390R
R2-R8	3.3K
Capacitors	
C1	100 nF
C2	10 μF
C3-C7	1 μF
Semiconductors	
IC1	7805 1A +5V voltage regulator
IC2	74LS244
IC3	MAX238CNG
D1	5mm green LED
D2-D8	Low power 3mm red LEDs
Connectors	
J1	Four-way detachable screw terminal block set
J2	Fuse holder
J3	Eight-way detachable screw terminal block set
J4	Ten-way PCB connector set
SK1	2.5mm male power connector
Others	
SW1	PCB mounting miniature SPDT switch
Fuse	1A 25mm length
Heat sink	(5 deg/watts)
PCB boards	
Holders for 3mm LEDs	
PCB pilar & screws	
9 pin female D-type connector and housing	
1m 9 core digital signal cable	

2.4.3 Game port experimental board

The circuit diagram of the game experimental board is given in Figure 2.21. The four resistance inputs are connected to an eight-way screw terminal (J3). The +5V voltage from the computer is connected to the terminal via a protection fuse rated at 25 mA. The +5V voltage is not intended to be used as a power supply. It is only used for connecting resistors. The four digital inputs are first fed into the 74LS244 Schmitt trigger buffers (IC2). The outputs from the buffers are connected to the four input bit of the game port via 100R resistors. Their logic status is monitored by LEDs. The power supply system is the same as that for the Centronic experimental board.

Some game ports on a PC only support one joystick. In this case, only two resistance channels and two digital input channels are used. The components utilized on the game port experimental board are listed in Table 2.3.

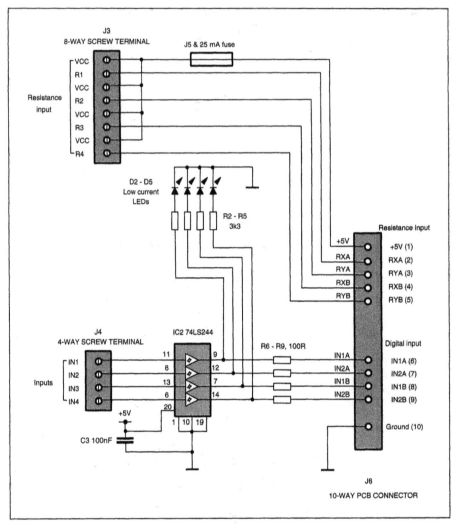

Figure 2.21 Circuit diagram of the game port experimental board

Table 2.3

Resistors (all 1% 0.25W metal film resistors)

R1	390R
R2-R5	3K3
R6-R9	100R

Capacitors

C1, C3	100 nF
C2	10 µF

Semiconductors

IC1	7805 1A +5V voltage regulator
IC2	74LS244
D1	5mm green LED
D2-D5	Low power 3mm red LEDs

Connectors

J1	Four-way detachable screw terminal block set
J2	Fuse holder
J3	Eight-way detachable screw terminal block set
J4	Four-way detachable screw terminal block set
J5	Fuse holder
J6	Ten-way PCB connector set
SK1	2.5mm male power connector

Others

SW1	PCB mounting miniature SPDT switch
Fuse 1	1A 25 mm length
Fuse 2	25mA 25mm length
Heat sink	(5 deg/watts)
PCB boards	
Holders for 3mm LEDs	
PCB pillar & screws	
15 pin D-type male connector with housing	
1m 10 core screened digital signal cable	

2.4.4 Construction of the experimental boards

The artwork of the PCBs for the three experimental boards is shown in Figures 2.22 to 2.24. The component layouts for the experimental boards are shown in Figures 2.25 to 2.27.

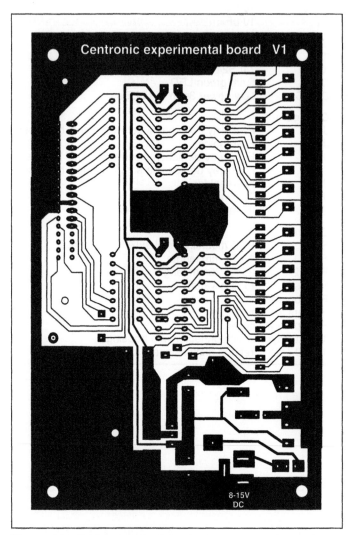

Figure 2.22 PCB artwork of the Centronic experimental board

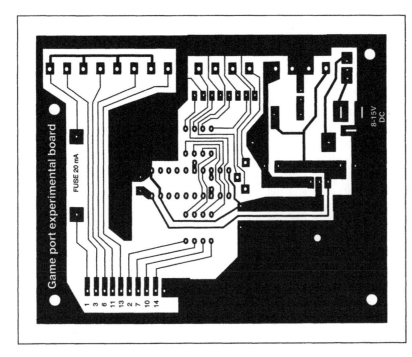

Figure 2.24 PCB copper track of the game experimental board

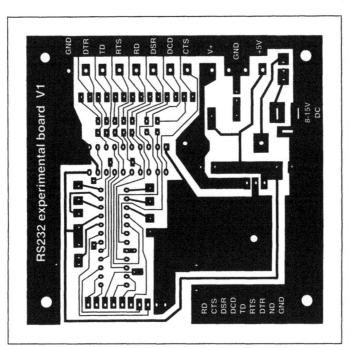

Figure 2.23 PCB artwork of the RS232 experimental board

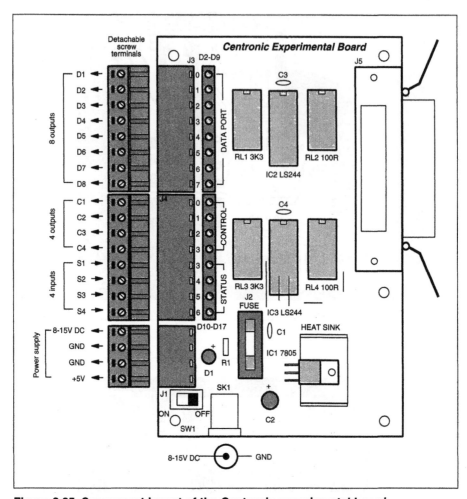

Figure 2.25 Component layout of the Centronic experimental board

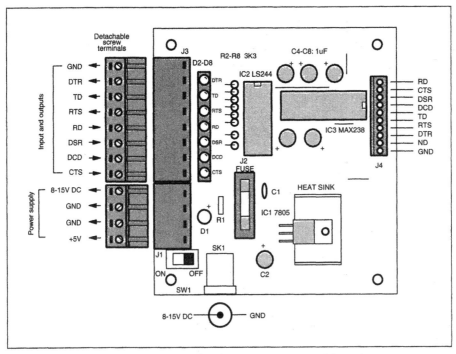

Figure 2.26 Component layout of the RS232 experimental board

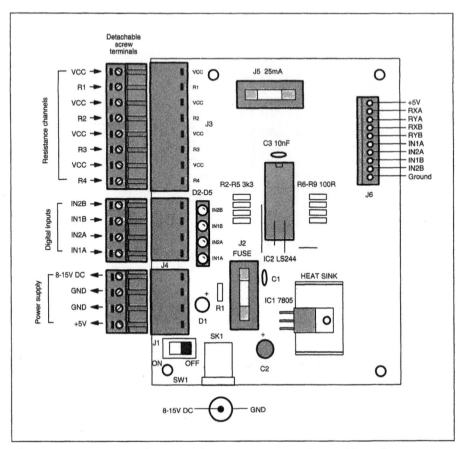

Figure 2.27 Component layout of the game port experimental board

2.5 Circuit making tools

The circuit making tools are bread boards, strip boards and PCBs. Using the bread board is the quickest way of making temporary experimental circuits. Stripe boards and PCBs are used for making permanent circuits.

Software drivers for the experimental boards

This chapter describes software drivers for the Centronic, the RS232 and the game port experimental boards. Three programming languages, Borland Turbo Pascal 6 for DOS (TP6), Borland Turbo Pascal for Windows (TPW) and Microsoft Visual Basic 3 (VB3), are used for developing the programs. The complete software package has two parts: driver programs and programming resource libraries. The software drivers include:

TP6 driver for the Centronic experimental board, CENTEXP.PAS
VB3 driver for the Centronic experimental board, CENTEXP
TP6 driver for the RS232 experimental board, RS232EXP.PAS
VB3 driver for the RS232 experimental board, RS232EXP
TP6 driver for the Game experimental board, GAMEEXP.PAS
VB3 driver for the Game experimental board, GAMEEXP

The programming libraries include:

TP6 Programming Resource Library – 1, TPLIB1.PAS
TP6 Programming Resource Library – 2, TPLIB2.PAS
Window DLL library – 1 (written in TPW), WLIB1.PAS

The TP6 programming resource libraries contain a collection of procedures and functions for basic I/O operations of the Centronic, RS232 and game ports and for detecting keyboard strokes and showing messages on screens, etc. The libraries can be included in users' TP6 program. Procedures and functions can then be called elsewhere in the program. The Windows DLLs library contains functions for I/O operations of the three ports and it is written in Turbo Pascal for Windows. The DLLs can be called by other Windows programs which may be written in Visual Basic and Visual C, etc.

The TP6 drivers for the boards run in the DOS environment and the VB3 drivers run in the Windows 3.1 and Windows 95 environments. The drivers allow users to understand basic I/O operations of the ports and to perform simple interfacing experiments using the ports. They also demonstrate how to integrate the resource libraries into users' programs.

3.1 Software drivers for the Centronic experimental board

3.1.1 DOS TP6 software driver CENTEXP.PAS

The driver provides the following functions:

- reports the number of installed Centronic ports on your computer
- allows you to select a Centronic port (LPT1 to LPT4) to be used
- changes the bit status of the data port (8 bits) and Control port (4 bits)
- reads data from the status port (4 lines)

After typing in the name of the program, path + CENTEXP, followed by a return in the DOS prompt, the following messages appear on the screen:

```
Number of LPT installed:  2
Addresses for LPT1 to LPT4: 888  632  0  0
Select LPT to be used (1,2,3 or 4)
```

The first line shows the number of LPT(s) installed on your computer. In this example there are 2 LPTs installed. The second line shows the base addresses for the installed LPTs. The third line allows users to select a Centronic port. Once an LPT is selected, a virtual control panel (Figure 3.1) appears

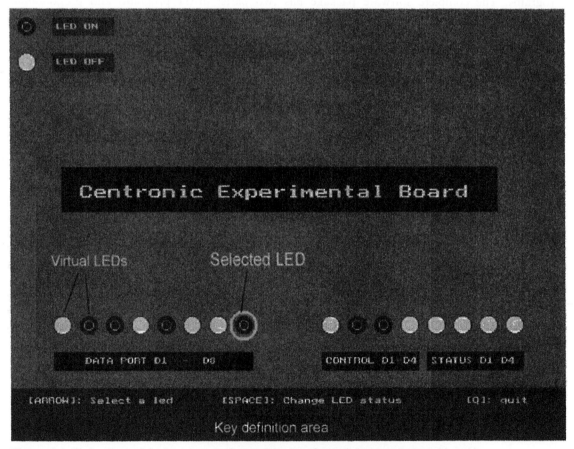

Figure 3.1 Turbo Pascal 6 virtual control panel for the Centronic experimental board

on the screen. There are 16 virtual LEDs on the panel corresponding to the 16 real LEDs on the Centronic experimental board. Eight of them represent the outputs of the data port; four of them represent the outputs of the control port and the other four represent the four inputs to the status port. At the bottom of the control panel, a key definition window is provided to show key functions.

[ARROW KEYS] to select an output line
[SPACE] to toggle the logic status of the selected output line
[Q or q] to quit the program

By pressing the left or right arrow keys, one of the 12 output lines can be selected. A selected line is indicated by a circle around the virtual LED. The status of the LED is toggled by pressing the space. A red LED indicates the logic high state. Every time the arrow keys or the space is pressed, the 4-bit data at the inputs of the status port is read into the computer and its status is shown on the screen. The program list is given below:

TP 6 program list of CENTEXP.PAS

```
Program Centronic_Experimental_Board;
(* Software driver for the Centronic experimental board *)


uses

    graph,crt,dos;
var

    i,led_selected:integer;

    ch:char;

    status:array[1..18] of integer;

    key_pressed:string[10];


(* include two included libraries: TPLIB1 and TPLIB2 *)
{$I c:\ioexp\tplib1.pas}
{$I c:\ioexp\tplib2.pas}


procedure Draw_panel;
(* draw the control panel of the Centronic experimental board on the screen *)
begin
    (* draw 16 LEDs on the screen *)
    setbkcolor(cyan);
    for i:=1 to 16 do status[i]:=0;
    for i:=1 to 8 do draw_led(30+i*30,  350, status[i]);
    for i:=1 to 8 do draw_led(340+i*30, 350, status[8+i]);

    (* draw captions *)
    draw_led(20,20,1); draw_message(50,20,70,20,lightblue,'LED ON',0,1,yellow);
    draw_led(20,60,0); draw_message(50,60,70,20,lightblue,'LED OFF',0,1,yellow);
    draw_message(50,390,230,20,blue,'    DATA PORT D1  -  D8  ',0,1,yellow);
```

```
     draw_message(360,390,110,20,blue,'CONTROL D1-D4',0,1,yellow);
     draw_message(480,390,110,20,blue,'STATUS D1-D4',0,1,yellow);

     (* draw bottom help bar *)
     setfillstyle(1,magenta);
     bar(1,420,800,480);
     settextstyle(0,0,1);
     outtextxy(20,430,'[ARROW]: Select a led        [SPACE]: Change LED status        [Q]: quit');

     (* draw central message box *)
     draw_message(60,200,500,50,blue,' Centronic Experimental Board',0,2,yellow);

     (* initialize the outputs *)
     Write_data_port(P_address, 0);
     Write_control_port(P_address, 0);
end;


Procedure Output_Input;
(* output and input procedure *)
var
   Output_byte, Input_byte:byte;
begin
     (* to calculate the value of data to be sent to the Data port *)
     Output_byte:=0;
     for i:=1 to 8 do Output_byte:=Output_byte + Status[i] * bit_weight(i);
     Write_data_port(P_address, Output_byte);

     (* to calculate the value of dta to be sent to the Control port *)
     Output_byte:=0;
     for i:=9 to 12 do Output_byte:=Output_byte + Status[i]*bit_weight(i-8);
     write_control_port(P_address, Output_byte);

     (* to input data from the Status port and calculate status for LEDs *)
     input_byte:=read_status_port(P_address);
     for i:=1 to 4 do status[12+i]:=round ((input_byte and bit_weight(i)) / bit_weight(i));
end;


Procedure scan_keyboard;
(* scan the keyboard and detect the keystroke *)
var
   led_selected_old:integer;
begin
     led_selected_old:=led_selected;
```

```
(* detect the keystrokes *)
key_pressed:=getkey;
if key_pressed='LEFT'  then led_selected:=led_selected-1;
if key_pressed='RIGHT' then led_selected:=led_selected+1;
if key_pressed=' ' then status[led_selected]:=1 - status[led_selected];


(* show virtual LEDs with status on the screen *)
setbkcolor(cyan);
for i:=1 to 8 do draw_led(30+i*30,  350, status[i]);
for i:=1 to 4 do draw_led(340+i*30, 350, status[8+i]);
Output_input;
for i:=5 to 8 do draw_led(340+i*30, 350, status[8+i]);
if led_selected>12 then led_selected:=12;
if led_selected<1 then   led_selected:=1;


(* display a circle around the virtual LEDs *)
setlinestyle (0,0,3);
setcolor(cyan);
if led_selected_old<=8 then circle(30+30*led_selected_old, 350,15)
   else circle(340+30*(led_selected_old-8),350,15);
setcolor(yellow);
if led_selected<=8 then circle(30+30*led_selected, 350,15)
   else circle(340+30*(led_selected-8),350,15);
end;


(* Main program *)
begin
    centronic_address;  (* input centronic address *)
    initialize_graph;   (* initilize the graphics mode *)
    draw_panel;         (* draw the virtual panel *)
    led_selected:=1;
repeat
    scan_keyboard;      (* scan the keyboard and detect keystrokes *)
until (key_pressed='Q') or (key_pressed='q');
    closegraph;   (* Close graphics mode *)
end.
```

The program first includes two libraries, TPLIB1.PAS and TPLIB2.PAS, using the TP6 INCLUDE instruction.

```
{$I C:\IOEXP\TPLIB1.PAS}
{$I C:\IOEXP\TPLIB2.PAS}
```

The program contains three main procedures. *Draw_panel* draws the virtual panel of the experimental board on the screen. *Draw_led()* and *Draw_message()* are two procedures in TPLIB2.PAS library. *Output_input* deals with I/O operations of the Centronic port. *Write_data_port()*, *write_control_port()* and *Read_status_port()* are procedures or functions in the TPLIB1.PAS library. *Scan_keyboard* scans the keyboard. It detects four keystrokes 'left', 'right', 'space' and 'q' and carries out corresponding tasks. It uses the *getkey* function in the TPLIB2.PAS library.

3.1.2 Windows VB3 software driver

The VB3 software driver provides the following functions:

- reports the number of the installed Centronic ports on your computer
- allows you to select a Centronic port (LPT1 to LPT4) to be used
- changes the bit status of the data port (8 bits) and control port (4 bits)
- reads data from the status port (4 lines)

In Windows 95, Click the START button and then select RUN. Next type in the name of the software driver: path + CENTEXP. After clicking the OK button, the screen shown in Figure 3.2 appears. It

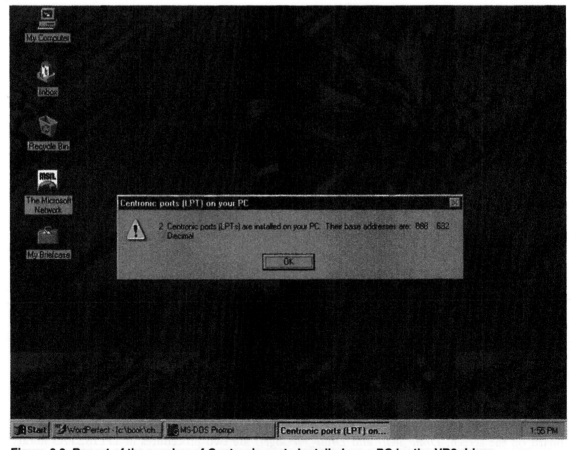

Figure 3.2 Report of the number of Centronic ports installed on a PC by the VB3 driver

reports the number of LPTs installed on your PC and their base addresses. Click OK to clear the screen. Another screen appears (see Figure 3.3). This screen asks you to select an LPT port to which the experimental board is to be connected. Key in the number of the LPT ports (1, 2, 3 or 4) and click the OK button. After this, a virtual control panel for the experimental board appears on the screen (Figure 3.4). By clicking the '0-1' buttons, the status of the corresponding output toggles. A red LED indicates the logic high state. Clicking the 'Get it' button updates the input data. The selected Centronic port and its base address are also shown in the panel. Users can re-select the Centronic port by clicking the 'Change' button. At the bottom of the panel, an information bar is provided to show the function of a control button when the mouse pointer moves over it.

The control panel consists of a number of objects. It has 15 command buttons which have the following functions.

COMMAND1: 'Get it' to get the status of the inputs
COMMAND2(0-7): '0-1' to toggle status of the Data port outputs
COMMAND2(8-11): '0-1' to toggle status of the Control port outputs

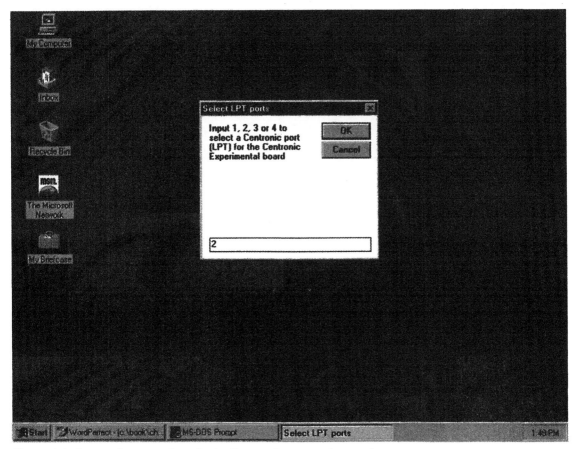

Figure 3.3 Screen for users to select a Centronic port to be used

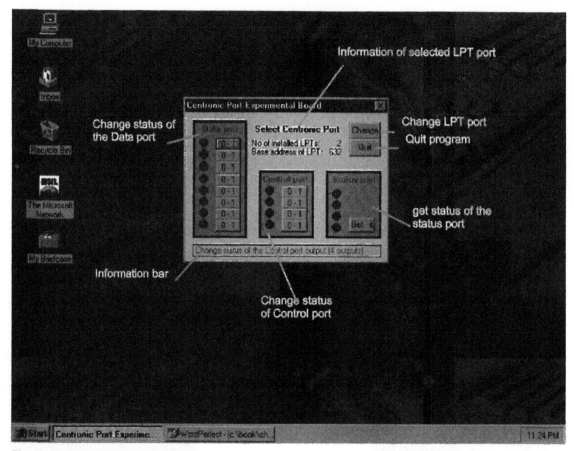

Figure 3.4 Visual Basic 3 virtual control panel for the Centronic experimental board

COMMAND3: 'Change' to re-select an LPT port
COMMAND4: 'Quit' to quit the program

The panel also has 19 shapes showing virtual LEDs and other graphic objects and seven labels showing various information. The complete program list is given below. Some explanations are given within the program list.

VB3 program list of CENTEXP.FORM

```
'Declare functions in the dynamic link library, WLIB1.DLL

'Declared functions: Centronic(), Bit_weight(), Read_status_port()
'                     Write_data_port() and write_control_port()

Declare Function Centronic Lib "C:\Ioexp\Wlib1.dll" (ByVal X As Integer) As Integer

Declare Function Bit_weight Lib "C:\Ioexp\Wlib1.dll" (ByVal X As Integer) As Integer

Declare Function Read_status_port Lib "C:\Ioexp\Wlib1.dll" (ByVal address As Integer) As Integer
```

```
Declare Function Write_data_port Lib "c:\Ioexp\Wlib1.dll" (ByVal address As Integer, ByVal Output_data As
Integer) As Integer
Declare Function write_control_port Lib "c:\IOEXP\Wlib1.dll" (ByVal address As Integer, ByVal Output_data As
Integer) As Integer

Sub Command1_Click ()
    input_byte = Read_status_port(P_address)
    For i = 12 To 15
    status(i) = (input_byte And Bit_weight(i - 11)) / Bit_weight(i - 11)
    If status(i) = 1 Then Shape1(i).BackColor = &HFF& Else Shape1(i).BackColor = black
    Next i

End Sub

Sub Command1_MouseMove (Button As Integer, Shift As Integer, X As Single, Y As Single)
     Label3.Caption = " Get the status of the Status port inputs (4 inputs)"
End Sub

Sub Command2_Click (index As Integer)
    'Change status of the outputs of Data port and Control port
    status(index) = 1 - status(index) 'toggle action
    If status(index) = 1 Then Shape1(index).BackColor = &HFF& Else Shape1(index).BackColor = black 'output
status to the virtual LEDs

    'Output data to the Data port
    Output_byte = 0
    For i = 0 To 7
    Output_byte = Output_byte + status(i) * Bit_weight(i + 1) 'form a byte to be output
    Next i
    dummy = Write_data_port(P_address, Output_byte) 'Output the byte to the Data port

    'Output data to the Data port
    Output_byte = 0
    For i = 8 To 11
    Output_byte = Output_byte + status(i) * Bit_weight(i - 7) 'form a byte to be output
    Next i
    dummy = write_control_port(P_address, Output_byte) 'output the byte to the Control port

    ' read the status port
    input_byte = Read_status_port(P_address)
    For i = 12 To 15
    status(i) = (input_byte And Bit_weight(i - 11)) / Bit_weight(i - 11) 'find the status of each bit
    If status(i) = 1 Then Shape1(i).BackColor = &HFF& Else Shape1(i).BackColor = black 'output status to the
virtual LEDs
```

```
    Next i

End Sub


Sub Command2_MouseMove (index As Integer, Button As Integer, Shift As Integer, X As Single, Y As Single)
    'show on-line help when mouse pointer movers across the buttons
    If index <= 7 Then
    Label3.Caption = " Change status of the Data port outputs (8 outputs)"
    Else
    Label3.Caption = " Change status of the Control port output (4 outputs)"
    End If
End Sub


Sub Command3_Click ()
    'Re-select a Centronic port
    dummy = MsgBox(Str(Centronic(0)) - 1 & "  Centronic ports (LPTs) are installed on your PC.  Their base
addresses are:  " & Format$(Centronic(1), "###") & "      " & Format$(Centronic(2), "###") & "      " &
Format$(Centronic(3), "###") & "      " & Format$(Centronic(4), "###") & "Decimal", 48, "Centronic ports (LPT)
on your PC") 'show information on installed LPTs
    lpt_number = Val(InputBox$("Input 1, 2, 3 or 4 to select a Centronic port (LPT) for the Mini-Lab Data
Logger/ Controller", "Select LPT ports")) 'Select a Centronic port
    P_address = Centronic(lpt_number) 'find the base address of the selected LPT port
    Label2.Caption = "Selected  LPT port :        " & Format(lpt_number) 'show the information on the selected
LPT port
    Label4.Caption = "Base address of LPT:    " & Format(P_address) 'show the information of the selected LPT
port
End Sub


Sub Command3_MouseMove (Button As Integer, Shift As Integer, X As Single, Y As Single)
     'show on-line help when mouse pointer moves across the button
     Label3.Caption = " re-select Centronic port"
End Sub


Sub Command4_Click ()
    'Quit the program
    End
End Sub


Sub Command4_MouseMove (Button As Integer, Shift As Integer, X As Single, Y As Single)
    Label3.Caption = " Quit the program"
End Sub


Sub Form_Load ()
    'initialize status()
```

```
For i = 0 To 11
    status(i) = 0
Next i


'show Centronic port information and allow user to select an LPT
    dummy = MsgBox(Str(Centronic(0)) - 1 & "  Centronic ports (LPTs) are installed on your PC.  Their base
addresses are:  " & Format$(Centronic(1), "###") & "     " & Format$(Centronic(2), "###") & "     " &
Format$(Centronic(3), "###") & "     " & Format$(Centronic(4), "###") & "Decimal", 48, "Centronic ports (LPT)
on your PC")
    lpt_number = Val(InputBox$("Input 1, 2, 3 or 4 to select a Centronic port (LPT) for the Centronic
Experimental board", "Select LPT ports"))
    P_address = Centronic(lpt_number)
    Label2.Caption = "No of installed LPTs:         " & Format(lpt_number)
    Label4.Caption = "Base address of LPT:    " & Format(P_address)
    dummy = Write_data_port(P_address, 0)
    dummy = write_control_port(P_address, 0)
End Sub
```

3.2 Software drivers for the RS232 experimental board

3.2.1 DOS TP6 software driver RS232EXP.PAS

The functions of the driver are shown below:

- reports the number of the installed COM ports on your computer
- selects an RS232 port (COM)
- configures the serial data transmission format
- inputs a byte and transmits the serial data from TD
- changes status of modem control lines, DTR and RTS
- reads a serial data from RD
- reads status of modem status lines, DSR, DCD and CTS

After typing in the name of the program, path + RS232EXP, in the DOS prompt followed by a return, the following message appears:

```
Number of COM installed:  4
Addresses for COM1 to COM4: 1016  760  1000  744
Select a COM to be used (1,2,3 or 4):
```

The first line shows the number of COMs installed. The second line shows the base address of the installed COMs. The third line asks users to select an RS232 port. Once a COM number is typed in, a virtual control panel as shown in Figure 3.5 appears on the screen. There are seven virtual LEDs corresponding to the seven real LEDs on the RS232 experimental board. Three LEDs represent the three outputs of the RS232 port and four LEDs represent the four inputs. At the bottom of the screen a help window is provided to show functions of keys.

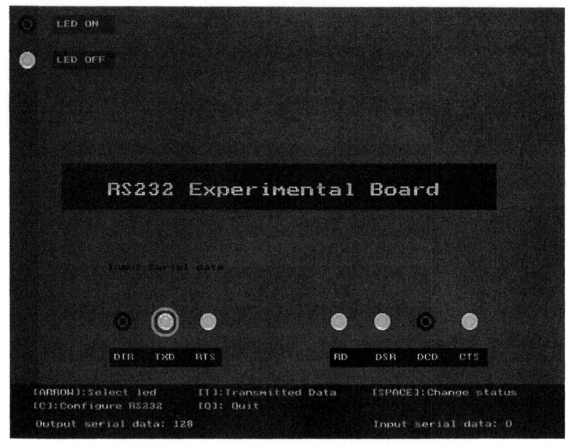

Figure 3.5 Turbo Pascal 6 virtual control panel for the RS232 experimental board

[ARROW KEYS]	left and right arrow keys to select an output
[T or t]	to input a data from the keybord and transmit the data from the TD line
[SPACE]	to change the status of the selected output line
[C or c]	to configure the serial data format
[Q or q]	to quit the program

By pressing the left or right arrow keys, an output line can be selected. A selected output is indicated by a circle around the LED. To change the status of the output, press the space. This has a toggle action. When an arrow key or the space is pressed, data at the inputs are read into the computer and shown on the screen. If the TD and RD lines are wired together, a loop test can be performed. The values of the output serial data and the input one should be the same.

TP6 program list of RS232EXP.PAS

```pascal
Program RS232_tester;
(* Software driver for the RS232 Experimental Board *)


uses

    graph,crt,dos;
var

    i,led_selected,Serial_input_byte, Baud_rate_byte,

    Data_length_byte, Stop_length_byte, Parity_byte :integer;

    Serial_output_string, Serial_input_string, Old_serial_input_string :string[5];

    ch:char;

    status:array[1..18] of integer;

    key_pressed:string[10];


(* to load two library files *)
{$I c:\ioexp\tplib2.pas}
{$I c:\ioexp\tplib1.pas}


procedure Draw_panel;
(* draw the control panel of the Centronic experimental board on the screen *)
begin
    for i:=1 to 16 do status[i]:=0;
    setbkcolor(cyan);
    for i:=1 to 3 do draw_led(80+i*50,  350, status[i]);
    for i:=4 to 7 do draw_led(180+i*50,  350, status[i]);
    draw_led(20,20,1);
    draw_message(50,20,70,20,lightblue,'LED ON',0,1,yellow);
    draw_led(20,60,0);
    draw_message(50,60,70,20,lightblue,'LED OFF',0,1,yellow);
    setfillstyle(1,magenta);
    bar(1,420,800,480);
    settextstyle(0,0,1);
    outtextxy(10,425,' [ARROW]:Select led      [T]:Transmitted Data      [SPACE]:Change status');
    outtextxy(10,440,' [C]:Configure RS232     [Q]: Quit');
    draw_message(60,200,500,50,blue,'   RS232 Experimental Board',0,2,yellow);
    draw_message(115,390,130,20,blue,'DTR    TXD    RTS ',0,1,yellow);
    draw_message(370,390,180,20,blue,'RD    DSR    DCD    CTS ',0,1,yellow);
end;


Procedure Output_Input;
var

    Output_byte, Input_byte:byte;
```

```
    code:integer;
begin
    (* to calculate the value of data to be sent to the Data port *)
    write_modem_status(RS232_address, status[3], status[1]);
    val (serial_output_string, output_byte, code);
    Status[5]:=read_modem_status(RS232_address,2);
    Status[6]:=read_modem_status(RS232_address,1);
    Status[7]:=read_modem_status(RS232_address,3);
    if status[2]=1 then
      begin
            repeat
                write_transmit_buffer(RS232_address, output_byte);
            until keypressed;
            status[2]:=0;
      end;
    delay(50);
    serial_input_byte:=read_receive_buffer(RS232_address);
    setcolor(magenta);
    outtextxy(420,460, 'Input serial data: '+ Old_serial_input_string);
    setcolor(yellow);
    str(serial_input_byte, serial_input_string);
    outtextxy(420,460, 'Input serial data: ' + serial_input_string);
    old_serial_input_string:=serial_input_string;
    setbkcolor(cyan);
end;


Procedure Scan_keyboard;
begin
    key_pressed:=getkey;
    if key_pressed='LEFT'  then led_selected:=led_selected-1;
    if key_pressed='RIGHT' then led_selected:=led_selected+1;
    if key_pressed=' ' then status[led_selected]:=1 - status[led_selected];
    if (key_pressed='T') or (key_pressed='t') then
    begin
        setcolor(magenta);
        outtextxy(30,460, 'Output serial data: ' + serial_output_string);
        draw_message(100,290,100,60,cyan,' Input Serial data ',0,1,yellow);
        gotoxy(22, 20); readln(Serial_output_string);
        draw_message(100,290,100,60,cyan,' Input Serial data ',0,1,blue);
        setcolor(yellow);
        outtextxy(30,460, 'Output serial data: ' + serial_output_string);
    end;
    if (key_pressed='C') or (key_pressed='c') then
    begin
```

```
                closegraph;
                Writeln('Configure RS232 port');
                Write('Input Baud Rate (115200-9600-4800-2400-1200): '); readln(Baud_rate_byte);
                Write('Input Parity (0=None, 1=Even, 3=Odd)        : '); readln(Parity_byte);
                Write('Input data bit length (5, 6, 7, 8)          : '); readln(Data_length_byte);
                Write('Input Stop bit length (2, 1)                : '); readln(stop_length_byte);
                write_data_format(RS232_address, Baud_rate_byte, Parity_byte, Data_length_byte, Stop_length_byte);
                initialize_graph;
                draw_panel;
                led_selected:=1;
            end;
    end;


procedure Draw_led_status;
var
        led_selected_old:integer;
begin
            led_selected_old:=led_selected;
            scan_keyboard;
            for i:=1 to 3 do draw_led(80+i*50,   350, status[i]);
            Output_input;


            for i:=4 to 7 do draw_led(180+i*50, 350, status[i]);

            if led_selected>3 then led_selected:=3;
            if led_selected<1 then  led_selected:=1;

            setlinestyle (0,0,3);
            setcolor(cyan);
            if led_selected_old<=3 then circle(80+50*led_selected_old, 350,15);
            setcolor(yellow);
            if led_selected<=3 then circle(80+50*led_selected, 350,15);
end;


(* Main program *)
begin
        COM_address;
        initialize_graph;
        draw_panel;
        led_selected:=1;
repeat
        draw_led_status;
```

```
until (key_pressed='Q') or (key_pressed='q');

    closegraph;      (* Close graphics mode *)
end.
```

The program contains four procedures. *Draw_panel* is used to draw the virtual panel of the experimental board on the screen. *Output_input* is a procedure for outputting and inputting data thought the RS232 port. *Write_moden_stauts(), write_transmit_buffer(), Read_modem_port()* and *Read_receiver_buffer()* are procedures or functions included in TPLIB1.PAS library. *Scan_keyboard* scans the keyboard. It detects six keystrokes: 'left', 'right', 'space', 't', 'c' and 'q' and carries out corresponding tasks.

3.2.2 Windows VB3 software driver

The driver provides the following functions:

- reports the number of the installed COM ports on your computer
- selects an RS232 port (COM)
- configures the serial data transmission format
- inputs a byte and transmits the serial data from TD
- changes status of modem control lines, DTR and RTS
- reads serial data from RD
- reads the status of modem status lines, DSR, DCD and CTS

Click the START button in Windows 95 and then select RUN. Next input the name of the software driver: path + RS232EXP. After clicking the OK button, the screen shown in Figure 3.6 appears. The screen reports the number of COMs installed on your computer and their base addresses. Click the OK button to clear the screen. Another screen appears (see Figure 3.7). It asks users to select a COM port to which the experimental board is connected. Type in the number of the COM port (1, 2, 3 or 4) and click the OK button. After this, the control panel of the experimental board appears on the screen (Figure 3.8). By clicking the '0-1' buttons of the DTR and RTS, the status of the corresponding line toggles. Logic high is indicated by a red LED. Users can input a serial data to be transmitted in the data field on the panel. If the button for the TD line is clicked, the data will be transmitted from the TD line continuously until the button is clicked again. Clicking 'Get it' updates the status of DSR, DCD and CTS inputs. The serial data received at RD is also shown on the screen. Users can re-select the COM port by clicking the 'Change Port' button and re-define the baud rate, parity, data bit length and the stop bit length. At the bottom of the control panel, there is an information window which displays the function of a control button when the pointer of the mouse moves over it.

A loop test can be carried out by connecting the TD and RD lines together. In this case the value of the input serial data should be the same as that of the output data. When the program outputs serial data, it will continuously transmit the data at the TD line. The waveform of the serial data transmission can be observed by using an oscilloscope. Users can output different values and change the baud rate, parity check and the data bit length. This can help users to understand serial data transmission.

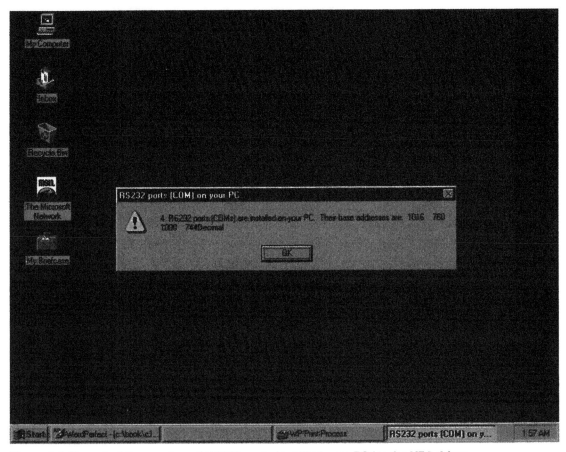

Figure 3.6 Report of the number of RS232 ports installed on a PC by the VB3 driver

VB3 program list of RS232EXP

```
'declare functions in DLL, WLIB1.DLL
'declared functions:    RS232(), Bit_weight(), Write_interrupt_enable()
'                       Read_interrupt_indentification()
'                       write_data_format(), write_transmit_buffer(), write_modem_status()
'                       write_receive_buffer(), read_modem_status()
Declare Function RS232 Lib "C:\Ioexp\Wlib1.dll" (ByVal X As Integer) As Integer
Declare Function Bit_weight Lib "C:\Ioexp\Wlib1.dll" (ByVal X As Integer) As Integer
Declare Function Write_interrupt_enable Lib "C:\Ioexp\Wlib1.dll" (ByVal address As Integer, ByVal datax As
Integer) As Integer
Declare Function Read_interrupt_indentification Lib "C:\Ioexp\Wlib1.dll" (ByVal address As Integer) As Integer
Declare Function write_data_format Lib "c:\IOEXP\Wlib1.dll" (ByVal address As Integer, ByVal Baud As Integer,
```

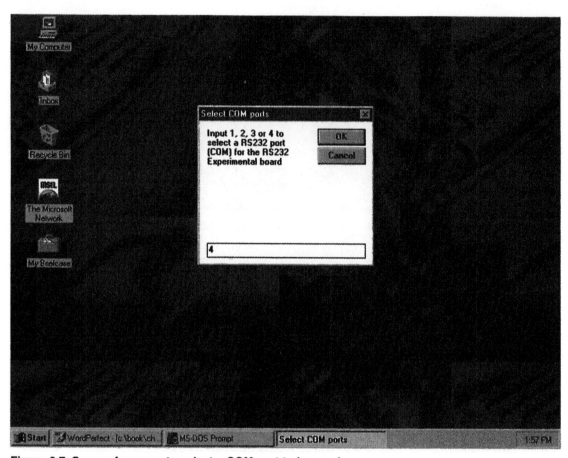

Figure 3.7 Screen for users to select a COM port to be used

```
ByVal parity As Integer, ByVal Data_byt As Integer, ByVal Stop_bit As Integer) As Integer
Declare Function Write_transmit_buffer Lib "C:\Ioexp\Wlib1.dll" (ByVal address As Integer, ByVal datax As
Integer) As Integer
Declare Function Write_modem_status Lib "C:\Ioexp\Wlib1.dll" (ByVal address As Integer, ByVal RTS As Integer,
ByVal DTR As Integer) As Integer
Declare Function Read_receive_buffer Lib "C:\Ioexp\Wlib1.dll" (ByVal address As Integer) As Integer
Declare Function Read_modem_status Lib "C:\Ioexp\Wlib1.dll" (ByVal address As Integer, ByVal X As Integer) As
Integer

Sub Command1_Click ()

    status(4) = Read_modem_status(RS232_address, 2)
    status(5) = Read_modem_status(RS232_address, 1)
    status(6) = Read_modem_status(RS232_address, 3)
```

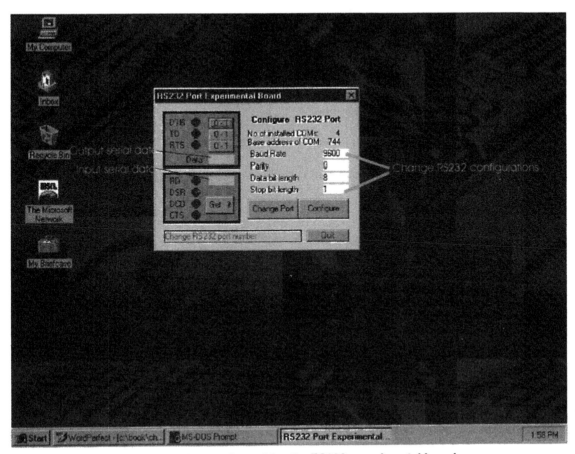

Figure 3.8 Visual Basic 3 virtual control panel for the RS232 experimental board

```
    For iq = 4 To 6
    If status(iq) = 1 Then Shapel(iq).BackColor = &HFF& Else Shapel(iq).BackColor = black
    Next iq

    Label3.Caption = Format$(Read_receive_buffer(RS232_address))
End Sub

Sub Command1_MouseMove (Button As Integer, Shift As Integer, X As Single, Y As Single)
    label7.Caption = "Get the status and read the serial data"
End Sub

Sub Command2_Click (index As Integer)
    'toggle the status of the output lines
    status(index) = 1 - status(index)
```

```
    If status(index) = 1 Then Shape1(index).BackColor = &HFF& Else Shape1(index).BackColor = black


    'output data to the Modem status register
    dummy = Write_modem_status(RS232_address, status(2), status(0))


    'updata the input lines
    status(4) = Read_modem_status(RS232_address, 2)
    status(5) = Read_modem_status(RS232_address, 1)
    status(6) = Read_modem_status(RS232_address, 3)
    For iq = 4 To 6
    If status(iq) = 1 Then Shape1(iq).BackColor = &HFF& Else Shape1(iq).BackColor = black
    Next iq


    'read and show the serial input data
    Label3.Caption = Format$(Read_receive_buffer(RS232_address))


    'output serial data
    If status(1) = 1 Then
        Do
        dummy = Write_transmit_buffer(RS232_address, Val(text1.Text))
        DoEvents
        Loop While status(1) = 1
    End If
End Sub


Sub Command2_MouseMove (index As Integer, Button As Integer, Shift As Integer, X As Single, Y As Single)
    'show the help information
    label7.Caption = "Change the status of the output line"
End Sub


Sub Command3_Click ()
    'configure the selected RS232 port
    baud_rate = Val(text2(0).Text) 'assign baud rate
    parity = Val(text2(1).Text) 'assign parity
    data_bit_length = Val(text2(2).Text)'assign length of data bits
    stop_bit_length = Val(text2(3).Text) 'assign length of stop bits
    dummy = write_data_format(RS232_address, baud_rate, parity, data_bit_length, stop_bit_length)'write the
configuration to the serial data format register
End Sub


Sub Command3_MouseMove (Button As Integer, Shift As Integer, X As Single, Y As Single)
    label7.Caption = "Change the configuration of RS232 port"
End Sub
```

```
Sub Command4_Click ()
    End
End Sub


Sub Command4_MouseMove (Button As Integer, Shift As Integer, X As Single, Y As Single)
    label7.Caption = "Quit the program"
End Sub


Sub Command5_Click ()
    're-select the RS232 port
    dummy = MsgBox(Str(RS232(0)) & "  RS232 ports (COMs) are installed on your PC.  Their base addresses are:
" & Format$(RS232(1), "###") & "      " & Format$(RS232(2), "###") & "      " & Format$(RS232(3), "###") & "      "
& Format$(RS232(4), "###") & "Decimal", 48, "RS232 ports (COM) on your PC") 'show RS232 information
    RS232_number = Val(InputBox$("Input 1, 2, 3 or 4 to select a RS232 port (COM) for the Mini-Lab Data
Logger/ Controller", "Select COM ports")) 'select a RS232 port
    RS232_address = RS232(RS232_number) 'get the base address of the selected COM port
    Label2.Caption = "Selected  COM port :        " & Format(RS232_number) 'show information of the selected
port
    Label4.Caption = "Base address of COM:    " & Format(RS232_address)
End Sub


Sub Command5_MouseMove (Button As Integer, Shift As Integer, X As Single, Y As Single)
    label7.Caption = "Change RS232 port number"
End Sub


Sub Form_Load ()
    For i = 0 To 11
        status(i) = 0
    Next i

    dummy = MsgBox(Str(RS232(0)) & "  RS232 ports (COMs) are installed on your PC.  Their base addresses are:
" & Format$(RS232(1), "###") & "      " & Format$(RS232(2), "###") & "      " & Format$(RS232(3), "###") & "      "
& Format$(RS232(4), "###") & "Decimal", 48, "RS232 ports (COM) on your PC")
    RS232_number = Val(InputBox$("Input 1, 2, 3 or 4 to select a RS232 port (COM) for the RS232 Experimental
board", "Select COM ports"))

    RS232_address = RS232(RS232_number)
    Label2.Caption = "No of installed COMs:        " & Format(RS232_number)
    Label4.Caption = "Base address of COM:    " & Format(RS232_address)
    baud_rate = 9600
    parity = 0
    data_bit_length = 8
    stop_bit_length = 1
```

```
        text2(0).Text = Format$(baud_rate)

        text2(1).Text = Format$(parity)

        text2(2).Text = Format$(data_bit_length)

        text2(3).Text = Format$(stop_bit_length)


        dummy = write_data_format(RS232_address, baud_rate, parity, data_bit_length, stop_bit_length)


End Sub


Sub Label3_MouseMove (Button As Integer, Shift As Integer, X As Single, Y As Single)
        'show the received serial data
        label7.Caption = "Value of the serial input data"
End Sub


Sub Label6_MouseMove (index As Integer, Button As Integer, Shift As Integer, X As Single, Y As Single)
        Select Case index
        Case 0
        label7.Caption = "Baud rate = 115200, 19200, 9600, 2400, etc."
        Case 1
        label7.Caption = "0 = No Parity, 1 = Odd Parity, 3 = Even Parity"
        Case 2
        label7.Caption = "Input 5, 6,7 or 8 to select the data bit length"
        Case 3
        label7.Caption = "Input 1 or 2 to select Stop bit"
        End Select
End Sub


Sub Text1_MouseMove (Button As Integer, Shift As Integer, X As Single, Y As Single)
        'allow users to input the serial data to be transmitted
        label7.Caption = "Input the serial data to be sent out"
End Sub


Sub Text2_Change (index As Integer)
        Select Case index
        Case 0:
        Case 1:
        Case 2:
        Case 3:
        End Select
End Sub
```

3.3 Software drivers for the game port experimental board

3.3.1 DOS TP6 software driver GAMEEXP.PAS

The functions of the software driver include:

- reading the status of two (or four) digital inputs
- measuring the period of the multivibrators for two (or four) resistance channels
- calibrating resistance channels
- measuring resistance of a resistor

After typing in the name of the program, path + GAMEEXP, under the DOS prompt followed by a return, a control panel as shown in Figure 3.9 appears on the screen. There are four virtual LEDs and eight virtual terminals corresponding to the four real LEDs and eight terminals on the game port experimental board. At the bottom of the screen there is a help window to show the functions of keys.

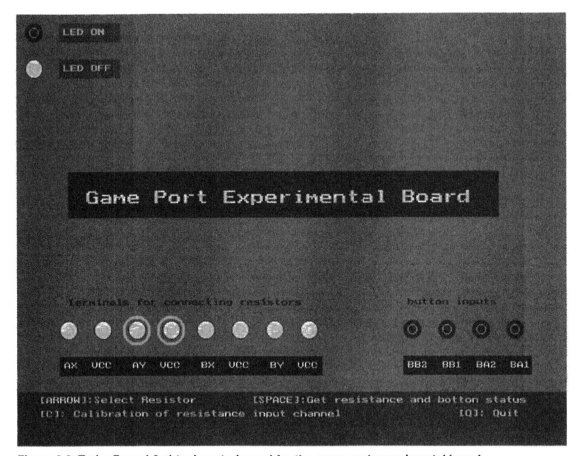

Figure 3.9 Turbo Pascal 6 virtual control panel for the game port experimental board

[ARROW KEYS]	left and right arrow keys to select a resistance channel
[SPACE]	to read resistance value of the selected channel and the status of the inputs
[C or c]	to calibrate the selected resistance input channel
[Q or q]	to quit the program

By pressing left or right arrow keys, a resistance input channel can be selected. The selected channel is indicated by two circles around the virtual terminals on the panel. After connecting a resistor to the terminals and pressing the space, the time period of the multivibrator is displayed. If that channel has been calibrated, the resistance of the resistor is also displayed. Calibration of a channel is carried out by pressing 'c'. During the calibration, users are asked to short the input terminals first and then to connect a resistor of a known resistance to the terminals. After calibration, the resistance of any resistors can be measured. The data present at the digital inputs is also read into the computer. The bit status of the data is indicated by the virtual LEDs.

TP6 program list of GAMEEXP.PAS

```
Program Game_tester;
(* Software driver for the Game Experimental Board *)
uses
     graph,crt,dos;
Const
     Game_address=513;
var
   i,led_selected,Time1, Time2 :integer;
   ch:char;
   status:array[1..18] of integer;
   period:real;
   Interval_0, Interval_R, Standard_R: array[1..4] of real;
   key_pressed:string[10];
   strx:string;


(* to load library files *)
{$I c:\ioexp\tplib2.pas}
{$I c:\ioexp\tplib1.pas}


Function Resistance(period:real; led_selected:integer):real;
(* calculate resistance knowing the period *)
(* a calibration is needed *)
var
   dummy, dummy2:real;
begin
     dummy2:=(Interval_R[led_selected] - Interval_0[led_selected]);
     if abs(dummy2)<0.0001 then dummy2:=1;
     dummy:=Standard_R[led_selected]/dummy2
                 *(period - Interval_0[led_selected]);
```

```
         if abs(dummy)>200 then resistance:=200 else resistance:=dummy;
end;


procedure Draw_panel;
(* draw the control panel of the Centronic experimental board on the screen *)
begin
       for i:=1 to 16 do status[i]:=0;
       setbkcolor(cyan);
       for i:=1 to 8 do draw_led(20+i*40,  350, status[i]);
       for i:=1 to 4 do draw_led(420+i*40,  350, status[i+8]);
       draw_led(20,20,1);
       draw_message(50,20,70,20,lightblue,'LED ON',0,1,yellow);
       draw_led(20,60,0);
       draw_message(50,60,70,20,lightblue,'LED OFF',0,1,yellow);
       setfillstyle(1,magenta);
       bar(1,420,800,480);
       settextstyle(0,0,1);
       outtextxy(10,425,' [ARROW]:Select Resistor          [SPACE]:Get resistance and botton status');
       outtextxy(10,440,' [C]: Calibration of resistance input channel             [Q]: Quit');
       draw_message(60,200,500,50,blue,' Game Port Experimental Board',0,2,yellow);
       draw_message(50,390,305,20,blue,'AX  VCC   AY  VCC   BX  VCC   BY  VCC',0,1,yellow);
       draw_message(450,390,149,20,blue,'BB2  BB1  BA2  BA1',0,1,yellow);
       draw_message(55,320,280,20,cyan,'Terminals for connecting resistors',0,1, red);
       draw_message(450,320,120,20,cyan,'button inputs',0,1,red);
end;



Procedure Output_Input;
var
   Output_byte, Input_byte:byte;


begin
       (* read the botton status *)
       Status[9]:=read_game_port(8);
       Status[10]:=read_game_port(7);
       Status[11]:=read_game_port(6);
       Status[12]:=read_game_port(5);
end;


Procedure Scan_keyboard;
begin
       key_pressed:=getkey;
       if key_pressed='LEFT'  then led_selected:=led_selected-1;
       if key_pressed='RIGHT' then led_selected:=led_selected+1;
```

```
    if key_pressed=' ' then
      begin
        period:=interval_game_port(led_selected);
        str(period*0.838:10:2, strx);
        draw_message(25,460,250,10,magenta, 'Interval [us]: '+strx,0,1,lightcyan);
        str(resistance(period,led_selected):10:2, strx);
        draw_message(370,460,250,10,magenta, 'Resistance [kOhm]: '+strx,0,1,lightcyan);
      end;
    if (key_pressed='C') or (key_pressed='c') then
      begin
          closegraph;
          clrscr;
          writeln('Calibration of resistance input channels   CH ',led_selected:4);
          writeln('Short the input terminal for the selected channel');
          writeln('Press RETURN to continue');
          readln;
          interval_0[led_selected]:=interval_game_port(led_selected);
          Writeln('Connect the standard resistor to the selected channel');
          write('Input the resistance of the resistor: ');readln(Standard_R[led_selected]);
          interval_R[led_selected]:=interval_game_port(led_selected);
          initialize_graph;
          draw_panel;
      end;
end;


procedure Draw_led_status;
var
    led_selected_old:integer;
begin
    led_selected_old:=led_selected;
    scan_keyboard;
    Output_input;
    for i:=1 to 4 do draw_led(420+i*40,  350, status[i+8]);

    if led_selected>4 then led_selected:=4;
    if led_selected<1 then  led_selected:=1;

    setlinestyle (0,0,3);
    setcolor(cyan);
    if led_selected_old<=4 then
    begin
        circle(-20+80*led_selected_old, 350,15);
        circle(-20+80*(led_selected_old)+40, 350,15);
    end;
```

```
        setcolor(yellow);

        if led_selected<=4 then

        begin

                circle(-20+80*led_selected, 350,15);

                circle(-20+80*(led_selected)+40, 350,15);

        end;

end;


(* Main program *)

begin

        initialize_graph;

        draw_panel;

        init_8253;

        led_selected:=1;

repeat

            draw_led_status

until (key_pressed='Q') or (key_pressed='q');

        closegraph;     (* Close graphics mode *)


end.
```

The program contains four procedures and one function. Procedures and functions in the programming resource libraries are also used. *Draw_panel* draws the virtual panel of the experimental board on the screen. *Draw_led()* and *Draw_message()* are two procedures in the library TPLIB2.PAS. *Output_input* is a procedure for inputting data through the game port. *Scan_keyboard* scans the keyboard. It detects five keystrokes: 'left', 'right', 'space', 'c' and 'q' and carries out corresponding tasks. It uses the *getkey* function in the library TPLIB2.PAS. *Read_game_port()* and *Interval_game_port* are from the TPLIB1.PAS programming resource library. *Function Resistance()* calculates the resistance value using the calibration parameters which are obtained during the calibration.

3.3.2 Windows VB3 software driver

The VB3 software driver provides the following functions:

● inputing the status of two (or four) digital inputs
● measuring the period of the multivibrators for two (or four) resistance channels
● calibrating each resistance channel
● measuring resistance of a resistor

Click the START button and then select RUN. Next input the name of the software driver, path + GAMEEXP. After clicking the OK button, the control panel for the game port experimental board appears on the screen (see Figure 3.10). The functions of this software are similar to those of the DOS version.

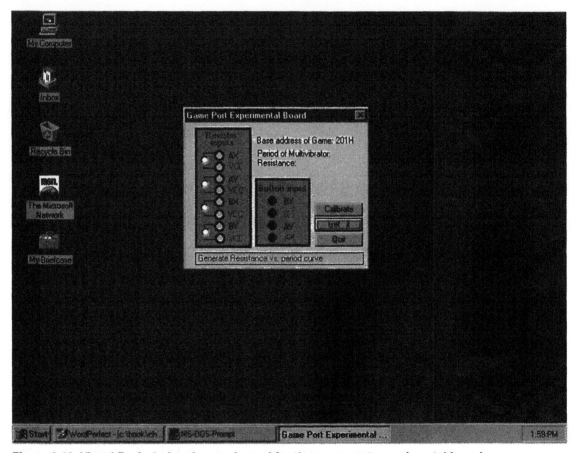

Figure 3.10 Visual Basic 3 virtual control panel for the game port experimental board

VB3 program list of GAMEEXP

```
Declare Function Bit_weight Lib "C:\Ioexp\Wlibl.dll" (ByVal X As Integer) As Integer

Declare Function read_game_port Lib "C:\Ioexp\Wlibl.dll" (ByVal X As Integer) As Integer

Declare Function Write_game_port Lib "c:\Ioexp\Wlibl.dll" () As Integer

Declare Function Interval_game_port Lib "c:\Ioexp\Wlibl.dll" (ByVal led_selected As Integer) As Integer


Sub Command1_Click ()
    DoEvents
    For i = 12 To 15
    status(i) = read_game_port(20 - i)
    If status(i) = 1 Then Shape1(i).BackColor = &HFF& Else Shape1(i).BackColor = black
    Next i
    DoEvents
```

```
    period = Interval_game_port(led_selected) * .838
    If period <> 0 Then
    Label2.Caption = "Period of Multivibrator: " & Format(period, "#####.#")
    Else
    Label2.Caption = "Error reading Multivibrator"
    End If


    Label5.Caption = "Resistance: " & Format(resistance(period), "###.#")
End Sub


Sub Command1_MouseMove (Button As Integer, Shift As Integer, X As Single, Y As Single)
    label16.Caption = " Get button status and period of multivibrators"
End Sub


Sub Command2_Click (index As Integer)

    status(index) = 1 - status(index)
    If status(index) = 1 Then Shape1(index).BackColor = &HFF& Else Shape1(index).BackColor = black


    For i = 12 To 15
    status(i) = (read_game_port(i - 11) And Bit_weight(i - 11)) / Bit_weight(i - 11)
    If status(i) = 1 Then Shape1(i).BackColor = &HFF& Else Shape1(i).BackColor = black
    Next i
End Sub


Sub Command3_Click ()
    MsgBox ("Short the terminals of the selected resistance input. The selected channel is " & led_selected)
    interval_0(led_selected) = Interval_game_port(led_selected) * .838
    MsgBox ("Connect a standard resistor to the selected resistance input. The selected channel is " &
led_selected)
    Standard_r(led_selected) = InputBox("Input the Resistance: ", "Calibration of resistance input", "1")
    interval_R(led_selected) = Interval_game_port(led_selected) * .838
End Sub


Sub Command3_MouseMove (Button As Integer, Shift As Integer, X As Single, Y As Single)
    label16.Caption = " Generate Resistance vs. period curve"
End Sub


Sub Command4_Click ()
    End
End Sub


Sub Command4_MouseDown (Button As Integer, Shift As Integer, X As Single, Y As Single)
    label16.Caption = " Quit the program"
```

```
End Sub


Sub Form_Load ()
    For i = 0 To 16
        status(i) = 0
    Next i


End Sub


Sub Option1_Click (index As Integer)
    led_selected = index + 1
End Sub


Sub Option1_MouseMove (index As Integer, Button As Integer, Shift As Integer, X As Single, Y As Single)
    label16.Caption = " Select No." & index + 1 & " resistance input channel"
End Sub


Function resistance (ByVal period As Single) As Single
    dummy2 = (interval_R(led_selected) - interval_0(led_selected))
    If Abs(dummy2) < .001 Then dummy2 = 1
    dummy = Standard_r(led_selected) / dummy2 * (period - interval_0(led_selected))
    If Abs(dummy) > 200 Then resistance = 200 Else resistance = dummy
End Function
```

3.4 Programming resource libraries

The program lists of the resource libraries, TPLIB1.PAS and TPLIB2.PAS for DOS TP6, and WLIB.PAS (Windows DLLs) are shown below. Detailed explanations of the procedures and functions are given within the program lists.

TP6 Programming Resource Library-1, TPLIB1.PAS

```
(* Turbo Pascal 6 Programing Resource Library 1 *)
(* Library name: TPLIB1.PAS *)
(* Procedures for controlling the Centronic, RS232 and Game port *)
(* This library can be included in user's program *)


Var
    P_address, RS232_address:integer;

(* ——Resource Library No. A1 (Detection of LPT base addresses)—— *)
Procedure Centronic_address;
(* $000:$0408 holds the printer base address for LPT1
```

```
    $000:$040A holds the printer base address for LPT2
    $000:$040C holds the printer base address for LPT3
    $000:$040e holds the printer base address for LPT4
    $000:$0411 number of parallel interfaces in binary format *)
var
    lpt:array[1..4] of integer;
    number_of_lpt,LPT_number,code:integer;
    kbchar:char;
begin
    clrscr;
    LPT_number:=1;                         (* to set default printer *)
    number_of_lpt:=mem[$0000:$0411];  (* to read number of installed Centronic ports *)
    number_of_lpt:=(number_of_lpt and (128+64)) shr 6;  (* Bit manipulation *)
    lpt[1]:=memw[$0000:$0408];         (* Memory read procedure *)
    lpt[2]:=memw[$0000:$040A];
    lpt[3]:=memw[$0000:$040C];
    lpt[4]:=memw[$0000:$040E];
    textbackground(blue); clrscr;
    textcolor(yellow); textbackground(red); window(10,22,70,24); clrscr;
    writeln('Number of LPT installed    :  ',number_of_lpt:2);
    writeln('Addresses for LPT1 to LPT 4:  ',lpt[1]:3,'   ', lpt[2]:3,'   ', lpt[3]:3,'   ', lpt[4]:3);
    write('Select LPT to be used (1,2,3,4)    :  ');
    delay(1000);
    if number_of_lpt>1 then begin    {select LPT1 through LPT4 if more than 1 LPT installed}
       repeat
          kbchar:=readkey;                  (* read input key *)
          val(kbchar, LPT_number, code);  (* change character to value *)
       until (LPT_number>=1) and (LPT_number<=4) and (lpt[LPT_number]<>0);
                             end;
    clrscr;
    P_address:=lpt[LPT_number];
    writeln('Your selected printer interface:  LPT',LPT_number:1);
    write('LPT  Address                :  ',RS232_address:3);
    delay(1000);
    textbackground(black); window(1,1,80,25); clrscr;
end;


(* ----Resource Library No. A2 (Find bit weight for a bit)---- *)
Function bit_weight(bit:byte):byte;
var
    i,dummy:integer;
begin
    if bit=1 then bit_weight:=1
```

```
            else begin
                dummy:=1;
                for i:=1 to bit-1 do dummy:=2*dummy;
                if dummy=0 then dummy:=1;
                bit_weight:=dummy;
                end;
end;


(* ──Resource Library No. A3 (Read data into pc)── *)
Function Read_status_port(P_address:integer):byte;
var
   byte1:byte;
begin
        byte1:=port[P_address+1];           (* read a byte from the status port *)
        byte1:=byte1 and 120;               (* 01111000 (MSB to LSB) and 0dddd... = 0dddd000 *)
        Read_status_port:=byte1 shr 3;      (* shift 3 bit right, Read_status_port = 0000hhhh *)
end;


(* ──Resource Library No. A4 (Write data to DATA port of pc)── *)
Procedure Write_data_port(P_address:integer; port_data:byte);
(* no lines in the Data port are not inverted *)
begin
        port[P_address]:=port_data;     (* output a byte to the data port *)
end;


(* ──Resource Library No. A5 (Write data to CONTROL port of pc)── *)
Procedure Write_control_port(P_address:integer; port_data:byte);
(* Bit 0, Bit 1 and Bit 3 are inverted. Bit manipulation is required *)
begin
        if port_data and 1 =1 then port_data:=port_data and (255-1)
           else port_data:=port_data or 1;
        if port_data and 2 =2 then port_data:=port_data and (255-2)
           else port_data:=port_data or 2;
        if port_data and 8 =8 then port_data:=port_data and (255-8)
           else port_data:=port_data or 8;
        port[P_address+2]:=port_data;  (* output a byte to the control port *)
end;


(* ──Resource Library No. A6 (detection of COM base address)── *)
Procedure COM_address;
```

```
(* $0000:$0400 holds the printer base address for COM1

   $0000:$0402 holds the printer base address for COM2

   $0000:$0404 holds the printer base address for COM3

   $0000:$0406 holds the printer base address for COM4

   $0000:$0411 number of parallel interfaces in binary format *)
var
    COM:array[1..4] of integer;

    COM_number, number_of_com, code: integer;

    kbchar:char;
begin
      clrscr;

      COM_number:=1; (*default printer *)

      number_of_COM:=mem[$0000:$0411]; (* read number of parallel ports *)

      number_of_COM:=(number_of_COM and (8+4+2)) shr 1;

      COM[1]:=memw[$0000:$0400];          (* Memory read procedure *)

      COM[2]:=memw[$0000:$0402];

      COM[3]:=memw[$0000:$0404];

      COM[4]:=memw[$0000:$0406];

      textbackground(blue); clrscr;

      textcolor(yellow); textbackground(red); window(10,22,70,24); clrscr;

      writeln('Number of COM installed    : ',number_of_COM:2);

      writeln('Addresses for COM1 to COM4: ',COM[1]:3,'   ', COM[2]:3,'   ', COM[3]:3,'   ', COM[4]:3);

      write('Select COM to be used (1,2,3,4)    : ');

      delay(1000);

      if number_of_COM>1 then begin    (* select COM1 through COM4 if more than 1 LPT installed *)

        repeat

            kbchar:=readkey;                 (* read input key *)

            val(kbchar, COM_number, code);   (* change character to value *)

        until (COM_number>=1) and (COM_number<=4) and (COM[COM_number]<>0);

                                end;

      clrscr;

      RS232_address:=COM[COM_number];

      writeln('Your selected RS232 interface:  COM',COM_number:1);

      write('RS232   Address                 : ',RS232_address:4);

      delay(1000);

      textbackground(black); window(1,1,80,25); clrscr;

end;



(* ——Resource Library No. A7 (to write to the interrupt enable register)—— *)
Procedure Write_interrupt_enable(RS232_address, Output_byte: integer);
begin
      Port[RS232_address+1]:=Output_byte;
end;
```

```
(* ----Resource Library No. A8 (to read from the interrupt identification register)--- *)
Function Read_interrupt_identification(RS232_address:integer):integer;
begin
      Read_interrupt_identification:=Port[RS232_address+2]
end;
```

```
(* ----Resource Library No. A9 (write to data serialization register)--- *)
Procedure Write_data_format(RS232_address, Baud, Parity, Data_bit, Stop_bit:integer);
var
      byte1, byte2, output_byte: byte;
         divisor: integer;
begin
         divisor:=115200 div Baud;
         if divisor<=255 then begin byte1:=divisor; byte2:=0 end;
         if divisor>255 then begin byte2:=divisor div 256; byte1:=divisor mod 256; end;
         output_byte:=(data_bit-5) + 4*(stop_bit-1) + 8*(parity);
      port[RS232_address+3]:=128;{Loading serial data format, first bit of the register is 1}
         port[RS232_address+0]:=Byte1;         {LSB of the divisor is 1}
         port[RS232_address+1]:=Byte2;         {MSB of the divisor is 0}
         port[RS232_address+3]:=output_byte;   {Load divisor and other parameters}
end;
```

```
(* ----Resource Library No. A10 (to write to the transmit buffer register)--- *)
Procedure write_transmit_buffer(RS232_address, Output_byte: integer);
begin
      port[RS232_address]:=Output_byte;
end;
```

```
(* ----Resource Library No. A11 (to write to the modem status register)--- *)
Procedure Write_modem_status(RS232_address, RTS, DTR:integer);
(* RTS and DTR = 0 or 1, RTS and DRT are inverted by MAX238 on the experimental board *)
(* RTS=bit 1, DTR=bit 0 of Modem control register, offset 04 *)
begin
      RTS:=1-RTS;
      DTR:=1-DTR;
      Port[RS232_address+4]:=RTS*2 + DTR  (* to output to the register 04 *)
end;
```

```
(* ——Resource Library No. A12 (to read data from receive buffer register)—— *)
Function Read_receive_buffer(RS232_address:integer):integer;
begin
     Read_receive_buffer:=port[RS232_address];
end;
```

```
(* ——Resource Library No. A13 (to read modem status register)—— *)
Function Read_modem_status(RS232_address, x:integer):integer;
(* X=1 select DCD bit, x=2 select DSR bit, x=3 select CTS bit *)
(* DCD=bit 7, DSR=bit 5, CTS=bit 4 of Modem status register, offset 06h *)
(* All bits are inverted by the Max238 on the experimental board *)
var
    input_byte:byte;
begin
     input_byte:=port[RS232_address+6];
     case x of
     1:    Read_modem_status:=1-round((input_byte and 128)/128);
     2:    Read_modem_status:=1-round((input_byte and 32)/32);
     3:    Read_modem_status:=1-round((input_byte and 16)/16);
     end;
end;
```

```
(* ——Resource Library No. A14 (to read Game port register)—— *)
Function Read_Game_port(Bitx:integer):integer;
(* Game port address: 201H
   X (1 to 8) selects status of AX, AY, BX, BY, BA1, BA2, BB1 and BB2 *)
var
    input_byte:byte;
begin
     input_byte:=port[$201];
     Read_game_port:=round((input_byte and bit_weight(bitx))/bit_weight(bitx));
end;
```

```
(* ——Resource Library No. A15 (to write to Game port register)—— *)
Procedure Write_Game_port;
(* output byte 0 to the game port to start the multi-vibrators *)
begin
     port[$201]:=0;
end;
```

```
(* ——Resource Library No. A16 (to get time interval of the multivibrator after one shot)—— *)
Function Interval_Game_port(x:integer):integer;
```

```
(* x selects AX (x=1), AY (x=2), BX (x=3), BY (x=4) *)
var
    Time1, Time2, dummy: integer;


Procedure init_8253;
(* Initialize 8253 *)
begin
(*  Control word= b6H = 10110111b
        10  = select counter 2
        11  = read/write low count byte first then high byte
        011 = mode 3
        0   = binary counting with 16-bit *)
        Port[$43]:=$b6; (* load control word to the control register of 8253 *)
        Port[$42]:=255; (* load low count byte *)
        port[$42]:=255; (* load high count byte *)
        port[$61]:=port[$61] or 1; (* disable speaker *)
        port[$43]:=$80; (* 80H is the counter latch command for counter 3 *)
end;


Function read_8253:integer;
(* read low order and high order bytes of the counters *)
var
    low_byte, high_byte:byte;
begin
        low_byte:=port[$42];
        high_byte:=port[$42];
        read_8253:=low_byte + 256* high_byte;
end;


Var
        i:integer;
begin
        init_8253;
        for i:=1 to 100 do i:=i;
        i:=0;
        dummy:=bit_weight(x);
        port[$201]:=0;
        Time1:=read_8253;
        repeat i:=i+1 until (port[$201] and dummy=0) or (i>=5000);
        Time2:=read_8253;
        Interval_game_port:=time1-time2;
        if i>=5000 then Interval_game_port:=0;
end;
```

TP6 Programming Resource Library-2, TPLIB2.PAS

```
(* Turbo Pascal Program Resource Library 2 *)
(* Library name: TPLIB0.PAS *)
(* graphics and read keyboard procedures*)
(* This library can be included in user's program *)
.
(* ----Resource Library No. 01 (initialize graph mode)---- *)
Procedure initialize_graph;
var
  Gd, Gm: Integer;
  Radius: Integer;
begin
  Gd := Detect; InitGraph(Gd, Gm, '');
end;


(* ----Resource Library No. 02 (draw a led on the screen)---- *)
Procedure draw_led(x,y: integer; status:byte);
(* x, y = centre position. status = ON or OFF *)
begin
     setcolor(red);
     setlinestyle(1,1,2);
     if status=1 then setfillstyle(1,red)
        else
            begin
                 setcolor(white);
                 setfillstyle(1,white);
            end;
     pieslice(x,y,0,360,10);
     setcolor(magenta);
     circle(x,y,10);
     setcolor(yellow);
     circle(x,y,5);
end;


(* ----Resource Library No. 03 (draw a text box and show message)---- *)
procedure draw_message(x1,y1,width,height,color_box:integer; message:string; font, size_text,
color_text:integer);
(* x1,y1 = left side position
   Width, height = width and height of the text box
   Color_box = color of the text box
   Message= message to be shown on the screen
   Font, size_text, color_text = font, size and color of the text *)
begin
     setfillstyle(1,color_box);
```

```
        bar(x1,y1-round(height/2),x1+width,y1+round(height/2));
        setcolor(color_text);
        settextstyle(font,0,size_text);
        outtextxy(x1+5,y1-4,message);
end;


(* ---Resource Library No. 04 (read some keystrokes)--- *)
Function getkey:string;
var
    ch:char;
begin
        ch:=readkey;  (* to read a character from the keyboard *)
        if ch=#0 then (* if an extended character is keyed, start the following procedures *)
        begin
            ch:=readkey; (* to read keyboard again to get the key code of the extended key *)
            if ch=#72 then getkey:='UP'    (* UP arrow =      #72 *);
            if ch=#80 then getkey:='DOWN'  (* DOWN arrow =    #80 *);
            if ch=#75 then getkey:='LEFT'  (* LEFT arrow =    #75 *);
            if ch=#77 then getkey:='RIGHT' (* RIGHT arrow =   #77 *);
            if ch=#82 then getkey:='INSERT'(* INSERT arrow = #82 *);
            if ch=#83 then getkey:='DELETE'(* DELETE arrow = #83 *);
            if ch=#71 then getkey:='HOME'  (* HOME arrow =    #71 *);
            if ch=#79 then getkey:='END'   (* END arrow =     #79 *);
            if ch=#71 then getkey:='HOME'  (* HOME arrow =    #71 *);
            if ch=#79 then getkey:='END'   (* END arrow =     #79 *);
        end
            else
                (* the pressed key is not an extended key *)
                begin
                    if ch=#13 then getkey:= 'RETURN'
                        else if (ch=#8) or (ch=#127) then getkey:='BACKSPACE'
                        else getkey:=ch;
                end;
end;


Procedure init_8253;
begin
(*  Control word= b6H = 10110111b
     10  = select counter 2
     11  = read/write low count byte first then high byte
     011 = mode 3
     0   = binary counting with 16-bit *)
     Port[$43]:=$b6; (* load control word to the control register of 8253 *)
     Port[$42]:=255; (* load low count byte *)
```

```
        port[$42]:=255; (* load high count byte *)

        port[$61]:=port[$61] or 1; (* disable speaker *)

        port[$43]:=$80; (* 80H is the counter latch command for counter 3 *)

end;


Function read_8253:integer;

var

    low_byte, high_byte:byte;

begin

        low_byte:=port[$42];

        high_byte:=port[$42];

        read_8253:=low_byte + 256* high_byte;

end;


Function find_period(Address:integer; Bit_weight:integer):real;

(* find the period of an input digital signal.

    Input signal is specified by Input port address (Address) and bit.

    Bit 0, Bit_weight=1

    Bit 1, Bit_weight=2

    .....

    Bit 7, Bit_weight=128 *)

var

    count, Average_number,time1,time2:integer;

begin

        (* Testing the period of low state of a digital signal. This will be used

        for calculating Average_number *)

        repeat until port[Address] and Bit_weight=Bit_weight; (* signal state high *)

        repeat until port[Address] and Bit_weight=0;          (* signal state low *)

        time1:=read_8253;                                  (* read counts in 8253 first time*)

        repeat until port[Address] and Bit_weight=Bit_weight; (* signal state high again *)

        time2:=read_8253;                                  (* read counts in 8253 the second time *)

        Average_number:=round(10000/(Time1-Time2));        (* find Average_number *)

        if Average_number=0 then Average_number:=1;

        repeat until port[Address] and Bit_weight=Bit_weight; (* signal state high *)

        repeat until port[Address] and Bit_weight=0;          (* signal state low *)

        time1:=read_8253;                                  (* read counts in 8253 first time *)

        for count:=1 to Average_number do                  (* find low going edge of a digital signal *)

        begin

        repeat until port[Address] and Bit_weight=Bit_weight;  (* signal state high *)

        repeat until port[Address] and Bit_weight=0;           (* signal state low *)

        end;

        Time2:=read_8253;                                  (* read counts in 8253 the second time *)

        Find_period:=((Time1-time2)*1/(2*1193180)*1e6/Average_number);

end;
```

Windows Programming Resource Library, WLIB.PAS

```
(* Windows Programming Resource Library A *)
(* Input and Output procedures for the Centronic port, RS232 and Game ports *)


Library libA;

uses
     Wincrt;


(* ----Windows Resource Library No. A1 (Detection of LPT base address)---- *)
Function Centronic(x:integer):integer; export;
(* $000:$0408 holds the printer base address for LPT1
   $000:$040A holds the printer base address for LPT2
   $000:$040C holds the printer base address for LPT3
   $000:$040e holds the printer base address for LPT4
   $000:$0411 number of parallel interfaces in binary format *)
var
     number_of_LPT, LPT1, LPT2, LPT3, LPT4 :integer;
begin
     number_of_LPT:=mem[$40:$11];                      (* read number of parallel ports *)
     number_of_LPT:=(number_of_lpt and (128+64)) shr 6;
     lpt1:=0; lpt2:=0; lpt3:=0; lpt4:=0;
     LPT1:=memw[$40:$08];                              (* Memory read procedure *)
     LPT2:=memw[$40:$0A];
     LPT3:=memw[$40:$0C];
     LPT4:=memw[$40:$0E];
     case x of
        0:   centronic:=number_of_LPT;
        1:   centronic:=lpt1;
        2:   centronic:=lpt2;
        3:   centronic:=lpt3;
        4:   centronic:=lpt4
     end;
end;




(* ----Windows Resource Library No. A2 (Find bit weight for a bit)---- *)
Function bit_weight(bit:integer):integer; export;
var
   i,dummy:integer;
begin
     if bit=1 then bit_weight:=1
        else begin
```

```
                dummy:=1;
                for i:=1 to bit-1 do dummy:=2*dummy;
                bit_weight:=dummy;
                end;

end;


(* ——Windows Resource Library No. A3 (Read data into pc)—— *)
Function Read_status_port(P_address:integer):integer; export;
var
   byte1:byte;
begin
        byte1:=port[P_address+1];        (* read a byte from the status port *)
        byte1:=byte1 and 120;            (* 01111000 (MSB to LSB) and 0dddd... = 0dddd000 *)
        Read_status_port:=byte1 shr 3;   (* shift 3 bit right, Read_status_port = 0000hhhh *)
end;


(* ——Resource Library No. A4 (Write data to DATA port of pc)—— *)
Function Write_data_port(P_address:integer; port_data:integer):integer; export;
(* no lines in the Data port are not inverted *)
begin
        port[P_address]:=port_data;    (* output a byte to the data port *)
end;


(* ——Resource Library No. A5 (Write data to CONTROL port of pc)—— *)
function Write_control_port(P_address:integer; port_data:integer):integer;export;
(* Bit 0, Bit 1 and Bit 3 are inverted. Bit manipulation is required *)
begin
        if port_data and 1 =1 then port_data:=port_data and (255-1)
           else port_data:=port_data or 1;
        if port_data and 2 =2 then port_data:=port_data and (255-2)
           else port_data:=port_data or 2;
        if port_data and 8 =8 then port_data:=port_data and (255-8)
           else port_data:=port_data or 8;
        port[P_address+2]:=port_data;  (* output a byte to the control port *)
end;


(* ——Resource Library No. A6 (detection of COM ports)—— *)
Function RS232(x:integer):integer; export;
{Universal auto detection of COM base address}
```

```
{ $0000:$0400 holds the printer base address for COM1
  $0000:$0402 holds the printer base address for COM2
  $0000:$0404 holds the printer base address for COM3
  $0000:$0406 holds the printer base address for COM4
  $0000:$0411 number of parallel interfaces in binary format}
var
      number_of_COM, COM1, COM2, COM3, COM4 :integer;
begin
      number_of_COM:=mem[$40:$11]; {read number of parallel ports}
      number_of_COM:=(number_of_COM and (8+4+2)) shr 1;
      COM1:=0; COM2:=0; COM3:=0; COM4:=0;
      COM1:=memw[$40:$00];            {Memory read procedure}
      COM2:=memw[$40:$02];
      COM3:=memw[$40:$04];
      COM4:=memw[$40:$06];
      case x of
          0:    RS232:=number_of_COM;
          1:    RS232:=COM1;
          2:    RS232:=COM2;
          3:    RS232:=COM3;
          4:    RS232:=COM4
         end;
end;


(* ——Resource Library No. A7 (to write to the interrupt enable register)—— *)
Function Write_interrupt_enable(RS232_address, Output_byte: integer):integer;Export;
begin
      Port[RS232_address+1]:=Output_byte;
end;


(* ——Resource Library No. A8 (to read from the interrupt identification register)—— *)
Function Read_interrupt_identification(RS232_address:integer):integer; Export;
begin
      Read_interrupt_identification:=Port[RS232_address+2]
end;


(* ——Resource Library No. A9 (write to data serialization register)—— *)
Function Write_data_format(RS232_address, Baudx, Parity, Data_bit, Stop_bit:integer):integer; Export;
var
      byte1, byte2, output_byte: byte;
         divisor: integer;
```

```
        baud:longint;
begin
    Baud:=baudx * 100 ;
        divisor:=115200 div Baud;
        if divisor<=255 then begin byte1:=divisor; byte2:=0 end;
        if divisor>255 then begin byte2:=divisor div 256; byte1:=divisor mod 256; end;
        output_byte:=(data_bit-5) + 4*(stop_bit-1) + 8*(parity);
    port[RS232_address+3]:=128;{Loading serial data format, first bit of the register is 1}
        port[RS232_address+0]:=Byte1;        {LSB of the divisor is 1}
        port[RS232_address+1]:=Byte2;        {MSB of the divisor is 0}
        port[RS232_address+3]:=output_byte;   {Load divisor and other parameters}
end;


(* ——Resource Library No. A10 (to write to the transmit buffer register)—— *)
Function write_transmit_buffer(RS232_address, Output_byte: integer):integer; Export;
begin
    port[RS232_address]:=Output_byte;
end;


(* ——Resource Library No. A11 (to write to the modem status register)—— *)
Function Write_modem_status(RS232_address, RTS, DTR:integer):integer; Export;
(* RTS and DTR = 0 or 1, RTS and DRT are inverted by MAX238 on the experimental board *)
(* RTS=bit 1, DTR=bit 0 of Modem control register, offset 04 *)
begin
    RTS:=1-RTS;
    DTR:=1-DTR;
    Port[RS232_address+4]:=RTS*2 + DTR  (* to output to the register 04 *)
end;


(* ——Resource Library No. A12 (to read data from receive buffer register)—— *)
Function Read_receive_buffer(RS232_address:integer):integer; Export;
begin
    Read_receive_buffer:=port[RS232_address];
end;


(* ——Resource Library No. A13 (to read modem status register)—— *)
Function Read_modem_status(RS232_address, x:integer):integer; Export;
(* X=1 select DCD bit, x=2 select DSR bit, x=3 select CTS bit *)
(* DCD=bit 7, DSR=bit 5, CTS=bit 4 of Modem status register, offset 06h *)
(* All bits are inverted by the Max238 on the experimental board *)
```

```
var
    input_byte:byte;
begin
    input_byte:=port[RS232_address+6];
    case x of
    1:    Read_modem_status:=1-round((input_byte and 128)/128);
    2:    Read_modem_status:=1-round((input_byte and 32)/32);
    3:    Read_modem_status:=1-round((input_byte and 16)/16);
    end;
end;


(* ----Resource Library No. A14 (to read Game port register)---- *)
Function Read_Game_port(Bitx:integer):integer;Export;
(* Game port address: 201H
    Bitx selects status of AX, AY, BX, BY, BA1, BA2, BB1 and BB2 *)
var
    input_byte:byte;
begin
    input_byte:=port[$201];
    Read_game_port:=round((input_byte and bit_weight(bitx)/bit_weight(bitx)));
end;


(* ----Resource Library No. A15 (to write to Game port register)---- *)
Function Write_Game_port:integer;Export;
(* output byte 0 to the game port to start the multi-vibrators *)
begin
    port[$201]:=0;
end;


(* ----Resource Library No. A16 (to get time interval of the multivibrator after one shot)---- *)
Function Interval_Game_port(x:integer):integer;Export;
(* x selects AX (x=1), AY (x=2), BX (x=3), BY (x=4) *)
var
    Time1, Time2, dummy: integer;


Procedure init_8253;
(* Initialize 8253 *)
begin
(*  Control word= b6H = 10110111b
    10 = select counter 2
    11 = read/write low count byte first then high byte
```

```
        011 = mode 3
        0   = binary counting with 16-bit *)
        Port[$43]:=$b6; (* load control word to the control register of 8253 *)
        Port[$42]:=255; (* load low count byte *)
        port[$42]:=255; (* load high count byte *)
        port[$61]:=port[$61] or 1; (* disable speaker *)
        port[$43]:=$80; (* 80H is the counter latch command for counter 3 *)
end;


Function read_8253:integer;
(* read low order and high order bytes of the counters *)
var
    low_byte, high_byte:byte;
begin
        low_byte:=port[$42];
        high_byte:=port[$42];
        read_8253:=low_byte + 256* high_byte;
end;


Var
        i:integer;
begin
        init_8253;
        for i:=1 to 10 do i:=i;
        i:=0;
        dummy:=bit_weight(x);
        port[$201]:=0;
        Time1:=read_8253;
        repeat i:=i+1 until (port[$201] and dummy=0) or (i>=10000);
        Time2:=read_8253;
        Interval_game_port:=time1-time2;
        if i>=10000 then Interval_game_port:=0;
end;


exports
        Centronic           Index 1,
            Bit_weight          Index 2,
            Read_status_port    Index 3,
            Write_data_port         Index 4,
            Write_control_port      Index 5,
            RS232           Index 6,
            Write_interrupt_enable      Index 7,
            Read_interrupt_indentification  Index 8,
            Write_data_format       Index 9,
```

```
        Write_transmit_buffer      Index 10,
        Write_modem_status         Index 11,
        Read_receive_buffer        Index 12,
        Read_modem_status          Index 13,
        Read_game_port             Index 14,
        Write_game_port            Index 15,
        Interval_game_port         Index 16;
Begin
end.
```

Expanding the Centronic, RS232 and game ports

In many applications, the number of I/O lines provided by the Centronic, RS232 and game port is not enough. Expansion of the I/O lines is required.

4.1 Expanding the Centronic port

One method for expanding I/O lines of the port is to use the 74LS TTL or 4000 CMOS series logic chips. The other is to use dedicated peripheral programmable interface (PPI) chips such as the 8255, 8155 or others. Using the logic chips is simple and economical. A huge number of inputs and outputs can be expanded. The disadvantage is that the hardware is not configurable. Using interface chips makes the expansion configurable. For example, the 8255 PPI provides 24 I/O lines which are arranged in three groups, A, B and C. Each group has eight I/O lines and can be configured as an input or an output port.

4.1.1 I/O expansion using logic ICs

(a) Reading 8-bit data

Figure 4.1 shows an experimental circuit to allow the Centronic port to read 8-bit data using a 74LS241 octal buffer. The pin-out of the 74LS241 is shown in Figure 4.1. When pin 1 is taken *low*, the four buffers on the left hand side are enabled (the outputs follow the inputs). Otherwise the outputs are in the high the impedance state. When pin 19 goes *high* the four buffers on the right hand side are enabled. If pins 1 and 19 are connected together to form a data selection line (DSL), by putting it low and then high, you can read the four bits connected to the buffers on the left and then the other four bits connected to the buffers on the right in turns. Operating in such a manner, 8-bit data can be read into the computer via only four lines. The DSL line can be controlled by bit 0 of the data port.

Figure 4.1 also shows how the 74LS241 is connected to the Centronic experimental board. D1, S1 to S4 are terminals on the experimental board. Eight-bit input data is loaded into a computer in two consecutive readings. When SEL is low, bit 0 to bit 3 of the input data are read into the computer. When SEL is high, bit 4 to bit 7 are read into the computer. To get the original 8-bit byte (bit 0 to bit 7), manipulation of the two bytes is performed. The TP6 and VB3 software drivers for the board (see Chapter 3) can be used for testing the circuit.

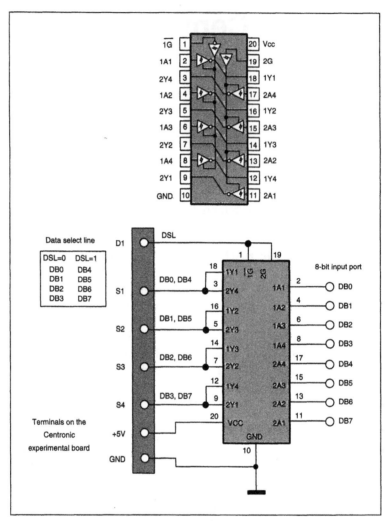

Figure 4.1 Circuit for expanding an 8-bit input port using a 74LS241

(b) Expanding outputs

The way to expand output lines is to use latches such as the 74LS373 or 74LS374 ICs. The pin-out and an experimental circuit using the 74LS374 are shown in Figure 4.2. The inputs to the 74LS374 are connected to bit 0 to bit 7 of the DATA port. Latching data into the IC is controlled by the CLK pin (pin 11). At the low-to-high transition, the input data is latched to the outputs. The CLK pin is controlled by one output line of the CONTROL port. In Figure 4.2, D1 to D8 and C1 are terminals on the Centronic experimental board. A TP6 software driver is listed below.

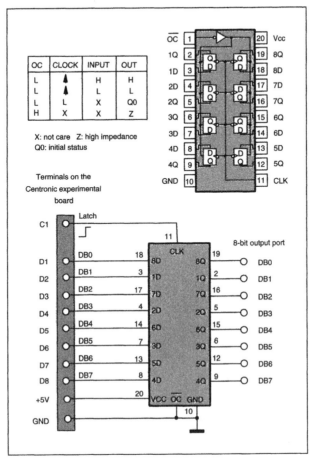

Figure 4.2 Circuit for expanding an 8-bit output port using 74LS374

TP6 program list of LS374.PAS

```
Program Centronic_Output_Expander_using_74LS374;
(* Software driver for expanding output ports using 74LS374 *)

uses
    graph,crt,dos;
var
    ch:char;

(* include two included libraries: TPLIB0 and TPLIB1 *)
{$I c:\ioexp\tplib1.pas}
```

```
Procedure Load_data_to_LS374;
(* load data to 74LS374 *)
var
    Output_byte :byte;
begin
    (* to output data to the Data port *)
    write_control_port(P_address,0);
    Write('Input the output data: '); readln(output_byte);
    Write_data_port(P_address, Output_byte);
    write('Press RETURN to load the input data to the output of 74LS374');
    readln;
    write_control_port(P_address,1);
    writeln('1st line of the Control port goes from low to high to latch data');
    delay(2000);
    write_control_port(P_address,0);
end;


(* Main program *)
begin
    centronic_address;   (* input centronic address *)
repeat
    clrscr;
    load_data_to_LS374;
    write('Continue (Y/N) : '); readln(Ch);
until upcase(ch)='N'
end.
```

4.1.2 I/O expansion using 8255 PPI chips

Figure 4.3 shows the pin-out and the internal block diagram of the 8255 PPI. It has 24 input/output lines which are arranged in three 8-bit ports, ports A, B and C. The 8255 has four internal registers. Three of them are called peripheral registers which are associated with the ports A, B and C. The fourth one is the control register. The peripheral registers are used for data transfer through the port. The control register is used to store the configuration parameters of the 8255. There is an 8-bit bidirectional data bus (bits 0–7, pins 34–27) through which data are written to or read from the 8255 under the control of -WR (pin 36) and -RD (pin 5) lines. The address lines A0 (pin 9) and A1 (pin 8) are used to select a particular internal register.

A0=0, A1=0,   select the register A
A0=1, A1=0,   select the register B
A0=0, A1=1,   select the register C
A0=1, A1=1,   select the control register

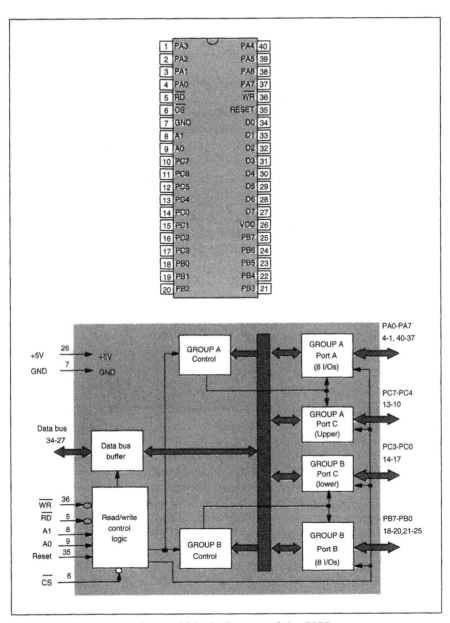

Figure 4.3 Pin-out and internal block diagram of the 8255

-CS (pin 6) line must be taken low to enable the IC. RESET (pin 35) is active high. After reset all the I/O lines of ports A, B and C are configured as inputs. In normal operations, The RESET line must be held low. The 8255 has three operation modes:

- In Mode 1, the ports A can be configured as an 8-bit input or output port. Mixture of inputs and outputs is not possible. Port B is the same as port A. Port C is split into two halves (the upper four bits and lower four bits). Each half can be configured as either input or output. The mixture of inputs and outputs within each half is not possible. All the outputs are latched.
- Mode 2 configures the 8255 PPI as strobed I/O ports. Ports A and B are configured as two independent 8-bit input or output ports. Each of them has a 4-bit control port associated with it. The control ports are formed by the lower and upper four bits of port C, respectively.
- In Mode 3, port A can be configured as a bidirectional port.

The modes of the 8255 are configured by writing an 8-bit control word to the control register. The bit function of this control word is shown below:

bit 7 (mode set flag)	always 1
bit 6, Bit 5 (mode selection bits)	00=Mode 1, 01=Mode 2, 1x=Mode 3
bit 4 (mode of port A)	1=input, 0=output
bit 3 (mode of upper half of C)	1=input, 0=output
bit 2 (mode selection for Mode 3)	1=Mode 1, 0=Mode 0
bit 1 (Mode of port B)	1=input, 0=output
bit 0 (Mode of lower half of C)	1=input, 0=output

A circuit diagram of an 8255 connected to a Centronic port is shown in Figure 4.4. The data port of the Centronic port sends data to the 8255. Data transfer is facilitated by IC2 and IC3 (the 74LS241 and the 74LS244 tri-state buffers). The status port reads data from the 8255. Two lines of the control port are connected to A0 and A1 of the 8255 and the other two lines are connected to -RD and -WR.

To write data to an 8255 register, firstly the required data is written to the data port and A0 and A1 are written to the control port, then a high-to-low-then-high pulse is issued from the -WR line. This enables the data buffers of IC3. The low-going transition on -WR writes the data into the selected register of the 8255. Reading data from the 8255 is accomplished by IC2 (the 74LS241). The data selection line (DSL) is controlled by bit 0 of the data port. When reading data from an 8255 register, firstly an address (A0 and A1) is written to the control port and -RD line is held low. This makes the 8255 output data onto its data bus. Then the DSL line is first set low and the status port reads the first reading. Then the DSL line is set high, the port reads the second one. The two readings are combined to reproduce the original 8-bit data.

A control software is written in Turbo Pascal 6. It configures all the ports as outputs (Mode 0, control word=128). The program contains all the necessary procedures and functions which allow users to develop their own software. *Write_control(Control_word:byte)* writes the control word into the internal control register of 8255. *Write_port (port_number, output_byte:byte)* writes a byte to a port A, B or C which has been configured as an output. *Inputbyte (port_number :byte):byte* reads data from a port A, B or C which is configured as an input.

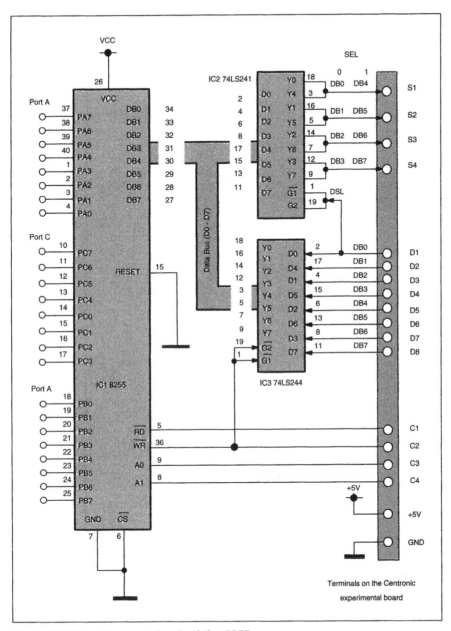

Figure 4.4 Experimental circuit of the 8255

TP6 Program list of 8255.PAS

```
Program Centronic_8255_interface;
(*Some useful control words: 128(decimal): Port A, B and C all as output
                             155(decimal): Port A, B and C all as input
                             144(decimal): Port A as input; Port B and C as output
                             146(decimal): Port A and B as input; Port C as output*)
uses
    crt,dos,graph;
var
    command,output_byte,input_byte,bitnumber,portnumber,outputbyte:byte;
    P_address,delaynumber:integer;
{$I c:\ioexp\tplib1.pas}
Procedure find_delay_number;
(* Check pc speed and find the delaynumber for 1 ms*)
var
    time1,time2,dt:real;
    t,h1,m1,s1,s1001,h2,m2,s2,s1002:word;
begin
    clrscr;
    gotoxy(25,24); write('Checking computer speed');
    gettime(h1,m1,s1,s1001);
    time1:=3600*h1+60*m1+s1+s1001/100;
    for t:=1 to 1000 do delay(1);
    gettime(h2,m2,s2,s1002);
    time2:=3600*h2+60*m2+s2+s1002/100;
    dt:=time2-time1;
    delaynumber:=round(1000/dt*0.001);
    clrscr;
    gotoxy(30,24); write('Finished...');
    clrscr;
end;


Function convert(bytex:byte):byte;
(*CONVERT THE bytex INTO THE BYTE TO BE SENT INTO THE 8255 REGISTERS*)
(*byte received by the 8255:          (byte into 8255 = B8 B7 B6 B5 B4 B3 B2 B1)
 byte output from the Centronic port: (data from Centronic port = B8 B4 B7 B3 B6 B2 B5 B1)
 The difference in bit sequence is due to hardware connection of the board. To sent a byte
 into the 8255, data from the Centronic port should take the above form*)
begin
    convert:=    ((bytex and 1) + ((bytex and 2) shl 1)+
                 ((bytex and 4) shl 2) + (bytex  and 8) shl 3+
                 ((bytex and 16) shr 3) + ((bytex  and 32) shr 2) +
                 (bytex and 64)  shr 1 + ((bytex  and 128)));
end;
```

```
Procedure write_control(Control_word:byte);
(*WRITE CONTROL_WORD INTO 8255 IC CONTROL REGISTER*)
(*Control_word is output by port [P_address], 8255 R/W is controlled by port [P_address+2]*)
(*Port [P_address+2] bit configuration, -1(-Read) -2(-Write) 3(A0) -4(A1)*)
begin
     Control_word:=convert(Control_word);(*Convert the word*)
     port[P_address]:=Control_word; delay(delaynumber*10); (*Control word output from port [P_address]*)
     port[P_address+2]:=0+0+4+0; delay(delaynumber*3); (*-Read=1, -Write=1, A0=1, A1=1, delay=10 ms*)
     port[P_address+2]:=0+2+4+0; delay(delaynumber*3); (*-Read=1, -Write=0, A0=1, A1=1, delay=10 ms*)
     port[P_address+2]:=0+0+4+0; delay(delaynumber*3); (*-Read=1, -Write=1, A0=1, A1=1, delay=10 ms*)
end;


Procedure write_port (port_number,output_byte:byte);
(*WRITE A BYTE (output_byte) TO A 8255 IC PORT SPECIFIED BY port_number*)
(*Output byte is output by port [P_address], 8255 R/W is controlled by port [P_address+2]*)
(*Port [P_address+2] bit configuration, -1(-Read) -2(-Write) 3(A0) -4(A1)*)
begin
     Output_byte:=convert(Output_byte); (*Convert the word*)
     port[P_address]:=output_byte;          (*Output a byte from port [P_address]*)
     if (port_number=0) then begin  (*Output a byte to A register of 8255 IC*)
        port[P_address+2]:=0+0+0+8; delay(delaynumber*3);       (*-Read=1, -Write=1, A0=1, A1=0*)
        port[P_address+2]:=0+2+0+8; delay(delaynumber*3);       (*-Read=1, -Write=0, A0=1, A1=0*)
        port[P_address+2]:=0+0+0+8; delay(delaynumber*3);       (*-Read=1, -Write=1, A0=1, A1=0*)
                        end;
     if (port_number=1) then begin  (*Output a byte to B register of 8255 IC*)
        port[P_address+2]:=0+0+4+8; delay(delaynumber*3);
        port[P_address+2]:=0+2+4+8; delay(delaynumber*3);
        port[P_address+2]:=0+0+4+8; delay(delaynumber*3);
                        end;
     if (port_number=2) then begin  (*Output a byte to C register of 8255 IC*)
        port[P_address+2]:=0+0+0+0;  delay(delaynumber*3);
        port[P_address+2]:=0+2+0+0;  delay(delaynumber*3);
        port[P_address+2]:=0+0+0+0;  delay(delaynumber*3);
                        end;
end;


Function Inputbyte(port_number:byte):byte;
(*READ A BYTE (input_byte) FROM A 8255 IC PORT SPECIFIED BY port_number*)
(*Input byte is input from port [P_address+1], 8-bit byte is input into the Centronic
  port in two stages. In the first stage, bits 1,2,3 and 4 are read and in the
  second one bits 5,6,7 and 8 are read. This operation is controlled by bit 1
  of port [P_address]. 8255 R/W is controlled by port [P_address+2]*)
(*Port [P_address+2] bit configuration, -1(-Read) -2(-Write) 3(A0) -4(A1)*)
```

```
var
    byte_1st, byte_2nd:byte;
begin
      if (port_number=0) then begin  (*Read a byte from port A of 8255*)
          port[P_address]:=0;                              (*DSL=0, Prepare to read low 4 bits*)
          port[P_address+2]:=0+0+0+8;  delay(delaynumber*3);         (*-Read=1, -Write=1, A0=0, A1=0*)
          port[P_address+2]:=1+0+0+8;                      (*-Read=0, -Write=1, A0=0, A1=0*)
          byte_2nd:= port[P_address+1];        (*Read low 4 bits*)
          port[P_address]:=1;                  (*DSL=1, Prepare to read high 4 bits*)
          byte_1st:=port[P_address+1];         (*Read high 4 bits*)
          port[P_address+2]:=0+0+0+8;          (*-Read=1, -Write=1, A0=0, A1=0*)
                              end;
      if (port_number=1) then begin  (*Read a byte from port B of 8255*)
          port[P_address]:=0;
          port[P_address+2]:=0+0+4+8; delay(delaynumber*3);
          port[P_address+2]:=1+0+4+8;
          byte_2nd:=port[P_address+1];
          port[P_address]:=1;
          byte_1st:=port[P_address+1];
          port[P_address+2]:=0+0+4+8;
                              end;
      if (port_number=2) then begin  (*Read a byte from port C of 8255*)
          port[P_address]:=0;
          port[P_address+2]:=0+0+0+0; delay(delaynumber*3);
          port[P_address+2]:=1+0+0+0;
          byte_2nd:=port[P_address+1];
          port[P_address]:=1;
          byte_1st:=port[P_address+1];
          port[P_address+2]:=0+0+0+0;
                              end;
          (*Note:  Byte_1st  =(x B8 B7 B6 B5 x x x)
                   Byte_2nd  =(x B4 B3 B2 B1 x x x)
           x=don't care, B8 to B1: bit value 0 or 1*)

          byte_1st:=byte_1st and 120; (*x B8 B7 B6 B5 x x x and 01111000 = 0 B8 B7 B6 B5 0 0 0*)
          byte_1st:=byte_1st shl 1;   (*shift 1 bit left, byte_1st =B8 B7 B6 B5 0 0 0 0*)
          byte_2nd:=byte_2nd and 120; (*x B4 B3 B2 B1 x x x and 01111000 = 0 B4 B3 B2 B1 0 0 0*)
          byte_2nd:=byte_2nd shr 3;   (*shift 3 bit right, byte_2nd =0 0 0 0 B4 B3 B2 B1*)
          Inputbyte:=byte_1st or byte_2nd; (*byte_1st or byte_2nd = B8 B7 B6 B5 B4 B3 B2 B1*)
end;


(********************MAIN PROGRAM**********************)
begin
      find_delay_number;
```

```
        clrscr;

    Centronic_address

repeat

        clrscr;

        writeln('                        Centronic port - 8255 card testing program');

        writeln;

        writeln('                    Port A, B and C are all configured as Outputs');

        writeln('                The control word sent to the 8255 PPI is 128 decimal');

        write_control(128); (*Port A, B and C are configured as OUTPUTs*)

        write_control(128);

        writeln;

        write('              Input the bit number to be tested    (1 to. 8, 9 to quit)   :  ');

readln(Bitnumber);

        outputbyte:=bit_weigth(bitnumber)

        writeln;

        textcolor(yellow+blink);

        write('   The selected bit of Port A, B and C will change from 0 to 1 to 0 repeatly');

        write('                      You need a logic probe to test the card!');

        textcolor(white);

        repeat

                write_port(0, outputbyte);

                write_port(1, outputbyte);

                write_port(2, outputbyte); delay(delaynumber*300);

                write_port(0,0);

                write_port(1,0);

                write_port(2,0);                delay(delaynumber*300);

        until keypressed or (portnumber=9);

        readln;

    until bitnumber=9;

end.
```

4.2 Expanding the RS232 port

4.2.1 RS232/TTL line translators

The simplest way of converting the RS232 voltage level to the TTL voltage level is to use voltage clamp circuits as shown in Figure 4.5(a). The circuit consists of one resistor and a +5.1V Zener diode. When the input RS232 status is high, the output is +5V. When the status is low, the output voltage is –0.6V. The output can drive TTL or CMOS circuits. Another TTL/RS232 transceiver circuit is shown in Figure 4.5(b). The circuit does not require any external power supplies. It 'steals' the power from the RS232 port. It has an inverting action.

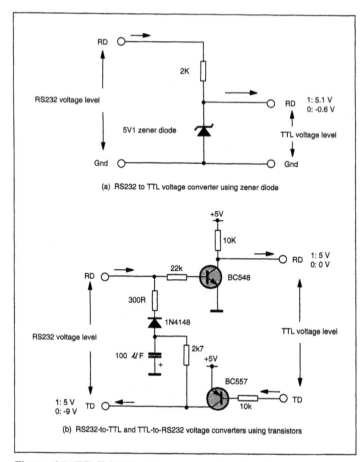

(a) RS232 to TTL voltage converter using zener diode

(b) RS232-to-TTL and TTL-to-RS232 voltage converters using transistors

Figure 4.5 TTL/RS232 voltage converter circuits

The TTL/RS232 transceiver ICs are widely used. The MAX232 (Maxim RS655–290) and the MAX238 (Maxim RS655–313) are two examples. The pin-out of the two ICs is given in Figure 4.6. The internal block diagram of the MAX232 is also shown in Figure 4.6. Both ICs require a signal rail +5V power supply. The MAX232 contains an on-board dual charge-pump DC-DC voltage converter, two RS232 drivers and two RS232 receivers. The dual charge-pumps convert the +5V supply voltage to +10V and –10V. Care should be taken not to load V+ and V– to a point that it violates the minimum RS232 (RS232C, V_{min} = 3V) voltage level. When a 20 mA current drawn from V+ and V–, the voltage at V+ and V– will be around 7V and –7V. The receiver inputs withstand a voltage up to ±25V. The maximum data transfer rate is 120 kbyte/s. The supply current of the MAX232 is 4 mA when the outputs have no load. The MAX238 has similar electrical characteristics and has four drivers and four receivers.

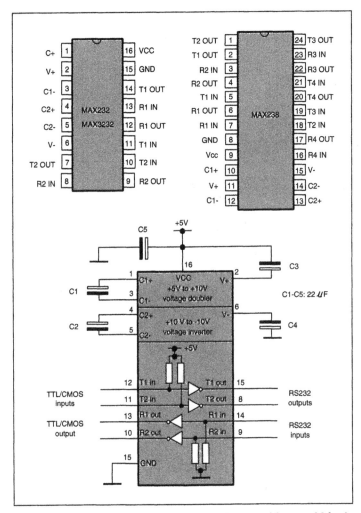

Figure 4.6 Pin-out of MAX232 and MAX238 and internal block diagram of MAX232

For battery-powered applications, a low power version MAX3232 (Maxim RS189–1453) can be used. It only consumes 250 µA. Other electrical characteristics are the same as those of the standard MAX232.

Isolated RS232 drivers/receivers are used to achieve high noise immunity and electrical isolation. A device such as the NM232DD (Newport RS264–412) provides two drivers and two transmitters and requires a single +5V power supply. The pin-out of the chip is shown in Figure 4.7. The IC has an isolated DC-to-DC converter and opto-isolators in one package. It provides an isolation of 1500V.

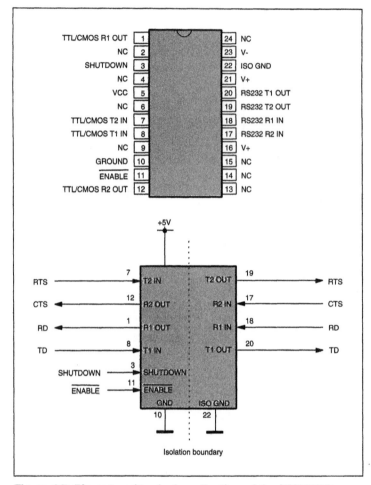

Figure 4.7 Pin-out and typical application of the NM232DD

4.2.2 Expanding RS232 ports using UARTs

The CDP6402 (Harris Semiconductors, RS 630-689) is a CMOS Universal Asynchronous Receiver/Transmitter for interfacing to asynchronous serial data channels. Its serial data format is programmable. It can have 5, 6, 7, or 8 bit length. The parity check can be odd, even or none. Stop bits can be 1, 1.5 or 2. The IC requires a power supply voltage 4 to 10 volts. The quiescent supply current is 1.5 mA for a supply voltage of 5V.

The pin-out and the internal block diagram are shown in Figure 4.8. Pin 21 is the Master Reset (MR), which should be at the logic low state in normal operations. Pins 35 through 39 control the serial data format. To enable the control pins, pin 34 (Control Register Load, CRL) must be at logic

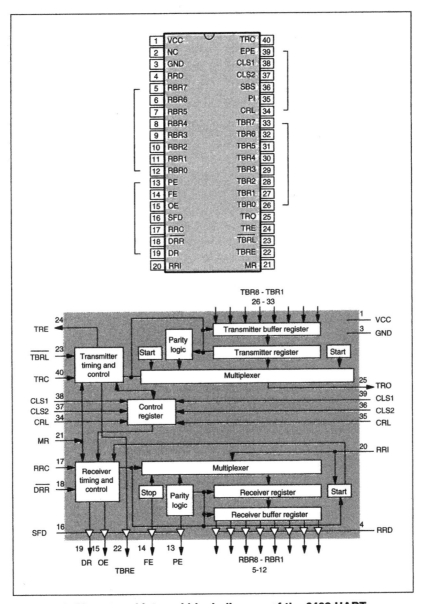

Figure 4.8 Pin-out and internal block diagram of the 6402 UART

high. A high level on pin 35 (Parity Inhibit, PI) inhibits parity generation and check. It also forces the Parity Error (PE, pin 13) pin to stay low. When PI is low, a high level on Even Parity Enable (EPE, pin 39) selects even parity. A low level on EPE pin selects odd parity. Pin 36 (Stop Bit Select) high selects 1.5 stop bits for 5 character format and 2 stop bits for other data lengths. If it is low, 1 stop bit is selected. Pins 37 (Character Length Selected, CLS2) and 38 (CLS1) select the data length: CLS1=0, CLS2=0 for 5 bits; CLS1=1, CLS2=0 for 6; CLS1=0, CLS2=1 for 7 and CLS1=1 and CLS2=1 for 8.

Pins 17 (Receiver Register Clock) and 40 (Transmitter Register Clock) are the clock inputs for the receiver and transmitter. The two inputs are driven by a clock which runs at 16 times the required baud rate. They are normally connected together.

Pin 20 (Receiver Register Input, RRI) is the serial data input. The received data is stored in the receiver buffer registers which are accessed via pins 5 to 12 (Receiver Buffer Registers). Pin 4 (Receiver Register Disable, RRD) should be low. When data is successfully received and loaded into the receiver buffer registers, pin 19 (Data Received) goes from low to high. It can be set to low by making pin 18 (-Data Received Reset) low. This enables the UART to receive the new data. Pins 13 (Parity Error), 14 (Framing Error) 15 (Overrun Error) give the status of errors occurring during a data transmission and they are all high active. To enable these status outputs, pin 16 (Status Flag Disable, SFD) should be low.

Pin 25 (Transmitter Register Output, TRO) is the serial data output. Data to be sent is written into the transmit buffer registers via pins 26 to 33 (Transmitter Buffer Registers). When pin 23 (-Transmitter Buffer Register Load, -TBRL) goes low, the data is loaded into the transmitter buffer registers and when it goes from low to high, it loads the data into the transmitter register and initiates the serial data transmission. Pin 22 is Transmitter Buffer Register Empty. A high level on this indicates that transmitter buffer register has transferred data into the transmitter register and is ready for new data. Pin 24 is Transmitter Register Empty. A high level on this pin indicates the completion of a serial data transmission.

A receive timing sequence is shown in Figure 4.9(a). Data is received at the RRI input. When no data is being received, RRI input must be high. At stage A, a low level on -DDR clears the DR line. At stage B, during the first stop bit of the transmission, the data is transferred from the receiver register to the receiver buffer registers. An overrun error occurs when DR has not been cleared before the present character is transferred to the registers. At stage C, 1/2 clock cycle after B, DR goes high, indicating that a new data is received. A logic high on FE indicates that an invalid stop bit has been received and a logic high on PE indicates a parity error. If the UART operates in a continuous mode, DDR can be pulled down to ground.

A transmit timing procedure is shown in Figure 4.9(b). At stage A, data is loaded into the transmitter buffer register from the inputs TBR1 through TBR8 at the high- to-low transition on the -TBRL input. Valid data must appear on TBR1–TBR8 before and after the rising edge of -TBRL. If the data bit length is less than 8, only the least significant bits are used. At stage B, the rising edge of -TBRL clears TBRE. After a short delay, data is transferred to the transmitter register and TRE is low. TBRE goes to a logic high showing that the transmit buffer registers are empty. Output data is clocked out by TRC. The clock rate is 16 times the data baud. At stage C, -TBRL goes from high to low then high again. This loads the second data to the transmit buffer register. Data transfer to the transmitter register is delayed until the transmission of the current character is complete. At stage D, data is automatically transferred to the transmitter registers and the transmission of the second data begins.

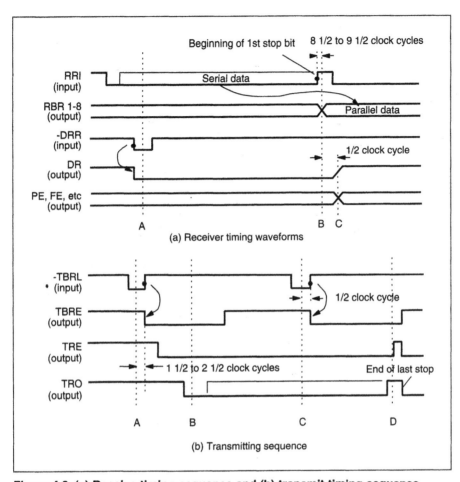

Figure 4.9 (a) Receive timing sequence and (b) transmit timing sequence

An experimental circuit of the 6402 connected to the RS232 experimental board is shown in Figure 4.10. RRI, TRO and -TBRL of the 6402 are connected to TD, RD and DTR terminals on the experimental board. The clock input to the UART is generated by a circuit using a CD4060 and a 2.4576 MHz crystal. From pins 7 of the CD4060, a clock signal at 153.6 kHz is generated, giving a baud rate of 9600. The serial data format is: baud rate = 9600; data bit length = 8; stop bit length = 1 and parity = none. Pin 18 (-DRR) is pulled to logic low. This causes the 6402 to receive serial data continuously.

The TP6 and VB3 software drivers for the RS232 experimental board (see Chapter 3) can be used for experimenting with the circuit. Users can send data from a computer to the 6402. By changing the status of DTR from high to low and then to high, the input data to the 6402 can be read into the computer. The eight outputs from the 6402 can be connected to the inputs to the IC for a loop test. In this case, the value of the received data should be equal to that of the output data.

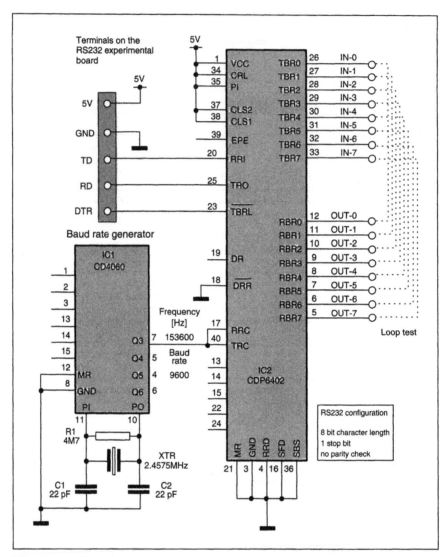

Figure 4.10 Experimental circuit diagram of the 6402 UART

4.2.3 New concepts for RS232 interfacing – ITC232-A

ITC232-A (Timely Technology, RS 213-7312) is a new peripheral chip which is designed for easy interfacing with the RS232 port on computers. It is connected to the RS232 port via three lines, TD, RD and ground. The IC has a powerful built-in control command set and a key stroke to machine code translator. Users can input command key strokes from the keyboard of a computer. The IC decodes the key strokes and performs the corresponding actions. This is advantageous over other I/O interfacing schemes. Firstly, there is no need for users to learn complicated low-level languages and hardware controls. Secondly, there is no need to compile the instructions.

The internal block diagram of the ITC232-A and a typical application circuit are given in Figure 4.11. The device has a 40-pin DIL package. The device requires a +5V power supply and consumes 50 mA. The RS232 serial I/O command port operates with a baud rate from 300 to 115,200. The

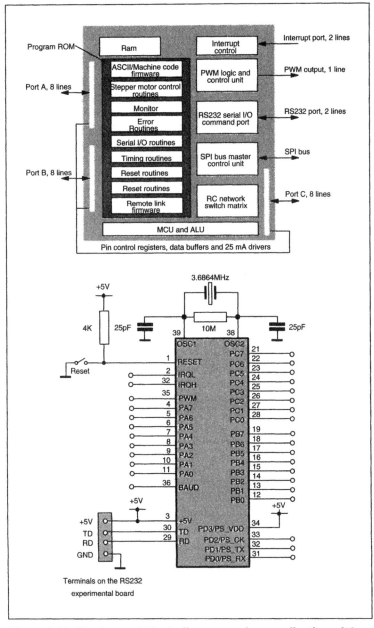

Figure 4.11 The internal block diagram and an application of the ITC232-A

IC has 24 digital I/O lines arranged in three ports A, B and C. They can be configured individually as input or output. Bits 4 to 7 of ports A, B and C can be used to drive three two-phase stepper motors. The stepping speed is in the range 10 to 4000 steps per second. Bits 0 to 3 of ports A, B and C can be used to measure resistance or capacitance. The device offers a pulse-width modulated output with a frequency range from 10 Hz to 10 kHz and a duty cycle range from 1 to 100%. The ITC232-A also equips a SPI bus from which various SPI compatible devices can be connected to the IC. One example of the device is the MC145041 10-channel A/D converter.

The ITC232-A can be connected to the RS232 experimental board as shown in Figure 4.11. If you send PWA254 followed by a return from the computer to the IC, you write 254 to port A. If you send SAL100 followed by a return to the IC, a stepper motor connected to the port A will turn 100 steps to the left. The W1000 command will cause the device to produce a 1 kHz tone at the PWM output. The full instruction set and application notes are available from the manufacturer.

Key stroke commands to the controller are typed at the command prompt of any terminal program. They can be also sent to the ITC232 from programs written in TP6 or VB3 programs.

4.3 Expanding the game port

The game port has two (or four) digital inputs and two (or four) resistance inputs and it has no output lines. The two digital input lines can read two digital inputs. The input can be serial encoded data and a software decoder is used inside the PC to convert the serial data into parallel data. Some application examples will be given later.

4.4 Serial-to-parallel interface

By using serial-in and parallel-out shift registers such as the 74LS164s, two output lines from a computer can generate an unlimited number of outputs. Figure 4.12(a) shows how a 74LS164 is used to generate eight output lines from two output lines of a PC. The 74LS164 has two gated serial data inputs, pins 1 and 2 (A and B) and eight shift register outputs (Qa to Qh). At the low-to-high transition of the CLOCK input, the serial data bit presented at the inputs A and B is shift to Qa. In the same time the value on Qa is shift to Qb, Qb to Qc, etc. After eight clock cycles, the 8-bit byte can be loaded into the outputs of the shift register with the first bit loaded to pin Qh. A logic low at pin 9 (-CLEAR) sets the eight outputs low. The maximum input clock frequency is 25 MHz. Several 74LS164s can be cascaded to generate more outputs.

The connection of the circuit to the RS232 experimental board is given in Figure 4.12(a). We can see that RTS is connected to the serial data in (pins 1 and 2) and DTR connected to the CLOCK (pin 8). When loading data into the 74LS164, first the serial data is present at the RTS and then a high-to-low-then-high pulse is applied to the DTR terminal. The TP6 and VB3 software drivers for the RS232 experimental board (see Chapter 3) can be used for experimenting with the circuit.

There are two problems associated with the serial-to-parallel interface. One is the data transfer rate. A Pentium computer can output a software-controlled clock signal at a frequency in the range from 0.1 MHz to 1 MHz. The period for loading 8-bit serial data can be calculated. The more outputs you have in the circuit, the slower the loading speed is. This is not a problem for low and medium speed interfacing applications. The other problem is that during data loading, each output changes status randomly. To solve this, data latches such as the 74LS374 can be used (see Figure 4.12(b)). After all data bits are loaded into the shift registers, they are loaded into the 74LS374 by applying a low-to-high signal to the CLOCK of the 74LS374 (pin 11). The circuit, however, requires another output line from the computer. For the RS232 port, TD line can be used.

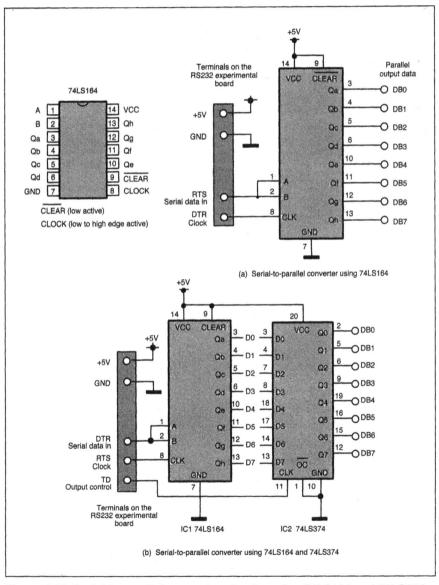

Figure 4.12 Serial-to-parallel converter circuits using 74LS164 and 74LS374

These circuits can be also used for the Centronic port. The three lines could be the output lines of the data port or the control port.

4.5 Parallel-to-serial interface

Using a parallel-in and serial-out shift register such as the CD4021, the number of inputs to a computer can be expanded. It requires two output lines from the computer (one to load parallel data and one to shift the data) and one input line to the computer to read data. Figure 4.13 shows a circuit for inputting eight bits of data. The pin-out of the CD4021 is also shown in Figure 4.13. The IC has a CLOCK input (pin 10), a parallel-in/serial-in control input (P/-S, pin 9), a serial data I/O (pin 11), eight parallel data inputs (D0 to D7) and three serial data outputs (Q6 to Q8). In operation, 8-bit data is present at the inputs. Then P/-S goes from low to high to load the 8-bit data into the internal register (parallel-in operation) regardless of the status of the clock. Next, P/-S is brought low to

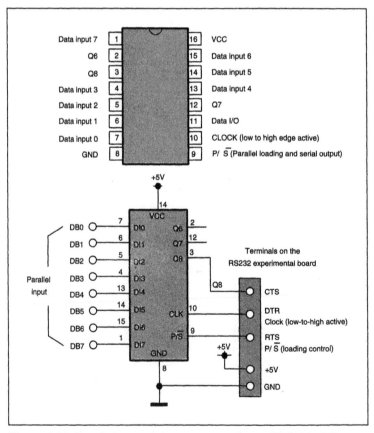

Figure 4.13 Parallel-to-serial converter using a CD4021 shift register

terminate the parallel-in operation and to start the serial-out operation. At the low-to-high transition of the clock input, the input data bits are shift out from pin Q7. After eight clock cycles, the 8-bit data is serially transmitted.

The connection of the IC to the RS232 experimental board is shown in Figure 4.13. CLOCK is connected to terminal DTR. P/-S control is connected to terminal RTS. Output Q8 is connected to CTS terminal. The TP6 and VB3 software drivers for the RS232 experimental board (see Chapter 3) can be used for experimenting the circuit. This circuit can be used with the Centronic port as well. Again there is a problem associated with the data transfer rate. It can be used only for medium to low speed interfacing applications.

4.6 Data encoders/decoders

Another method for expanding digital I/O lines is to use digital encoder/decoder ICs such as the HT-12 (Hotek) series or the MC1405XX (National Semiconductors) family. Encoders and decoders are ICs specially designed for digital data communication applications. Encoders are parallel-to-serial converters and decoders are serial-to-parallel converters. The link between the encoders and the decoders can be simply a wire link or other types of links such as infra-red, fibre optic, ultra-sonic and radio. Data transfer rate is low.

The pin-out and the internal block diagram of the HT-12E encoder are given in Figure 4.14. It transmits a serially encoded data upon the receipt of a low-going signal at the Transmit Enable pin (-TE, pin 14). The 12 bits of data consist of eight bits of address (A0 to A7, pins 1 to 8) and four bits of data (D0 to D3, pins 10 to 13). The total number of address combinations is 2^8. An external oscillator resistor (5% tolerance) is connected between pins 15 and 16. By selecting different resistance values, various rate of data transmission can be achieved. The serial data output is from pin 17. It has a wide operating voltage from 2.4 to 12V with a typical stand-by current of 1 µA.

Initially the encoder is in the stand-by mode. Upon the receipt of a low-going transition on -TE, it begins a four-word transmission cycle and repeats the cycle until -TE becomes high. Each word contains two periods: the pilot period and code periods as shown in Figure 4.15(a). The pilot period has a 12-bit length period and is at logic low. The code period also has a 12-bit length period. The encoder detects the logic state of the 12-bit inputs (A0-A7 and D0-D3) and transmits the information during the code period. The logic levels '0' and '1' are encoded in a manner as shown in Figure 4.15(b).

The pin-out and internal block diagram of the HT-12D decoder are given in Figure 4.16. The HT-12D receives the 12 bit word and interprets the first eight bits as the address and the last four bits as data. When the received address matches the decoder's preset address, the 4-bit data is stored in the internal register. This condition is checked three times. If the newly received address or data is different from that received previously, the HT-12D aborts the present process and resets itself. The preset address for the encoder is determined by the logic states at pins 1 to 8. The latched data is output from pins 10 to 13. The serial data is input at pin 14. An external oscillator resistor (5% tolerance) is connected between pins 15 and 16. Pin 17 is the valid transmission indicator output.

The resistors required by the devices are 5% resistors. The frequencies of the HT-12E and HT-12D should follow the following relationship:

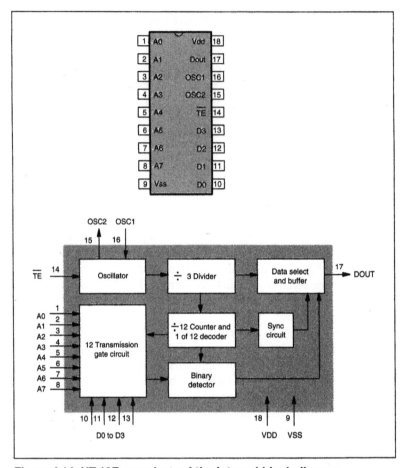

Figure 4.14 HT-12E encoder and the internal block diagram

$$F_{\text{osc, HT–12D}} = 50 \times F_{\text{osc, HT–12E}}$$

for a 3 kHz oscillation frequency of the encoder. The external resistor for the encoder is 1.1 MΩ and the resistor for the decoder (which should run at 150 kHz) is 62 kΩ. For other frequencies, refer to the manufacturer's data sheets.

The following TP6 program simulates the HT-12E to produce 12-bit serial encoded data. The data is output from the DTR terminal of the RS232 experimental board with a clock frequency of 1 kHz. The experimental circuit of the HT-12D is given in Figure 4.17. The external resistance is 220 kΩ, which gives a system clock frequency of 50 kHz. The data input (pin 14) is connected to the DTR terminal of the RS232 experimental board.

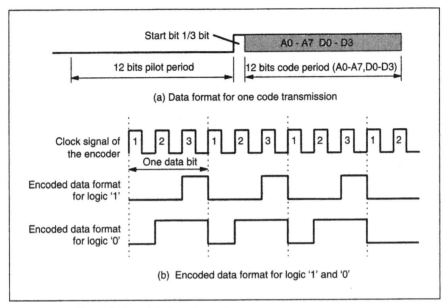

(a) Data format for one code transmission

(b) Encoded data format for logic '1' and '0'

Figure 4.15 Encoded serial data format

TP6 program list of HT_12E

```
Program HT_12_encoder;
(* software driver to transmit HT-12E signal *)


uses
    graph,crt,dos;
var
    addressx,datax:integer;
    bit:array [1..15] of byte;
    i,Serial_input_byte, Baud_rate_byte, Data_length_byte, Stop_length_byte, Parity_byte
:integer;
    Ch:char;


(* to load two included library files *)
{$I c:\ioexp\tplib1.pas}


Procedure transmit_serial_data(Port_address, Bit, Original_data, Address, data:integer;
invert_flag:boolean);
(* transmit serial data in HT-12 format, transmitter frequency 1000 Hz *)
(* Port_address: port I/O address, Bit: bit used for transmitting data
    Original_data: data originally appear on that port
    Address: 8-bit address to be transmitted
```

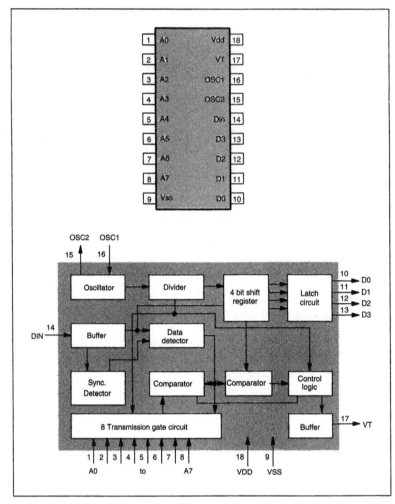

Figure 4.16 HT-12D encoder and its internal block diagram

```
    Data: 4-bit address to be transmitted
    invert_flag: =1 to invert the transmitted data *)
var
    i,Transmit_time:byte;
    data_bit: array [1..73] of byte;
begin
    (* HT-12 serial data format:
        first 36 clock cycles for pilot period,
        one 1/2 clock cycle for start bit,
        24 clock cycles for address (A0 to A7) and
        12 clock cycles for data (D0 to D3) *)
```

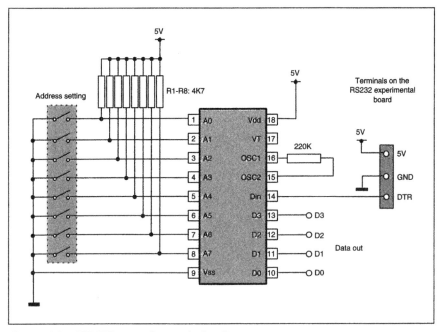

Figure 4.17 HT-12D experimental circuit

```
(* assign data_bit *)

(* pilot data bits *)
    for i:=1 to 36 do if not Invert_flag then data_bit[i]:=original_data and
(255-bit_weight(bit))
        else data_bit[i]:=original_data or bit_weight(bit);


(* start bit *)
    if not invert_flag then data_bit[37]:=original_data or bit_weight(bit)
        else data_bit[37]:=original_data and (255-bit_weight(bit));


(* address bits , Al transmitted first and A8 last *)
    for i:=1 to 8 do
    begin
        if not Invert_flag then
            begin
                data_bit[3*(i-1)+37+1]:=original_data and (255-bit_weight(bit));
                data_bit[3*(i-1)+37+2]:=original_data or bit_weight(bit);
                data_bit[3*(i-1)+37+3]:=original_data or bit_weight(bit);
            end
            else
            begin
```

```
                    data_bit[3*(i-1)+37+1]:=original_data or bit_weight(bit);

                    data_bit[3*(i-1)+37+2]:=original_data and (255-bit_weight(bit));

                    data_bit[3*(i-1)+37+3]:=original_data and (255-bit_weight(bit));

                end;

        If address and bit_weight(i) > 0 then

            begin

                if not invert_flag then data_bit[3*(i-1)+37+2]:=original_data and
(255-bit_weight(bit))

                        else data_bit[3*(i-1)+37+2]:=original_data or bit_weight(bit);

                end;

        end;

    (* data bits *)

    for i:=1 to 4 do

    begin

        if not Invert_flag then

            begin

                    data_bit[3*(i-1)+61+1]:=original_data and (255-bit_weight(bit));

                    data_bit[3*(i-1)+61+2]:=original_data or bit_weight(bit);

                    data_bit[3*(i-1)+61+3]:=original_data or bit_weight(bit);

            end

            else

            begin

                    data_bit[3*(i-1)+61+1]:=original_data or bit_weight(bit);

                    data_bit[3*(i-1)+61+2]:=original_data and (255-bit_weight(bit));

                    data_bit[3*(i-1)+61+3]:=original_data and (255-bit_weight(bit));

            end;

        If data and bit_weight(i) > 0 then

            begin

                if not invert_flag then data_bit[3*(i-1)+61+2]:=original_data and
(15-bit_weight(bit))

                        else data_bit[3*(i-1)+61+2]:=original_data or bit_weight(bit);

                end;

        end;

    (* transmit the code for 10 times *)

    for Transmit_time:=1 to 10 do

    begin

        for i:=1 to 73 do

        begin

            port[Port_address]:=data_bit[i];

            delay(11); (* a delay to give a 1 ms delay, oscillation frequency: 1 kHz *)

        end;

    end;

end;
```

```
(* Main program *)
begin
    COM_address;
    port[RS232_address]:=0;
    repeat
        clrscr;
        write('Input the address of receiver HT-12D (0-255): ');readln(addressx);
        write('Input the data to be transmitted (0-15)      : ');readln(datax);
        transmit_serial_data(RS232_address+4,0,0,addressx,datax,true);
        write('Quit the program [Y/N]: ');readln(ch);
    until upcase(ch)='Y'
end.
```

The encoder, HT-12E, can be used as a 12-bit parallel-to-serial data converter. The serial data can be read into a computer via one input line and software can be used to decode the serial data into a parallel data. The following Turbo Pascal 6 program reads serial data from an HT-12E encoder via the CTS line of the RS232 port, decodes the serial data and shows the parallel data (eight address bits and four data bits) on the screen. The experimental circuit is given in Figure 4.18. The external resistance is 2.5 MΩ, which gives a system clock frequency of 1 kHz. The Dout (pin 17) is connected to the CTS terminal of the RS232 experimental board. This circuit also works with the game port. The Dout can be connected to one of the digital inputs to the game port.

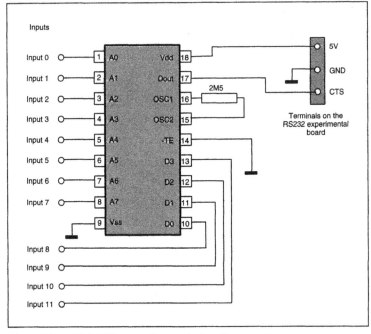

Figure 4.18 HT-12E experimental circuit

TP6 program list of HT-12D

```
Program HT_12_receiver;
(* Software driver for HT-12D series receiver *)


uses
    graph,crt,dos;
var
    Value, oldvalue:integer;
    bit:array [1..15] of byte;
    i,led_selected,Serial_input_byte, Baud_rate_byte,
    Data_length_byte, Stop_length_byte, Parity_byte :integer;


(* to load two included library files *)
{$I c:\ioexp\tplib1.pas}


Function Serial_data(x:byte):byte;
{decode the signal issued by HT-12E. Input connected to CTS line}
{x=1 for A0-A7, x=2 for D0-D3}
var
    Sdata, Saddress,i:byte;
    TimeI_0,TimeI_1,ClockI,TimeI:longint;
begin
    (* Find the time period (software count) for high state *)
    repeat delay(1) until Port[RS232_address+6] and 16=16;  {find the low state}
    repeat delay(1) until Port[RS232_address+6] and 16=0    {find the low-to-high
transition};
    ClockI:=0;
    repeat
         ClockI:=ClockI+1;
         delay(1);
    until Port[RS232_address+6] and 16=16;

    (* Find the pilot period, long period low state *)
    repeat
         repeat delay(1) until Port[RS232_address+6] and 16=16;
         TimeI_0:=0;
         repeat
              TimeI_0:=TimeI_0+1;
              delay(1);
         until Port[RS232_address+6] and 16=0;
    until TimeI_0>12*clockI;

    ClockI:=0; (* find the clock period of start bit *)
```

```
        repeat delay(1) until port[RS232_address] and 16 = 0;

    repeat

            ClockI:=ClockI+1;

            delay(1);

    until port[RS232_address+6] and 16=16     {find the low going transition};


    (* read the following 12 bits *)

    for i:=1 to 12 do

    begin

        TimeI_1:=0;

        repeat delay(1) until port[RS232_address+6] and 16 = 0;

        repeat

                TimeI_1:=TimeI_1+1;

                delay(1);

        until port[RS232_address+6] and 16=16;

        if abs(TimeI_1-ClockI)>clockI/2 then bit[i]:=0 else bit[i]:=1;

    end;

    Sdata:=0;

    Saddress:=0;

    for i:=1 to 8 do Saddress:=Saddress+bit[i]*bit_weight(i);

    for i:=9 to 12 do Sdata:=Sdata+bit[i]*bit_weight(i-8);

    if x=1 then Serial_data:=Saddress;

    if x=2 then Serial_data:=Sdata;

end;


(* Main program *)

begin

    COM_address;

repeat

    write('Received serial address= ',serial_data(1));

    delay(300);

    write('          Received serial data   = ',serial_data(2));

    readln;

until keypressed;

end.
```

4.7 I²C bus

I²C stands for Inter-IC-Communication bus which is a data bus designed by Philips and allows integrated circuits or modules to communicate with each other. The bus allows data and instructions to be exchanged between devices via only *two* wires! This greatly simplifies the design of complex electronic circuits. There is a family of I²C compatible devices available for various applications. They include I/O expansion, A/D and D/A conversion, time keeping, memory and frequency synthesis, etc. By implementing an I^2C bus to a computer, you can enjoy all the powerful features offered by the bus and its support ICs. Both the Centronic port and the RS232 port can be used to implement the I^2C bus.

4.7.1 Principles of the I^2C bus

The I^2C bus consists of two lines: a bi-directional data line (SDA) and a clock line (SCL). Both lines are connected to the positive power supply via pull-up resistors. An I^2C bus system is shown in Figure 4.19. The device generating the message is a 'transmitter'. The device receiving the message is the 'receiver'. The device that controls the bus operation is the 'master'. The devices which are controlled by the master are the 'slaves'. The following communication protocol is defined: (1) a data transfer may be initiated only when the bus is not busy and (2) during the data transfer, the data line must remain stable whenever the clock line is high. Changes in the data line while the clock line is high are interpreted as control signals. The following bus conditions can be defined (see Figure 4.20):

(i)   **Bus not busy:** Both data and clock lines remain *high*.
(ii)   **Start data transfer:** A change in the state of the data line *from high to low* while the clock is *high*, defines the START condition.
(iii)   **Stop data transfer:** A change in the state of the data line *from low to high* while the clock is *high* defines the STOP condition.
(iv)   **Data valid:** The state of the data line represents valid data after a start condition. The data line is *stable* for the duration of the *high period of the clock signal*. The data on the line may be changed during the low period of the clock signal. There is one clock pulse per data bit. Each data transfer is initiated with a START condition and terminated with a STOP condition. The number of data bytes transferred between the start and stop conditions is not limited. The information is transmitted byte-wise and the receiver acknowledges with a ninth bit.
(v)   **Acknowledge bit:** Each byte is followed by an acknowledge bit. The acknowledge bit is a high level put on the bus by the transmitter whereas the master generates an extra acknowledge related clock pulse. The acknowledge bit is a low level put on the bus by the receiver. A slave receiver which is addressed is obliged to generate an acknowledge bit after the reception of each byte.

The device that acknowledges has to pull down the SDA line during the acknowledge clock pulse in such a way that the SDA line is at a stable low state during the high period of the acknowledge related clock pulse. A master receiver must signal an end to the slave transmitter by not generating an acknowledge on the last byte that has been clocked out of the slave.

4.7.2 Operation of the I^2C bus

Before any data is transmitted on the bus, the device which should respond is addressed first. This is carried out with the 7-bit address byte plus R/-W bit transmitted after a start condition. A typical address byte has the following format:

Fixed address bits + Programmable address bits + R/-W bit (in total 8 bits)

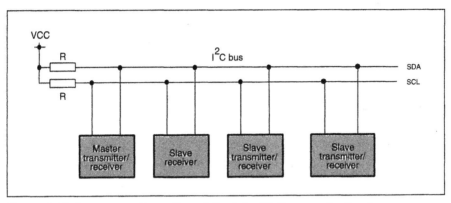

Figure 4.19 System configuration of the Inter-IC-Communication bus

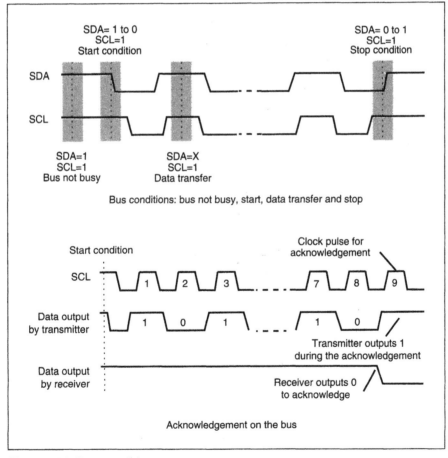

Figure 4.20 Bus conditions

The fixed address depends on the IC and it can not be changed. The programmable address bits can be set using the address pins on the chip. The last bit is the read/write bit which indicates the direction of data flow. The byte following the address byte is the control byte which depends on the IC used. Following the control byte are the data bytes. The serial data has the format shown in Figure 4.21.

4.7.3 Implementing I^2C bus on the Centronic and RS232 ports

An experimental circuit showing a simple I^2C bus on the Centronic port is given in Figure 4.22. The circuit only implements the I^2C bus standard with the computer being the master. Two transistors provide the open collection output for the data and clock lines. The voltage of the I^2C bus is 5V. The transistors could be any general purpose npn transistors with a switching frequency of 100 kHz. SCL is connected to D2 terminal of the Centronic experimental board (bit 1 of the data port). SDA is connected to D1 terminal (bit 0 of the data port). SDA is read into the computer via S1 terminal of the experimental board (bit 3 of the status port).The circuit can also use a 7407 open-collector buffer.

An experimental circuit of the I^2C bus for the RS232 port is also shown in Figure 4.22. DTR and RTS terminals on the experimental board control the SCL and SDA lines, respectively. SDA is read into the computer via CTS terminal. Software examples will be given in Chapter 7.

4.7.4 I^2C support chips

Some of the I^2C bus compatible chips are listed below:
LCD drivers: PCF8466, PCF8576, PCF8577, PCF8578/79, SAA1064
Memories: PCF8570, PCF8572/8573, PCF8582A, PCF8598-2T
Time keeping: PCF8583, 41T56C, PCF8593, PCF8598
I/O interface: PCF8574, PCF8584, PCF8582, PCF82B715
8-bit 4 channel A/D and D/A converters: PCF8591
RC-5 infra-red transmitter: SAA3028
DTMF/modem/tone generator: PCD3311/3312
Speech synthesizer: PCF8200
PCM audio interface: SAA1136

4.8 Serial peripheral interface (SPI)

The SPI bus allows peripheral integrated ICs to be connected to a host computer using only three wires. One is the system clock which is an input to the IC; another is the data input and the third is the data output from the IC. A number of SPI compatible ICs can be connected to the same SPI bus. The IC which is communicating with the computer should be selected. Ths is achieved by making the chip select on that IC (-CS) low. Various ICs including A/D and D/A converters, analogue multiplexers, etc. have the SPI bus.

Both the Centronic and RS232 port can be implemented with the SPI bus. By doing so, you can connect various ICs to your computer easily. Some examples will be given in later chapters.

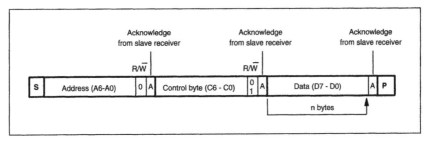

Figure 4.21 Serial data format on the bus

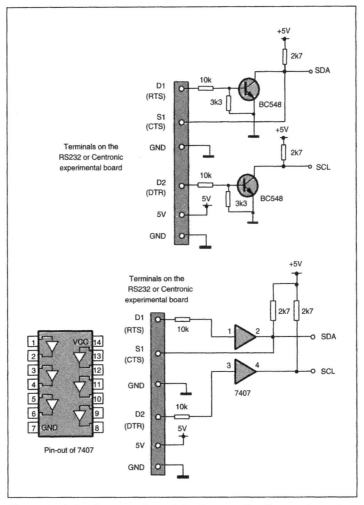

Figure 4.22 Implementation of the bus on the Centronic and RS232 ports

4.9 MicroLAN bus

The MicroLAN bus was introduced by Dallas Semiconductor. It requires only one wire and a ground reference. The cable could be an unshielded low-cost telephone wire. The bus has one master and multiple slaves with 2^{56} logical addresses. The maximum cable length is more than 300 meters without using any repeaters. The bus allows various devices to be connected together. These include data tags which store an identification number, EEPROMs, temperature sensors, real time clocks and sensing and/or activating switches, etc. Every device has a unique network identification number. The bus has the standard TTL/CMOS voltage level and all the devices in a network are powered by the data line. A voltage from 0 to 0.8V is interpreted as logic 0 and a voltage above 2.2V is interpreted as logic 1. A voltage of 2.8 is required to power all the devices. The data transfer rate is in the range from DC to 16300 bits per second. The bus can be implemented on the RS232 port of a computer. The computer is the master controller and all the devices are slaves.

4.10 Interfacing between TTL and CMOS gates

It is necessary to interface the output of TTL logic gates to the CMOS inputs and vice versa. Figure 4.23 shows the methods for connections. If the power supplies of the TTL and the CMOS gates are the same, a CMOS gate can drive one LS-TTL gate directly without using any external components. If more than one LS-TTL gates are to be driven, a CMOS buffer such as the 4049B should be used to boost up the current. When an LS-TTL gate drives a CMOS gate, a 2.2 kΩ pull-up resistor should be used.

4.11 Protecting digital I/O lines

The simplest way to protect an I/O line is to use a voltage clamping circuit in which a resistor and a Zener diode are used.

The ultimate protection of digital I/O lines is to use opto-isolators. A typical opto-isolator consists of an infra-red LED and a photo-transistor or a photo-diode. The isolation between the input and output could be as high as several kilovolts. A typical application is shown in Figure 4.24. There are various types of opto-isolators in terms of their electrical characteristics of the inputs and outputs and the number of opto-isolators. The input can be a standard LED type, low current LED type, AC type or CMOS/TTL type. The output can be transistor type, Darlington transistor type, CMOS/TTL type or Schmitt trigger type. The number of on-board opto-isolators pairs can be 1, 2 or 4.

An important parameter of the opto-isolator is the transfer ratio, which is the ratio of the output current to the input current expressed as a percentage. A transfer ratio of 100 percent will provide an output current of 1 mA for each 1 mA input current to the LED. The transistors type have a transfer ratio of 20%. The Darlington transistor type can have a transfer ratio of 500%.

The PC817, PC827 and PC847 (Sharp, RS175-110, RS175-126 and RS175-132) are 1-channel, 2-channel and 4-channel opto-isolators. The characteristics of the opto-isolators are the same. The maximum isolation voltage is 5000V rms. The transfer ratio is between 50% and 600%. The typical

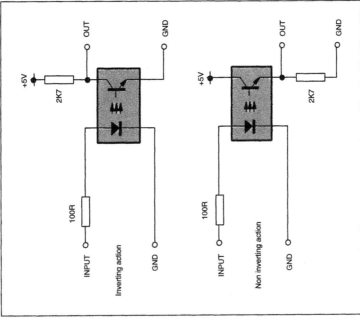

Figure 4.24 Applications of opto-isolators

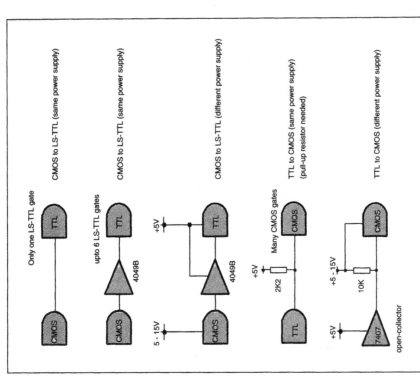

Figure 4.23 Interface between CMOS and TTL gates

forward voltage of the LED is 1.2V and the maximum forward current is 50 mA. The maximum voltage applied across the c and e of the transistor must not exceed 35V and the maximum forward current of the transistor is 50 mA. The rise and the fall time is typically 4 and 3 μs, respectively. The maximum frequency is 150 kHz. The pin-out is shown in Figure 4.25(a). The PC815, PC825 and PC845 (Sharp, RS175-198, RS175-205, RS175-211) are 1-channel, 2-channel and 4-channel Darlington opto-isolators. The isolation voltage is 5000V rms. The transfer ratio is 600–7500%. The typical forward voltage across the LED is 1.2V and the maximum forward current to the LED is 50 mA. The maximum voltage across c and e of the Darlington transistor is 35V and the maximum collector current is 80 mA. The rise time is typically 60 μs and the fall time is 53 μs. The pin-out is shown in Figure 4.25(b).

The HCPL-2630 (Toshiba, RS768-116) is a dual channel high speed TTL output compatible opto-isolator. It has a maximum isolation voltage of 2500V rms. The forward voltage for the LED is typically 1.5V and the maximum forward current is 15 mA. The IC requires a 5V power supply. The output transistor has a maximum collector current 50 mA. The rise and fall time are 30 ns and 30 ns, respectively. The highest data transfer rate is 10 Mbd. The fan-out of the output is 5. The pin-out and the internal block diagram is given in Figure 4.26(a) and (b).

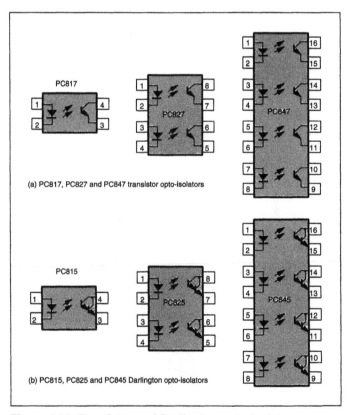

(a) PC817, PC827 and PC847 transistor opto-isolators

(b) PC815, PC825 and PC845 Darlington opto-isolators

Figure 4.25 Transistor and Darlington opto-isolators

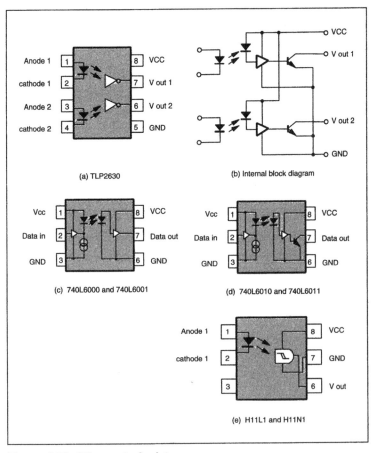

Figure 4.26 Other opto-isolators

The 74OL6000 series (Quality Technologies) are opto-isolators for TTL and CMOS logic circuits. They have a data transfer speed of typically 15 MBd and an isolation voltage of 2500V rms. The input and output are both TTL or CMOS compatible. The fan-out of the output is 10. The 74OL6000 (RS650-829) is an LSTTL to TTL buffer; the 74OL6001 (RS650-835) is an LSTTL to TTL inverter; the 74OL6010 (RS650-841) is an LSTTL to CMOS buffer and the 74OL6011 (RS650-857) is an LSTTL to CMOS inverter. The pin-out is given in Figure 4.26(c) and (d).

Some opto-isolators have a Schmitt trigger output type. The H11L1 (Isocom Components, RS585-292) and the H11N1 (Quality Technologies, RS577-875) are two examples. The former has a data transfer rate of 1 MHz and the latter has 5 MHz. The forward voltage of the LED is 1.5V with a maximum forward current of 60 mA for the H11L1 and 30mA for the H11N1. The maximum collector current is 50 mA. The pin-out is shown in Figure 4.26(e).

Drivers for external devices

In computer control applications, a computer must be able to drive various external devices. These may be lights, heaters, DC or stepper motors, speakers, visual displays, etc.

5.1 Power drivers

Logic and peripheral interface ICs are not able to provide high current to drive external devices. In digital control applications, power drivers are required to drive the devices.

5.1.1 Opto-isolator drivers

Opto-isolators can be used to drive low current external devices. They also provide electrical isolation in the same time. The maximum driving current is limited by the photo-transistors. For example the PC815 series Darlington opto-isolators (Sharp, RS175-198) have a maximum output current of 80 mA. This will be enough to drive a small relay, which could then control devices operating at higher voltages and currents (Figure 5.1). The PS2502 series Darlington opto-isolators

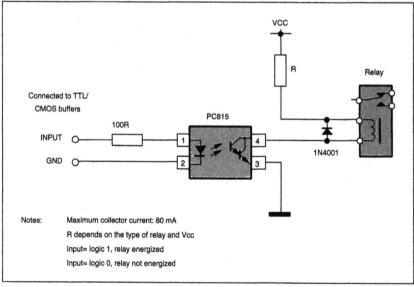

Figure 5.1 PC815 opto-isolator used for driving a relay

(NEC, RS590-424 and RS590-430) can supply a current up to 160 mA. The transfer ratio is typically 2000%. The forward voltage of the LED is 1.1V and the maximum forward current is 80 mA. The maximum voltage across c and e of the photo-transistor is 40V and the rise and fall time is typically 100 μs.

5.1.2 Transistor drivers

Transistor drivers are the simplest and the most economical way of driving external devices. A typical application is shown in Figure 5.2(a), in which a BC108C or a ZTX300 npn transistor is used. The BC108C and ZTX300 have a maximum collector current of 100 mA and 500 mA with a maximum

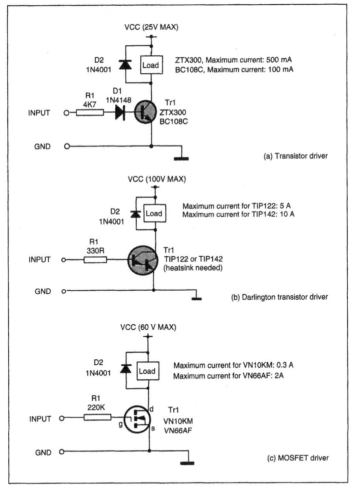

Figure 5.2 Transistor, Darlington transistor and MOSFET drivers

power rating of 300 mW and 500 mW. The maximum voltage that can be applied across c and e is 20V for the BC108C and 25V for the ZTX300. The maximum operation frequency is 300 MHz for the BC108C and 150 MHz for the ZTX300. Suppressor diodes must be used for inductive loads such as relays or electric motors. It is not necessary if the load is resistive such as light bulbs or electronic circuits.

5.1.3 Darlington drivers

Figure 5.2(b) shows a driver circuit using a Darlington power transistor, the TIP122 or TIP142. The TIP122 controls a voltage up to 100V and a current of 5 A. The maximum power rating is 65 W. Darlington transistors start to conduct for a base-to-collector voltage of 1.2V and have a typical current gain of 5000, therefore a base voltage slightly higher than 1.2V will cause the transistor to saturate in conduction. The base can be connected to a TTL gate via a resistor. The TIP142 is rated at 10 A. Both of them have a maximum operation frequency of 5 MHz. Protection diodes should be used for inductive loads.

5.1.4 MOSFET drivers

Figure 5.2(c) shows a circuit using VMOS transistors, the VN10KM or VN66AF. A VMOS transistor requires a forward gate-to-source bias voltage of about 0.8 volts before it starts to conduct. It is biased hard into conduction by a forward bias of about 5V. The input impedance of a MOSFET device is extremely high and the loading on the output port of the computer is negligible. Therefore, it can be driven directly by a TTL/CMOS gate without using any resistors. The VN10KM allows a maximum voltage of 60V and a current of 310 mA. The VN66AF can handle a maximum voltage of 60V and a current of 2 A. The rise and the fall time are around 15 ns.

5.1.5 PROFET drivers

The PROFET power drivers are so-called 'intelligent MOS' drivers and provide power switching for digital control applications. The input control is 5V logic level compatible. The driver features a built-in thermal shutdown facility which protects the chip from over-temperature, short-circuit and over-current conditions. The thermal protection turns off the MOS power output at a temperature of 140°C. When the temperature falls to 125°C, the switch is turned on again. The devices also have a status output to show the conditions of open circuit and over-temperature.

    The BTS410 is an example. Its pin-out is shown in Figure 5.3. It could control voltages in the range 4.9 to 40V and the over-voltage protection level is 42–52V. The maximum operation temperature is 150°C and the maximum over-current level varies from 3.1 to 21 A depending on its temperatures. It has a very small on-resistance over the full temperature range. The turn-on and turn-off periods are 60 and 50 μs. The input voltage for switch on is 2 to 5V and that for switch off is 0 to 0.8V. The input current is typically 25 μA for an input voltage of 3.5V.

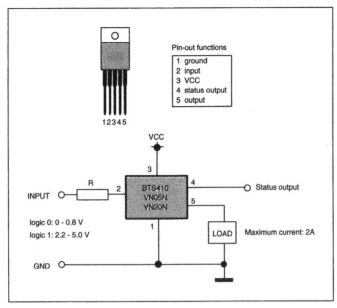

Figure 5.3 PROFET driver

The VN05N and VN20N are other two examples. The pin-out and a typical application circuit are shown in Figure 5.3. The VN05N is able to switch 12 A continuously and the VN20N to switch 28 A.

5.2 LED drivers

5.2.1 Standard LEDs

Standard LEDs require a current of 10 to 20 mA at a 2V potential to illuminate. Several LED drivers are shown in Figure 5.4. Figure 5.4(a) shows a driver using a transistor ZTX300. In the circuit, a resistor R should be used in series with the LED and its value should be chosen according to the voltage applied. LEDs can be also driven by TTL or CMOS gates directly (Figure 5.4(b) and (c)). An LSTTL gate (not a buffer) can sink 7–10 mA and source 0.4 mA. An LSTTL buffer can sink 24 mA and source 15 mA. The supply voltage for TTL ICs is 5V and the serial resistor R should be around 220 Ω. For CMOS buffers, R should be chosen according to the supply voltage (see Figure 5.4).

5.2.2 Low current LEDs

Low current LEDs require only 2 mA at 1.8V to illuminate. The LEDs can be driven using the circuits for the standard LEDs (Figure 5.4). The values of the serial resistor, however, should be changed. The relationship between the supply voltage (VCC) and the resistor value is shown below:

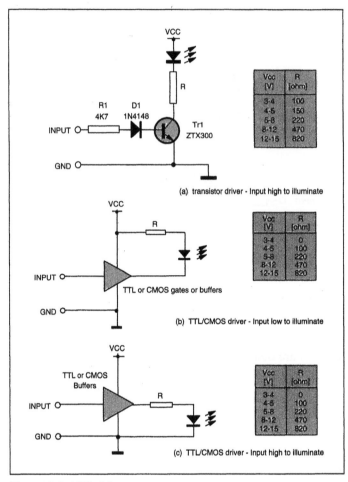

Figure 5.4 LED drivers

Vcc=3–4 V   R=600R
Vcc=4–5 V   R=1K6
Vcc=5–8 V   R=3K1
Vcc=8–12 V   R=5K1
Vcc=12–15V   R=6K6

5.2.3 Multi-colour LEDs

There are two types of multi-colour LEDs. One is the bi-colour type which has one red and one green LED packed in a single package. By changing the polarity, the colour can be changed from red to green or vice versa. The other type is the tri-colour type. It has three terminals. One is common, the other two are connected to the anodes of a red LED and a green LED. It gives four statuses: all off, red LED on, green LED on and two LEDs both on (which gives yellow). They can be driven using the LED drivers shown in Figure 5.4.

5.2.4 Infra-red LEDs

Most infra-red LEDs are high current types and are mostly used for remote control and communication applications. An example of these LEDs is the SFH485 series (Siemens). The maximum forward current through the LED is 100 mA with a forward voltage of 1.5V. The SFH485 (RS585-242) has a beam angle of 40° and the SFH485P (RS585-236) has an angle of 80°. The radiant intensity is 16–32 mW/Sr for the SFH485 and 3.15–6.3 mW/Sr for the SFH485P. The LED driver shown in Figure 5.4 can be used to drive the infra-red LEDs. Several LEDs can be connected in parallel or in series to boost the power of the infra-red light emission. Figure 5.5(a) shows such a driver circuit.

The OD880 series (Optek) offers higher light emitting power. The beam angles are 80° for the OD880W (RS195-439), 35° for the OD880L (RS195-445) and 8° for the OD880F (RS195-451). The maximum forward voltage is 1.9V and a continuous forward current is 100 mA. If a pulsed signal is used, the peak current would be as high as 3 A. The radiant power for these devices are 16, 50 and 135 mW/sr.

A pulsed infra-red emission scheme is often adopted for remote control applications. The electric current passing through the LED is a train of pulses instead of a continuous current. When the LED is switched on, a large current passes through the LED. Operating in such a manner, a large infra-red radiant flux can be produced. Figure 5.5(b) shows a 38 kHz pulse train generator. The transistor drivers with a suitable rating can be used to drive the LEDs.

5.3 Relay drivers

5.3.1 Dry reed relays

Low power dry reed relays operate with a voltage of about 3.7V and a current of 7.4 mA. They can be driven directly by TTL gates or buffers. Figure 5.6(a) shows such a circuit. The relay is energized when the TTL gate sources the current (the logic high state). A suppressor diode must be used to protect the TTL output. The maximum voltage of the relay contact is usually below 240V.

5.3.2 Transistor relay drivers

Medium and high power relays require a higher coil voltage and current. Figure 5.6(b) shows a circuit using a ZTX300 transistor. The driver operates for a maximum supply voltage of 25V and a maximum current of 0.5 A. The supply voltage is chosen according to the relay used.

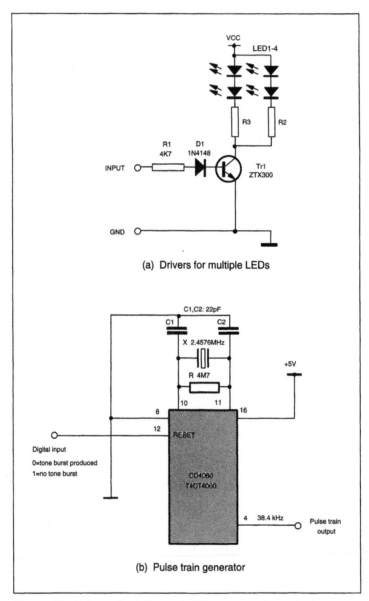

(a) Drivers for multiple LEDs

(b) Pulse train generator

Figure 5.5 Drivers for infra-red LEDs in remote control applications

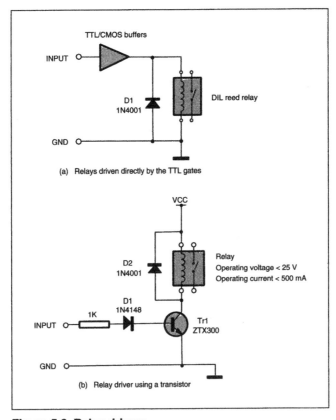

Figure 5.6 Relay drivers

5.4 Integrated power driver ICs

5.4.1 Multi-channel driver ICs

When a number of loads are required, integrated driver ICs such as the ULN2803A array (SGS-Thomson) can be used. It has eight separate Darlington transistor drivers. The pin-out and an application circuit are given in Figure 5.7. Each driver is capable of supplying 500 mA at up to 50V. The inputs of the IC can be connected directly to TTL/CMOS gates. The ULN2003A (Allegro Microsystems RS307–109) has seven drivers.

5.4.2 Latched drivers

The UCN5832A (Allegro Microsystems, RS426-755) is a 32-bit serial-input latched driver. The pin-out and the internal logic diagram are shown in Figure 5.8. The device has 32 bipolar npn open-

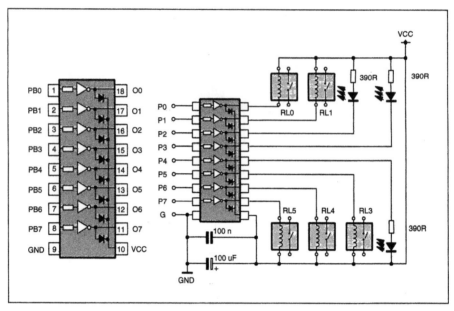

Figure 5.7 ULN2803 Darlington transistor array

collector drivers. Each is capable of driving 150 mA current with a maximum control voltage of 40V. The IC consists of a data latch for each driver, two high speed 16-bit shift registers and control circuitry. The device is controlled via four CMOS digital input lines, which can be driven directly by outputs from a computer. If they are connected to TTL outputs, pull-up resistors (4.7K) should be used. The maximum data input rate is 3.3 MHz.

The timing sequence is shown in Figure 5.9. Serial data present at the input is transferred to the shift register on the transition from 0 to 1 of the clock input. On the next clock pulses, the registers shift data towards the serial data output. The serial data must be stable at the input prior to the rising edge of the clock input. Information presented at any register is transferred to its respective latch when the strobe is high. The latch will continue to accept new data as long as the strobe is high. Data will be latched at the high-to-low transition of the strobe pulse. When the output enable input is low, all of the output buffers are turned off. When the output enable input is high, the output status is controlled by the content of the latches.

The experimental circuit using the Centronic experimental board is shown in Figure 5.10. The serial data input, clock and strobe are connected to D1, D2 and D3 terminals. The TP6 software driver is listed below:

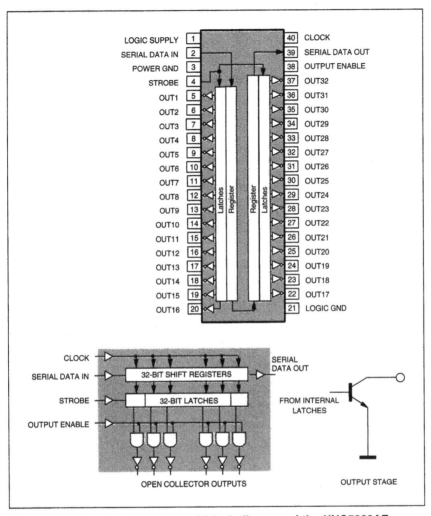

Figure 5.8 Pin-out and the internal block diagram of the UNC5832AF

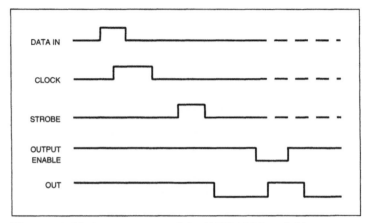

Figure 5.9 Timing sequence of the UCN5832A serial-input latched driver

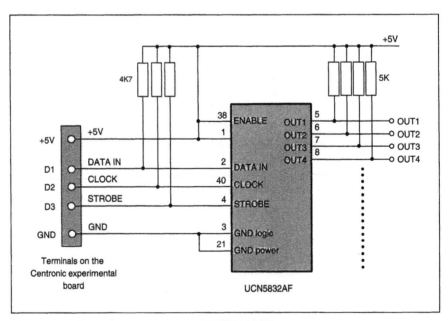

Figure 5.10 Experimental circuit of UNC5801AF

TP6 program list of 5832.PAS

```
Program UCN5832A;
(* software driver for the UCN5832 serial input latched driver *)
(* connected to the Centronic experimental board
    Serial data in connected to D1
    Clock connected to D2
    Strobe connected to D3 *)


uses
    crt, dos;


{$I c:\ioexp\tplib1.pas }


var
    bank1,bank2,bank3,bank4:byte;



Procedure load_data(x:byte);
(* load a data bit into the UCN5833A *)
begin
     write_data_port(P_address,x);      (* data=x, clock=0, strobe=0 *)
     write_data_port(P_address,x+2);    (* data=x, clock=1, strobe=0 *)
     write_data_port(P_address,x);      (* data=x, clock=0, strobe=0 *)
end;



Procedure strobe;
(* strobe the data *)
begin
     write_data_port(P_address,4); (* strobe=1 *)
     write_data_port(P_address,0);
end;



Procedure output_control(bank1,bank2,bank3,bank4:byte);
(* bank1: lowest 8-bit byte, bank4: highest 8-bit byte *)
var
    i:integer;
begin
     for i:=1 to 8 do load_data( round (bank4 and bit_weight(9-i) / bit_weight(9-i) ));
     for i:=1 to 8 do load_data( round (bank3 and bit_weight(9-i) / bit_weight(9-i) ));
     for i:=1 to 8 do load_data( round (bank2 and bit_weight(9-i) / bit_weight(9-i) ));
     for i:=1 to 8 do load_data( round (bank1 and bit_weight(9-i) / bit_weight(9-i) ));
```

```
        strobe; (* strobe the data into the UCN5833A *)
end;


(* Main program *)
begin
    centronic_address;
    writeln('UCN5832A demonstration program');
    writeln('Out1, Out9, Out17 and Out25 oscillating, other outputs = zero ');
    repeat
            output_control(1,1,1,1);  (* first output in each bank=1, output stage enabled (output
inverted) *)
            delay(1000);
            output_control(0,0,0,0);  (* output stage off *)
            delay(1000);
    until keypressed
end.
```

The UCN5810AF (Allegro Microsystems) is a 10-bit latched driver. Each driver has a 15 mA current rating. For a 5V digital power supply, when the 10 outputs are all turned on or all off, the quiescent current is 100 µA. The data loading procedure for the device is the same as for the UCN5832A. The pin-out and the internal logic diagram are shown in Figure 5.11. Unlike the UCN5832A, the outputs from the latches are not inverted.

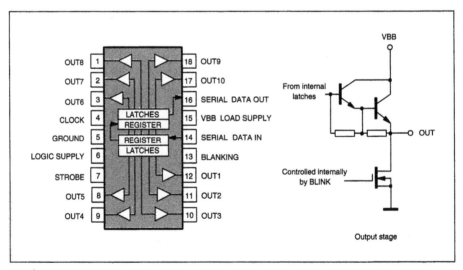

Figure 5.11 Pin-out and the internal block diagram of the UNC5810AF

5.5 Opto-isolated zero-crossing solid state relays

Zero-crossing solid state relays are suitable for AC switching applications. The input circuit is an LED. The LED turns on when a current passes through it. The light from the LED is focused on to a phototransistor connected to the triac control circuitry. Since the only connection between the input circuit and the output is a beam of light, they could achieve a voltage isolation as high as several thousand volts. The actual switching device is a triac. When it is triggered, the device conducts on either half of an AC cycle. The zero-voltage detector makes sure that the triac is only triggered when the voltage of the AC line is very close to zero.

The MOC3041 (ISOCOM Components, RS195-4122) incorporates an infra-red LED, a zero-crossing unit and a triac. The block diagram and an application circuit are given in Figure 5.12. It has a 400V rating and can handle a maximum current of 100 mA. A variety of high power solid state relays are available. Figure 5.13 shows a high power zero-crossing solid state relay.

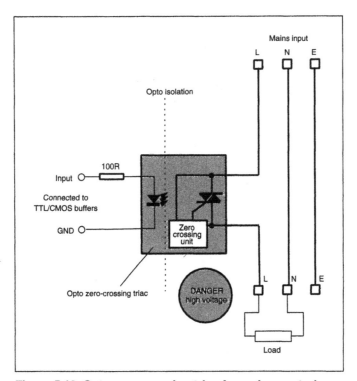

Figure 5.12 Opto zero-crossing triac for mains control applications

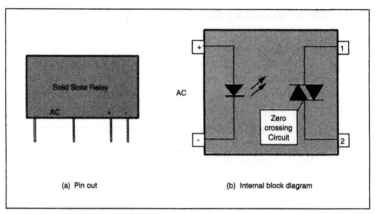

(a) Pin out   (b) Internal block diagram

Figure 5.13 High power zero-crossing solid state relay

5.6 DC motor drivers

DC motors can be driven by relays (Figure 5.6) or transistors (Figure 5.2). The on/off as well as the rotation direction of a motor can be controlled using a specially arranged relay driver. The circuit requires a single rail power supply and the circuit diagram is shown in Figure 5.14. The SPDT (single

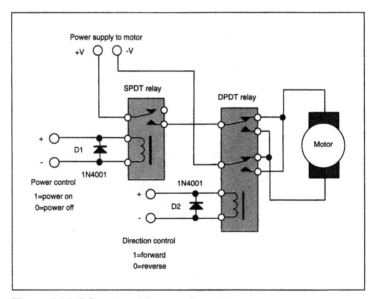

Figure 5.14 DC motor drivers using relays

pole double throw) relay controls the power on/off and the DPDT (double pole and double throw) relay controls the rotating direction of the motor.

Another method of controlling a DC motor is to use full-bridge drivers such as the L298N (SGS-Thomson, RS636-384). It is a high voltage (up to 46V) and high current (2 A DC for each channel) dual full-bridge driver which is designed to accept standard TTL logic levels. The pin-out and the internal block diagram are given in Figure 5.15. Vs (pin 4) is the power supply for the motors and Vss (pin 9) is the power supply for the logic circuitry which is +5V. Pins 6 and 11 enable the input signals to the two drivers. IN1 and IN2 (pins 5 and 7) control the first full-bridge driver and IN3 and IN4 control the second driver. The emitters of the transistors are connected together and the external terminals can be used for connecting an external sensing resistor.

A typical application is given in Figure 5.16. When ENA is low, the inputs are inhibited and the motor stops rotation. When ENA is high, the inputs are enabled. The two inputs IN1 and IN2 control the modes of the motor.

IN1=1, IN2=0,	motor turning clockwise
IN1=0, IN2=1,	motor turning anti-clockwise
IN1=IN2,	motor stop

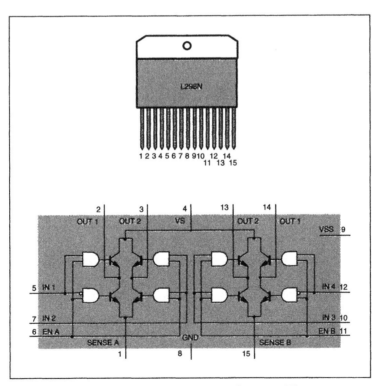

Figure 5.15 Pin-out and block diagram of the L298N

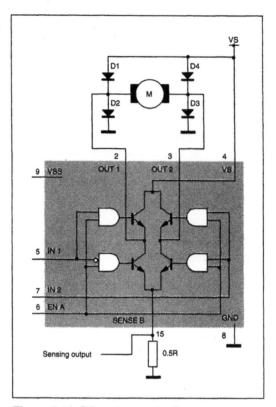

Figure 5.16 DC motor controller

5.7 Stepper motor drivers

There are two types of stepper motors: the uni-polar four phase and the two phase type (see Figure 5.17). Different driving schemes are required for these motors.

5.7.1 Drivers for four-phase uni-polar stepper motors

Three stepping sequences can be used. They are the wave drive, the full-step drive and the half-step drive. The sequences are shown in Figure 5.18.

The wave drive is the simplest way of driving stepper motors. Each winding is energized in sequences. By energizing the windings in the reverse order, the rotor rotates in the opposite direction. As only one winding is energized at a time, the torque of the motor is low. To improve this, the full step drive is used. The full-step drive involves a similar four-step sequence, but two windings are energized at a time. Because of this, the torque of the motor is improved. The half-step drive is a

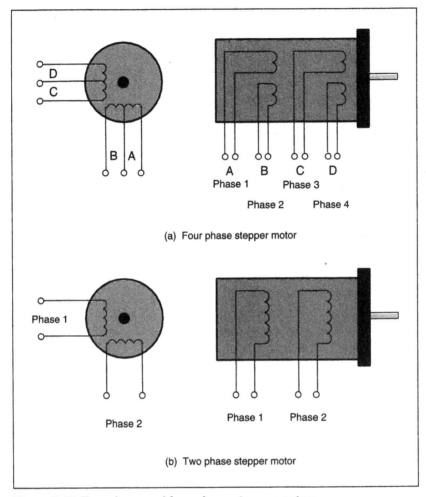

(a) Four phase stepper motor

(b) Two phase stepper motor

Figure 5.17 Two-phase and four-phase stepper motors

combination of the wave drive and the full-step drive, so as to double the number of steps available for one revolution. In this mode, the torque of the motor varies with steps, but the motor runs much smoother. Dedicated stepper motor control ICs are used to drive the motors.

The UCN5804 (Allegro Microsystems, RS653-531) can generate all three stepping sequences. The pin-out, the internal block diagram and the typical application of the IC are shown in Figure 5.19. The IC requires two power supplies, one for driving the logic circuits of the IC and one for driving the stepper motors. Pin 16 is connected to the positive rail of the power supply for logic circuits. The maximum voltage is 7V. Pin 2 and pin 7 are connected to the power supply of a motor. Pins 4, 5, 12 and 13 are the ground of the power supplies. The four outputs from the chip (pins 1, 3, 6 and 8) are internally connected to four Darlington transistors which have a maximum rating of 35V at 1.5 A.

(a) wave drive sequence

STEP	A	B	C	D
1	ON	OFF	OFF	OFF
2	OFF	ON	OFF	OFF
3	OFF	OFF	ON	OFF
4	OFF	OFF	OFF	ON

(c) half step drive sequence

STEP	A	B	C	D
1	ON	OFF	OFF	OFF
2	ON	ON	OFF	OFF
3	OFF	ON	OFF	OFF
4	OFF	ON	ON	OFF
5	OFF	OFF	ON	OFF
6	OFF	OFF	ON	ON
7	OFF	OFF	OFF	ON
8	ON	OFF	OFF	ON

(b) full step drive sequence

STEP	A	B	C	D
1	ON	OFF	OFF	ON
2	ON	ON	OFF	OFF
3	OFF	ON	ON	OFF
4	OFF	OFF	ON	ON

Figure 5.18 Stepping sequences for the four-phase stepper motors

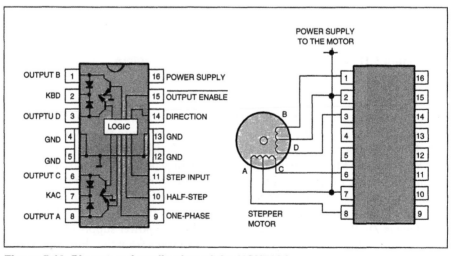

Figure 5.19 Pin-out and application of the UCN5804

The Output Enable (-OE, pin 15) controls the output of the IC. When it is at logic high, all outputs are turned off. Pin 14 (Direction) sets the rotation direction of the motor. Pin 11 is the Step Input. A high-to-low transition on the pin makes the stepper motor rotate one step. The stepping modes are configured by pin 9 (One-Phase) and pin 10 (Half-Step).

pin 9=L	pin 10=L:	to select the full step sequence
pin 9=H	pin 10=L:	to select the wave driving sequence
pin 9=L	pin 10=H:	to select the half-step driving sequence
pin 9=H	pin 10=H:	step inhibit

In operation, pins 9, 10 and 14 should only be changed when the Step Input is at the logic high state.

Another popular stepper motor driver is the SAA1027 (Philips Semiconductor, RS300-237). It can be used for driving four-phase motors. The supply voltage range is between 9.5 to 18V. The maximum current of the output is 500 mA. The input is not TTL compatible. A logic high will be a voltage above 7.5V and a logic low should be a voltage below 4.5V.

If high power stepper motors are used, high power Darlington transistors, such as the TIP122, can be used. It is rated at 5 A at a voltage up to 100V. The driver circuit is shown in Figure 5.20. The

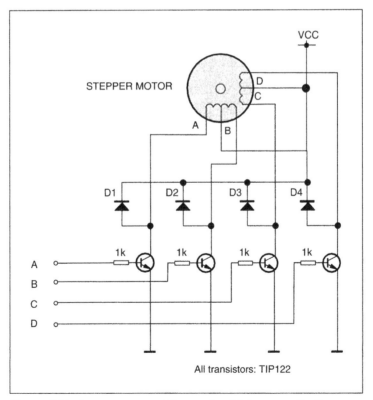

Figure 5.20 Stepper motor driver using high power Darlington transistors

inputs A, B, C and D can be connected to a computer port or connected to the UCN5804 or the SAA1027 via an interfacing circuit.

5.7.2 Drivers for two-phase stepper motors

A two-phase stepper motor driver is shown in Figure 5.21. The L298N full bridge driver is used as the power driver of the motor. An L297 stepper motor controller (SGS-Thomson, RS636-362) is used to generate the stepping sequences for the two-phase stepper motors.

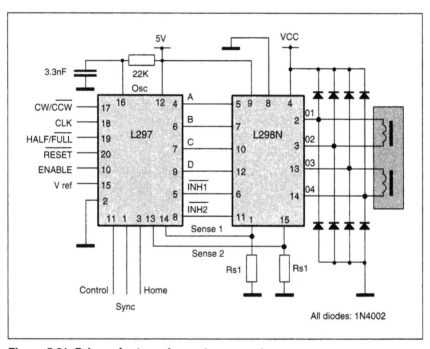

Figure 5.21 Drivers for two-phase stepper motors

5.8 Driving sounders

5.8.1 Drivers for sounders, buzzers and sirens

Piezo-electric sounders are devices to generate sounds. They have a maximum input voltage of 50V and a typical current of 10 mA. Figure 5.22(a) shows a circuit using a TTL/CMOS buffer to driver a sounder. Figure 5.22(b) shows a ZTX300 transistor driver. In order to give a sound, a pulse train

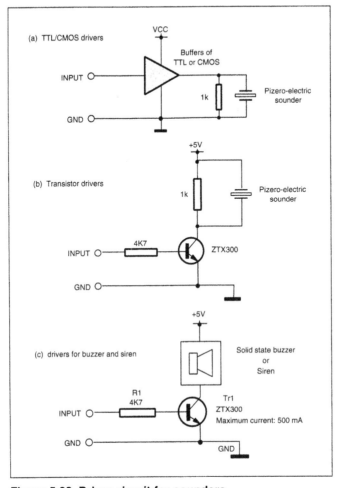

Figure 5.22 Driver circuit for sounders

signal should be supplied to the input. Solid state buzzers are standalone sounders which could give a single tone of sound at about 450 Hz. Figure 5.22(c) shows a transistor driver circuit using the ZTX300. To generate sound, the input to the base of the ZTX300 should be high. Sirens can be driven using the same circuit.

Ultrasonic transducers are used for generating ultrasonic sound, the frequency of which varies from 40 kHz to several MHz. The transducers are widely used in remote control, remote sensing and data communication applications. Ultrasonic range finders and object movement detectors are two examples. A driver circuit producing a precise 38.4 kHz signal is shown in Figure 5.23. In the circuit, when the Reset input is at the logic low state, an ultrasonic signal will be produced. When the Reset input is high, the signal will not be produced.

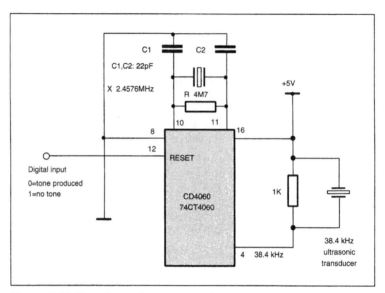

Figure 5.23 Tone burst for ultra-sonic transducers

5.8.2 Drivers for speakers

Figure 5.24(a) shows a speaker amplification circuit using a TBA820M. The IC requires a power supply from 3 to 12 V and provides an output power of 2 W RMS using an 8 Ω speaker. Pin 2 is the inverting input and there is an internal 6K resistor between the input and output of the IC. This allows the voltage gain of the amplifier to be adjusted by an external resistor and the voltage gain is equal to the value of the internal resistor divided by the external resistor. The resistor is recommended to be in the range from 22 to 220 Ω. The input sound signal generated by D/A converters is attenuated by a variable resistor RV2.

The LM380N-1 is another audio amplifier IC having a fixed gain of 50. The gain can be increased to 200 by using external components. The IC incorporates output current limiting and thermal shutdown. It needs a power supply 4 to 12V. The minimum load impedance is 8 Ω. A typical circuit is shown in Figure 5.24(b).

5.9 Drivers for displays

5.9.1 LED multi-digit displays with on-board driver

The TSM6734T (Three Five System) is a four-digit, 0.3 inch height green LED display with an on-board serial data input. The illumination current required by each segment is 2.0 mA. The pin-out

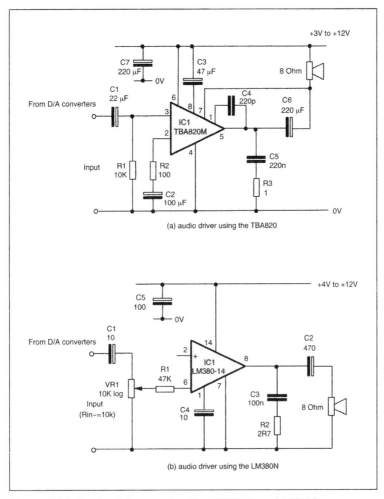

Figure 5.24 Audio drivers using the TBA820 and LM380

and the internal block diagram are shown in Figure 5.25. Current through the LEDs is determined by an external resistor and is typically 25 times greater than the current flowing through the brightness control pin (pin 7). A 100 nF capacitor should be connected from the brightness control pin to the ground. The device requires two power supplies, VDD and VLED. VDD is the power supply to the on-board control circuit and should be between 4.75 to 12V. The supply current is 7 mA for a 12V power supply. V LED is typically 5V, which supplies the power to the LED displays.

Serial data transfer is achieved via three TTL compatible lines: DATA IN (pin 4), -ENABLE (pin 3) and CLOCK (pin 5). Figure 5.26 shows the timing sequence for loading data into the display

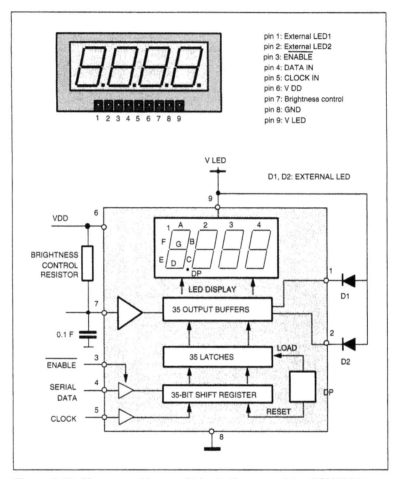

pin 1: External LED1
pin 2: External LED2
pin 3: ENABLE
pin 4: DATA IN
pin 5: CLOCK IN
pin 6: V DD
pin 7: Brightness control
pin 8: GND
pin 9: V LED

Figure 5.25 Pin-out and internal block diagram of the TSM6234

module. The data format consists of a leading '1' followed by 35 data bits. At the low-to-high transition of the clock, serial data presented at the data input is latched internally. -ENABLE should be low to enable the data input. At the 36th low-to-high clock transition, a load signal is generated internally, which loads the 35 bits in the shift registers into the latches. At the next high-to-low transition of the clock, a reset signal is generated which clears all the shift registers. When the chip is powered on, an internal power on reset is generated which resets all the registers and all latches. The start bit and the first clock return the chip to its normal operation. To clear the display, you should load a 1 followed by 35 zeros. This also resets the IC.

The function of the 35 bits of serial data is shown below. Bit 1 is the first bit following the start bit and determines the on/off state of the segment A of digit 1 (see Figure 5.25).

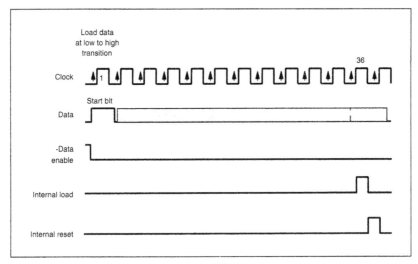

Figure 5.26 Timing sequence of the TSM6034

bits 1–8:   segments A to DP for digit 1
bits 9–16:   segments A to DP for digit 2
bits 17–24:   segments A to DP for digit 3
bits 25–32:   segments A to DP for digit 4

An experimental circuit using the RS232 experimental board is shown in Figure 5.27. The DATA IN and CLOCK are connected to RTS and DTR terminals of the board. -ENABLE is connected to GND to permanently enable the display module.

TP6 program list of TSM6234

```
program TSM6234;

(* software driver for the TSM6234 4 digits LED display *)

(* connected to the RS232 experimental board

   DATA connected to RTS

   CLOCK connected to DTR *)


uses

    crt, dos;


{$I c:\ioexp\tplib1.pas}


Procedure start;

(* load start bit:  data bit high, clock from low to high *)
```

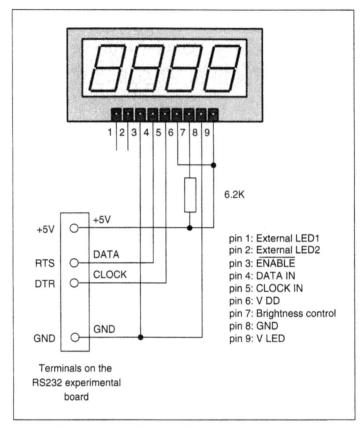

Figure 5.27 Experimental circuit

```
begin
     write_modem_status(RS232_address,1,0);
     write_modem_status(RS232_address,1,1);
     write_modem_status(RS232_address,1,0);
end;


Procedure load_bit(bitx:byte);
(* load a data bit, bitx *)
begin
     write_modem_status(RS232_address,bitx,0);
     write_modem_status(RS232_address,bitx,1);
     write_modem_status(RS232_address,bitx,0);
end;
```

```
Function segment_data(charx:char):byte;
(* charx is character to be displayed, 0,1, to 9, A,B, to F *)
(* this function calculates the binary value for the display *)
(* display binary data: segment a,b,c,d,e,f,dp = DB0,DB1,DB2...DB7 *)
begin
      if charx='0' then segment_data:=$3F;
      if charx='1' then segment_data:=$06;
      if charx='2' then segment_data:=$5B;
      if charx='3' then segment_data:=$4F;
      if charx='4' then segment_data:=$66;
      if charx='5' then segment_data:=$6D;
      if charx='6' then segment_data:=$7D;
      if charx='7' then segment_data:=$07;
      if charx='8' then segment_data:=$7F;
      if charx='9' then segment_data:=$6F;
      if upcase(charx)='A' then segment_data:=$77;
      if upcase(charx)='B' then segment_data:=$7C;
      if upcase(charx)='C' then segment_data:=$39;
      if upcase(charx)='D' then segment_data:=$5E;
      if upcase(charx)='E' then segment_data:=$79;
      if upcase(charx)='F' then segment_data:=$71;
      if upcase(charx)=' ' then segment_data:=$00;
end;


Procedure load_digits(strx:string);
(* load 34 bits of data *)
(* total clock pulses: 35 *)
var
   i,j:integer;
   bitvalue:byte;
begin
      for j:=1 to 4 do
      for i:=1 to 8 do
       begin
            load_bit( round( segment_data(strx[j]) and bit_weight(i) / bit_weight(i) ));
       end;
      for i:=1 to 2 do load_bit(0);
      load_bit(0);
end;


Procedure loaddata_test;
var
```

```
    i:integer;
    digit_string:string[4];

begin
    write_transmit_buffer(RS232_address,0);
    repeat
        clrscr;
        start;
        writeln('Input Q  or q to quit the program ');
        write('Input four digits (0,1,2..9,a,b..f): '); readln(digit_string);
        load_digits(digit_string);
    until upcase(digit_string[1])='Q';


end;


(* main program *)
begin
    COM_address;
    loaddata_test;
end.
```

5.9.2 LED dot matrix displays with on-board driver

The RS590-935 and RS590-941 are 2-inch 5 × 7 dot matrix displays which can be used to generate large display characters. The former is red and the latter is green. The pin-out is given in Figure 5.28. The built-in CMOS integrated circuit contains memory, ASCII character generator, LED multiplexing and drive circuitry. This allows the display to display 96 ASCII characters without the need of additional circuitry.

The I/O lines are TTL compatible and allow a number of displays to be connected together. The power supply is typically 5V and the device consumes 80 mA when all the LEDs are on at full brightness. The brightness can be reduced by half and by a quarter. Pin 3 is the -CHIP ENABLE and it is low active. This pin must be at low state when writing data into the display. Parallel data D0 to D6 should be present at pins 8 to 14 first. Then a high-to-low-then-high pulse is applied to the -WR input (pin 4). At the low-to-high transition, the data is latched to the display. The input digits D0 to D6 determine one of the 96 characters to be displayed. The characters are ASCII characters. No synchronization is necessary and each character will continue to display until it is replaced by another. BL0 and BL1 determine the brightness of the LED.

BL1=0, BL=0:   display blank
BL1=0, BL=1:   LEDs having 1/4 brightness
BL1=1, BL=0:   LEDs having 1/2 brightness
BL1=1, BL=1:   LEDs having full brightness

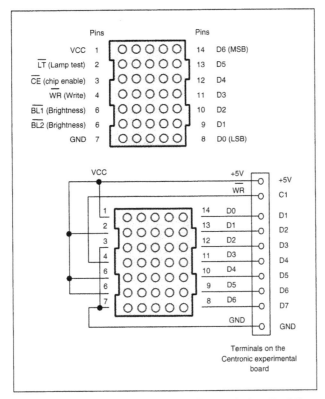

Figure 5.28 Pin-out and an experimental circuit of the matrix display

Pin 2 is the lamp test input (-LT). When it is low, all dots on the display illuminate at the quarter brightness. The lamp test function does not affect the character displayed previously.

An experimental circuit diagram is shown in Figure 5.28. D0 to D6 of the display are connected D1 to D7 terminals on the Centronic experimental board. -WR of the display is connected to the C1 terminal. Pins 2, 5 and 6 are all connected to the logic high state. Because the character set of the display board is the ASCII character set, which is also used in the computer system, an ASCII character can be converted into its binary code using a Turbo Pascal instruction: ORD(char). A TP6 software driver is shown below:

TP6 program list of RS590935.PAS

```
Program LED590935_Dot_metrix_display;
(* Driver for the RS590-935 2 inch intelligent dot matrix displays.
    Display connected to the Centronic experimental board
        D1 to D7 connected to D0 to D6 of the display
```

```
        C1 connected to -WR of the display *)
uses

    crt, dos;

var

    character:char;


{$I c:\ioexp\tplibl.pas }


Procedure display(character:char);
(* display the character on the display *)
var

    i:integer;
begin

    write_data_port(P_address,ord(character));   (* output binary data *)

    writeln('Output value for the character is : ', ord(character));

    write_control_port(P_address,1);   (* -WR high *)

    write_control_port(P_address,0);   (* -WR low  *)

    write_control_port(P_address,1);   (* -WR high again, data latched at low-to-high transition *)

end;


begin

    centronic_address;

    repeat

        Write('Input the character to be displayed: '); readln(Character);

        display(character);

    until ord(character)=13;

end.
```

5.9.3 LED multi-digit dot matrix character displays with on-board driver

The DLR1414 (Siemens, RS589-301) is a four digit, 5×7 dot matrix display module with a built-in CMOS driver circuitry. The on-board integrated circuit contains memory, ASCII ROM decoder, multiplexing circuitry and drivers. Inputs are TTL compatible and a single 5V supply is required. The device is stackable enabling a display system to be built using any number of the modules. The character size is 3.66 mm. The pin-out and the internal block diagram are shown in Figure 5.29. In operation, the data (D0 to D6) and digit address (A0 and A1) are held stable at the inputs. It is followed by a high-to-low pulse at -WR input. Digit 0 is defined as the right hand digit with A0 = A1 = 0.

An experimental circuit is shown in Figure 5.30. D0 to D6 on the display module are connected D1 to D7 terminals of the Centronic experimental board. -WR of the display is connected to the C1 terminal of the board. A0 and A1 are connected to C2 and C3 terminals. Because the character set of the display board is the ASCII character set, which is used in the computer system as well, an ASCII character can be converted into its binary code using the TP6 instruction: ORD(char). A software driver written in TP6 is shown below:

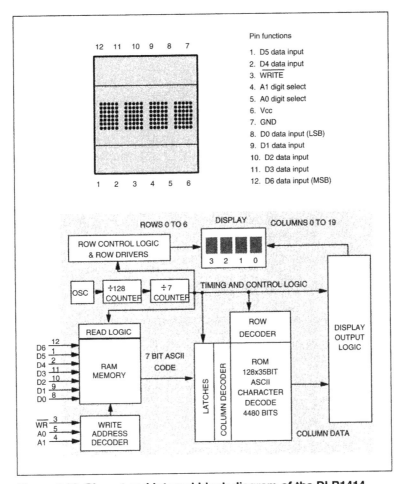

Figure 5.29 Pin-out and internal block diagram of the DLR1414

TP6 program list of 1414.PAS

```
Program RS1414_Dot_metrix_display;
(* Driver for the 1414 intelligent 4 digit dot matrix displays.
    Display connected to the Centronic experimental board
        D1 to D7 connected to D0 to D6 of the display
        C1 connected to -WR of the display
        A0 and A1 connected to C2 and C3 *)
uses
    crt, dos;
var
    ch1,ch2,ch3,ch4:char;
```

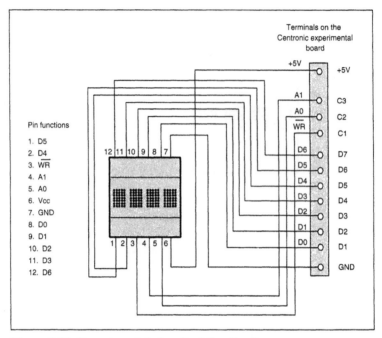

Figure 5.30 Experimental circuit of the display

Pin functions

1. D5
2. D4
3. $\overline{WR}$
4. A1
5. A0
6. Vcc
7. GND
8. D0
9. D1
10. D2
11. D3
12. D6

```pascal
{$I c:\ioexp\tplib1.pas }

Procedure display(character:char;digit:byte);
(* display the character on the display *)
var
    i:integer;
begin
    write_data_port(P_address,ord(character));   (* output binary data *)
    writeln('Output value for the character is : ', ord(character));
    write_control_port(P_address,1+digit*2);   (* -WR high *)
    write_control_port(P_address,0+digit*2);   (* -WR low  *)
    write_control_port(P_address,1+digit*2);   (* -WR high again, data latched at low-to-high
transition *)
end;

Procedure Load_digits(ch1,ch2,ch3,ch4:char);
(* display four digits *)
begin
    display(ch1,3);
    display(ch2,2);
    display(ch3,1);
    display(ch4,0);
end;
```

```
begin

    centronic_address;

    repeat

            Write('Input four character to be displayed (from left to right): ');

            readln(Ch1,ch2,ch3,ch4);

            load_digits(ch1,ch2,ch3,ch4);

    until ord(ch1)=13;

end.
```

5.9.4 LCD dot matrix character display modules

The HD44780 (Hitachi) is a liquid crystal character display module which can display two rows of characters. Each character can have 5×10 dots of matrix or 5×7 which is software selectable. The display has an instruction set which enables it to perform various display functions.

The pin-out and the internal block diagram of the module are shown in Figure 5.31. The I/O lines consist of an 8-bit bidirectional data bus, Register Select (RS), Read/-Write (R/-W) and -Enable

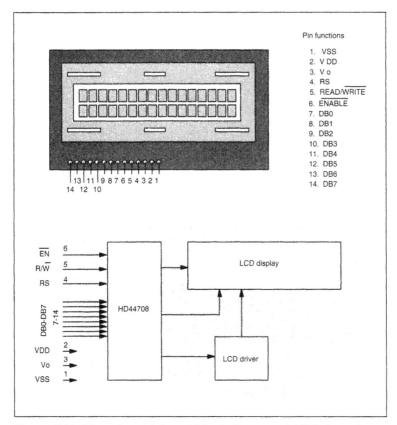

Figure 5.31 Pin-out and internal block diagram of LCD character display

inputs (-EN). RS indicates whether the data sent to the module is an instruction or data to be displayed (RS=0 for instruction, RS=1 for data). R/-W indicates whether the operation is a read or a write operation (R/-W=1 to read, R/-W =0 to write). Loading data into or reading data from the module are controlled by -EN. When writing data to the module, RS, R/-W, DB0 to DB7 are all stable. Then a high-to-low-then-high pulse is applied to the -EN pin. Data is latched at the high-to-low transition (Figure 5.32). The instruction set is summarized in Figure 5.33 and is explained in detail in the manufacturer's data sheet.

An experimental circuit diagram is shown in Figure 5.34. In this circuit, the 8-bit data operation mode is used. D0 to D7 of the display are connected to D1 to D8 terminals on the Centronic experimental board. -EN is connected to the C1 terminal of the board. RS and R/-W are connected to C2 and C3 terminals. Because the character set of the display board is the ASCII character set, which is also used in the computer system, an ASCII character can be converted into its binary code using the TP6 instruction: ORD (char). A TP6 software driver is shown below.

TP6 program list of LM016L.PAS

```
Program LM016L_Dot_matrix_display;
(* Driver for the LCD character display.

   Display connected to the Centronic experimental board

        D1 to D8 connected to D0 to D7 of the display

        C1 connected to E of the display

        RS and R/W connected to C2 and C3 *)

uses

     crt, dos;
```

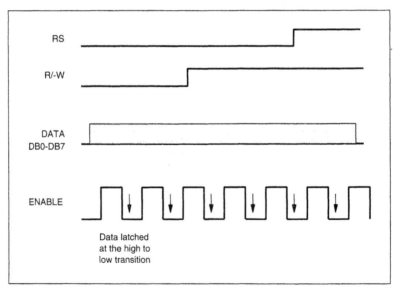

Figure 5.32 Timing sequence of the LCD matrix display module

Instructions	RS	R/W̄	DB 7	DB 6	DB 5	DB 4	DB 3	DB 2	DB 1	DB 0	Description
Clear display	0	0	0	0	0	0	0	0	0	1	clear displays and returns the cursor to home
Return home	0	0	0	0	0	0	0	0	1	0	return cursor to home. No change in DD RAM
Entry mode set	0	0	0	0	0	0	0	1	I/D	S	set the display mode (I/D and S to be selected)
Display on/off	0	0	0	0	0	0	1	D	C	B	display on/off, D:all display, C:cursor, B:cursor blink
Cursor shift	0	0	0	0	0	1	S/C	R/L	0	0	move cursor and shift display. DD RAM unchanged
Function set	0	0	0	0	1	DL	N	F	0	0	configure interface I/O
Set CGRAM address	0	0	0	1	A CG						set CGRAM address, data sent or received after
Set DDRAM address	0	0	1	A DD							set DDRAM address, data sent or received after
Read busy flag and address	0	1	BF	AC							read busy flag and address counter
Write data to CG or DD RAM	1	0	write data								write data into DD or CG RAM
Read data from CG or DD RAM	1	1	read data								read data from DD or CG RAM

I/D=1: increment; I/D=0: decrement	DD RAM: display data RAM
S=1: accompany display shift	CG RAM: character generator RAM
S/C=1: display shift; S/C=0: cursor move	A CG: address of CG RAM
R/L: shift to the right; R/L: shift to the left	A DD: Address of DD RAM, cursor address
DL=1: 8 bit; DL=0: 4 bit	AC: address counter used for DD and CG RAMs
N=1: 2 lines; N=0: 1 line	
F=1: 5 by 10 matrix; F=0: 5 by 7 matrix	
BF=1: internally operating	
BF=0: accept instruction	

Figure 5.33 Instruction set

```
var
    sen1,sen2:string[16];


{$I c:\ioexp\tplib1.pas }



Procedure control(command:byte);
(* output a control byte to the display *)
var
    i:integer;
begin
    write_data_port(P_address,command);   (* output binary data *)
    write_control_port(P_address,0+0+0);  (* E high, RS bit = 0, R/W bit = 0 *)
    write_control_port(P_address,1+0+0);  (* E low, 0=RS bit, 0=R/W bit  *)
    write_control_port(P_address,0+0+0);  (* E high again, data latched at low-to-high transition
```

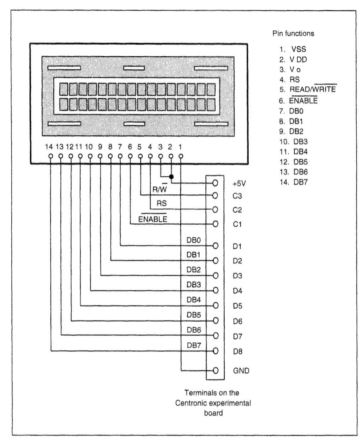

Figure 5.34 Experimental circuit of the LCD module

```
*)
     delay(100);
end;



Procedure clear;
(* clear all digits *)
begin
     control(1);
end;



Procedure home;
(* move cursor to home position *)
```

```
begin
     control(2);
end;



Procedure line1;
(* move cursor to the first display line *)
begin
     control(128);
end;



Procedure line2;
(* move cursor to the second display line *)
begin
     control(128+64);
end;



Procedure data(ch:char);
(* display a character on the display *)
var
   i:integer;
begin
     write_data_port(P_address,ord(ch));    (* output binary data *)
     write_control_port(P_address,0+2+0);   (* E high, RS bit =1, R/W bit = 0 *)
     write_control_port(P_address,1+2+0);   (* E low, 2= RS bit, 0=R/W bit   *)
     write_control_port(P_address,0+2+0);   (* E high again, data latched at low-to-high transition
*)
     delay(10);
end;



Procedure initialization;
begin
     control(16+32);       (* function set, 8-bit data length, 2 line, 5*7 dots *)
     control(16+32);       (* function set, as above *)
     control(16+32);       (* function set, as above *)

     control(16+32+8+4);(* function set, 8-bit data length, 2 line, 5*10 dots *)
     control(8+4+2+1);  (* 8=control bit, 4=digits on, 2=cursor on, 1=cursor character blink *)
     clear;             (* clear all digits *)
     control(4+2+0);    (* entry mode set, 4=contrl bit, 2=increment, 0=cursor display not shift
*)
```

```
end;


Procedure test;
(* a simple test program *)
var
    i:integer;
begin
        sen1:='                   ';
        sen2:='                   ';
        write('Input the first sentence (max 16 char): ');
        readln(sen1);
        write('Input the second sentence (max 16 char): ');
        readln(sen2);

        (* display the first line *)
        line1;
        for i:=1 to 16 do
        begin
        data(sen1[i]);
        end;

        (* display the second line *)
        line2;
        for i:=1 to 16 do
        begin
        data(sen2[i]);
        delay(10);
        end;

end;


begin
        centronic_address;
        initialization;
        test;
end.
```

5.10 Drivers for muscle wires

Muscle wires are made from shape memory alloys. Flexinol alloy is one of the most common materials used. These special metals undergo changes in shape when heated or cooled. Muscle wires pull with a large force. They are capable of lifting thousands of times of their own weight and operate smoothly and silently just by heating up the wire above a certain temperature. The heating can be caused by passing electricity through the wire. It can be used to generate a wide range of motions. The shape memory alloys have already been used in numerous applications.

The Flexinol muscle wires are available in various diameters: 25, 50, 100, 150 and 250 μm. Let us take an example of the 100 μm diameter wire. It has a linear resistance of 150 Ω per meter. The recommended current through the wire is 180 mA (the wire is in still air). It is capable of pulling a load of 150 g continuously without losing its shape memory functions. Depending on the local heating and cooling conditions, the typical cycle rate is about 30 cycles per minute. The temperature at which the wire starts to change its length is 68°C. At 78°C the wire has its maximum deformation. The maximum deformation ratio is 8%. This means that the wire is 8% shorter than its cold length.

When controlling the muscle wires, the current that goes through the wire should be limited below the recommended level. Any transistor drivers or relay drivers (Figures 5.2, 5.6 and 5.7) can be used to power the wire. A load resistor which is connected in series with the wire may be needed. A simple experiment (a muscle wire stepper motor) using the muscle wire is shown in Figure 5.35. The

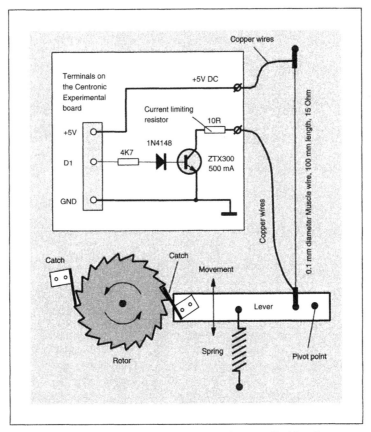

Figure 5.35 Muscle wire 'stepper motor' controlled by the Centronic port

experiment shows how a muscle wire is used to generate a rotational movement under the control of a computer. It is controlled by the Centronic experimental board.

5.11 Drivers for other devices

Using the drivers as described above, any devices you can think of can be controlled by a computer. Relays and the opto-isolated solid state relays can drive mains operated devices. Water pumps, solenoid valves, air extractors and high power lamps can all be controlled by computers.

Gathering information from the external world

6.1 Analogue-to-digital converters

An analogue-to-digital converter outputs a binary code to represent a voltage which is as near as possible to the applied input analogue voltage. It is one of the fundamental devices which enables a computer to read analogue signals from the external world. There are mainly three types of A/D converters: flash, successive approximation and dual-slope integrating converters. The flash converters offer the highest conversion rate, while the dual-slope converters have the highest conversion accuracy but a slow conversion rate. A good compromise on speed and accuracy is given by the successive approximation converters. The I/O interface between converters and external circuits can be one of two types: parallel and serial. For the parallel interface, the converted data is output from the converter via a parallel bus which consists of a number of data lines. For the serial interface, the data is output via one data line. In both cases, some control lines are required.

6.1.1 A/D converters with parallel I/O interface

(a) CA3306 flash converter

The principle of flash converters is that the input signal is compared with all possible subdivisions of a reference voltage at the same time (see Figure 6.1). The reference voltage (V ref) is divided by a series of resistors. The smallest step is 1 LSB in the middle and 1/2 LSB at the two ends. The reference input to the bottom comparator is 1/2 and the second one from the bottom is 1.5 LSB. An input signal of zero results in no comparator switching. An input of between 1/2 and 1.5 LSB causes the lowest comparator to switch. The code generated by the comparators is converted to a binary code by an encode circuit. The number of comparators grows rapidly with the number of bits. An n-bit converter requires 2^n comparators!

The CA3306CE (Harris Semiconductor, RS648-652) has a conversion rate of 15 MHz and a 6-bit conversion accuracy. It has 64 comparators and requires a power supply from 3 to 7.5V. The power consumption is about 50 mW. The pin-out of the chip is given in Figure 6.2. B1 through to B6 output the conversion data. Pin 2 is the overflow indication pin and is high active. There are two enable pins: CE2 (pin 5) and -CE1 (pin 6). When CE2=1 and -CE1=0, the conversion data appears on B1

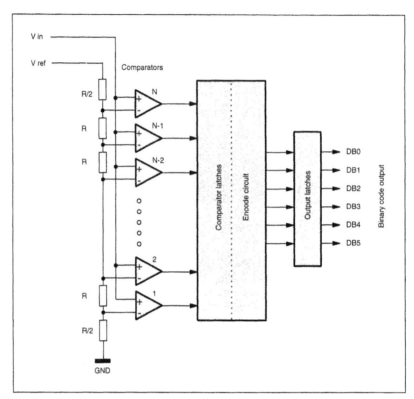

Figure 6.1 Principle of 6-bit flash A/D converters

to B6 outputs, otherwise the outputs are in the high impedance state. Pin 7 is a Clock input and pin 8 (Phase) controls the sequential operation of A/D conversion. When Phase is high, the *rising* edge of the clock starts a sampling cycle. When the clock is at the high state, comparators compare the input signal with the reference. At the falling edge of the clock, the converted data from the comparators is latched into the comparator latches. During the low state of the clock, the data propagates through the encode circuit and the encoded data appears at the input of the output latches. At the *next rising* edge of the clock, the data is latched into the output latches and appears on the pins. At the same time, it initializes a new sampling cycle. Therefore, the output of the converted data is for the previous clock cycle. V ref– (pin 10) and V ref+ (pin 9) are the voltage reference to the converter. V ref– is connected to the ground and V ref+ is connected to a voltage from 1 V to the power supply voltage.

The experimental circuit is given in Figure 6.2. It is connected to the Centronic experimental board. The circuit uses a 74LS241 buffer IC which allows the computer to read the 6-bit conversion data via four input lines. C1 from the Centronic experimental board is connected to the Clock input of the CA3306. To read the previous A/D conversion result and to start a new conversion, a low-to-high-then-low pulse is output from C1. After this, the previous conversion data appears at the output pins. The 74LS241 splits the 6-bit data into two parts: the upper two bits and the lower four bits.

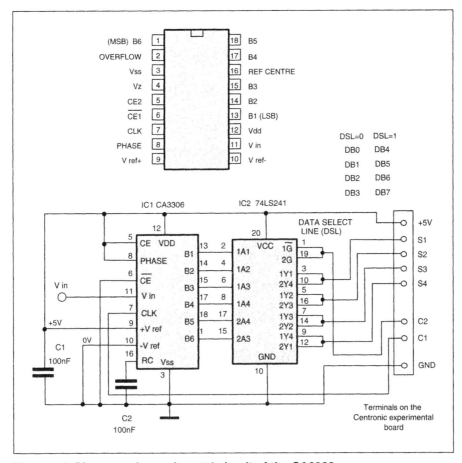

Figure 6.2 Pin-out and experimental circuit of the CA3306

The two parts are read into the computer in turns using the Data Select Line (DSL). The DSL is controlled by C2. The control program is written in TP6.

TP6 program list of CA3306C.PAS

```
Program Centronic_CA3306;
(* Software driver for the flash A/D CA3306 test circuit. CA3306 is connected to the Centronic experimental board
*)

uses
    crt, graph;
var
    byte_high,byte_low,truebyte     :byte;
```

```
(* include two included libraries: TPLIB2 and TPLIB1 *)
{$I c:\ioexp\tplib1.pas}
{$I c:\ioexp\tplib2.pas}


Function voltage:real;
(* function to read the analogue voltage *)
(* write_control_port, read_status_port are procedures in the TPLIB1.PAS library *)
begin
      (* start A/D conversion *)
      write_control_port(P_address,0);        (* CLOCK=0, SEL=0 *)
      delay(1);                                   (* delay a short time *)
      write_control_port(P_address,1);        (* CLOCK=1, SEL=0, previous data appears on the data bus
                                                  and a new conversion is started *)
      write_control_port(P_address,0);        (* CLOCK=0, SEL=0 *)

      (* read flash A/D conversion results *)
      byte_low:=read_status_port(P_address);   (* SEL=0, read low byte *)
      write_control_port(P_address,2);        (* CLOCK=0, SEL=1 *)
      Byte_high:=read_status_port(P_address);  (* SEL=1, read high byte *)
      truebyte:=byte_high*16+byte_low;         (* high and low bytes are combined *)
      Voltage:=truebyte/63*5.00;                (* convert a binary value into a voltage,
                                                  Reference voltage=power supply voltage=5.00 V *)
                                                  (* B0-B6, 6 bit, maximum value=63 *)
end;


{================main program==================}
begin
      clrscr;
      Centronic_address;         (* assign Centronic port address *)
repeat
      gotoxy(20, 10); write('Voltage at the Input:  ',Voltage:5:2, '  [V]');
      delay(1000);
until keypressed
end.
```

The experimental circuit can be simplified if the data port of the Centronic port is a bi-directional port. The 6-bit data from the CA3306 can be read into the computer in one go. This also increases the A/D conversion rate. Unfortunately, some Centronic ports do not allow the data port to read data.

A conversion rate of several hundred kHz can be achieved using the circuit. This is because of the fact that the data transfer between the CA3306 and the computer is too slow. A solution to this problem is to allow the flash A/D converter to write data temporally into memory buffers. The A/D conversion results can be stored in the buffer at a much higher speed. When the buffer is full, the data are downloaded into the computer.

(b) ZN449 successive approximation A/D converter

A successive approximation analogue-to-digital converter consists of the following parts: a digital-to-analogue converter, a comparator and a successive-approximation register. Figure 6.3 shows the internal block diagram of a typical 8-bit successive approximation converter. Each bit is brought to logic high successively to test if the output voltage from the D/A converter is higher or lower than the input voltage. If the DAC voltage is higher than the input voltage, the value of the tested bit should return to zero. If the DAC voltage is lower than the input, the value of the tested bit is 1. By testing each bit in such a manner, a value can be established. For an n-bit converter, one conversion needs n clock cycles.

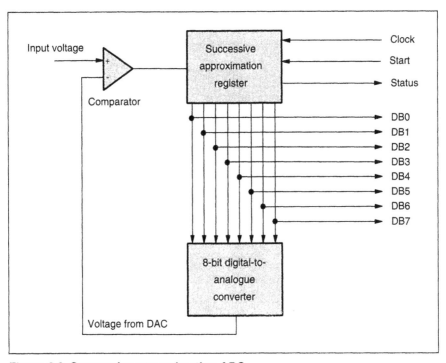

Figure 6.3 Successive approximation ADC

The ZN449 or ZN448 (GEC Plessey, RS301-729) is an 8-bit successive approximation A/D converter. It has a minimum conversion time of 9 μs. An on-board clock generator and a 2.5V bandgap voltage reference are provided on the chip. The pin-out of the converter is given in Figure 6.4. When the -CONVERT input (pin 4) receives a low-going signal, the A/D converter begins an A/D conversion and the -BUSY output (pin 1) becomes low. The -BUSY output will go high at the end of the conversion indicating that the conversion is completed. The -RD input (pin 2) is the data enable line which is taken low to enable the data on the output lines (DB0 to DB7, pins 18 to 11) which otherwise are in the high impedance state.

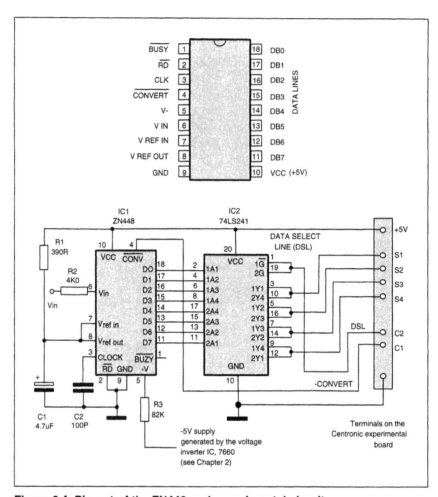

Figure 6.4 Pin-out of the ZN449 and experimental circuit

A clock capacitor (C2) is connected between pin 3 and the ground (pin 9) which enables the on-board clock generator to generate a clock signal. The maximum clock frequency is obtained with a capacitor value of 100 pF. A negative power supply ranging from –3V to –30V can be supplied to pin 5 (–V) via a resistor, the value of which has to be chosen according to the negative voltages. When the negative voltage is –5V, the resistor value is 82 K.

Pin 8 is the output of the on-board 2.5V reference $V_{ref,out}$. A resistor (R1) and a decoupling capacitor (C1) are required. $V_{ref,out}$ (pin 8) is connected to $V_{ref,in}$ (pin 7). The input voltage to be measured is fed to V_{in} (pin 6) via a 4K resistor. A 2.5V input voltage will produce a byte of 255 decimal at the output of the A/D converter. The decimal values for other input voltages are calculated using the following equation:

$$\text{Decimal value} = \frac{\text{Input voltage}}{2.5} \times 255$$

The experimental circuit is shown in Figure 6.4. The circuit is connected to the Centronic experimental board. The -CONVERT is connected to C1 terminal; Data Select Line for the 74LS241 is connected to C2 terminal of the experimental board. The data is read into the computer via S1 to S4. The −5V negative voltage is generated by the 7660 voltage converter circuit as described in Chapter 2. The software driver is written in TP6.

TP6 program list of ZN449.PAS

```
Program Centronic_ZN449;

(* Software driver for the ZN449 test circuit. ZN449 is connected to the Centronic experimental board *)


uses

    crt, graph;

var

    byte_high,byte_low,truebyte    :byte;


(* include two included libraries: TPLIB1 and TPLIB2 *)

{$I c:\ioexp\tplib2.pas}

{$I c:\ioexp\tplib1.pas}


Function voltage:real;

(* function to read the analogue voltage *)

(* write_control_port, read_status_port are procedures in the TPLIB1.PAS library *)

begin

    (* start A/D conversion *)

    write_control_port(P_address,0);       (* -Conversion=0, SEL=0 *)

    delay(1);                              (* delay a short time to wait for completion of A/D conversion
*)

    write_control_port(P_address,1);       (* -Conversion=1, SEL=0, stop a conversion *)

    delay(1);                                (* delay a short time *)


    (* read A/D conversion results *)

    byte_low:=read_status_port(P_address);   (* SEL=0, read low byte *)

    write_control_port(P_address,3);         (* -Conversion=1, SEL=1 *)

    Byte_high:=read_status_port(P_address);  (* SEL=1, read high byte *)

    truebyte:=byte_high*16+byte_low;         (* high and low bytes are combined *)

    Voltage:=truebyte/255*2.50;              (* convert a binary value into a voltage, Reference voltage=2.50V
*)

                                             (* on-board voltage reference = 2.50 V *)

end;
```

```
{================main program===================}
begin
      clrscr;
      Centronic_address;          (* assign Centronic port address *)
repeat
      gotoxy(20, 10); write('Voltage at the Input:  ',Voltage:5:2, '  [V]');
      delay(1000);
until keypressed
end.
```

(c) ICL7109 12-bit integrating A/D converter

The working principle of an integrating A/D converter is described in Figure 6.5. The technique involves an integrator and a negative reference voltage. The conversion is in two phases: the signal integration phase and reference de-integration phase. In the first phase, S1 is closed (S2 open) to supply the input voltage to the integrator for a fixed period of time, T_{INT}. After this, the reference de-integration phase starts. S1 is open and S2 is closed. This action supplies the input of the integrator with the negative reference. The capacitor of the integrator starts to discharge at a rate determined by the reference voltage. After a period of T_{DEINT}, the output of the integrator crosses the zero volt level. Knowing the two time periods, the input voltage can be calculated using the following equation:

$$\text{Input voltage} = V_{ref}\frac{T_{DEINT}}{T_{INT}}$$

An advantage of using a dual-slope converter is that the accuracy is unrelated to the accuracy of the values of the integrating resistor and capacitor as long as their values are stable during the

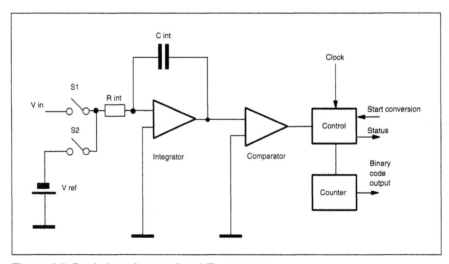

Figure 6.5 Dual-slope integrating A/D converter

conversion. It offers high noise immunity. Random noise can be averaged to zero during the signal integration phase. It also provides noise rejection automatically. Interference signals with a fixed frequency can be removed by choosing the right integrating period. The integrating converters often have an integration period to reject 50/60Hz mains frequency interferences.

The ICL7109ACPL (Telcom, RS207-0203) is a low-power, 12-bit integrating A/D converter. The pin-out is given in Figure 6.6. REF IN+ (pin 36) and REF IN– (pin 39) are connected to a bandgap voltage reference. The ICL7109 provides an on-board voltage reference which is normally 2.8V below V+. This reference voltage is output from the REF OUT (pin 29). IN HI (pin 35) and IN LO (pin 34) are pins for the input signal.

The analogue section of the ICL7109 needs four external components. They are the reference capacitor, C_{REF}, the auto-zero capacitor, C_{AZ}, the integrating capacitor C_{INT} and the integrating resistance R_{INT}. The values should be chosen according to the manufacturer's data sheet. The on-chip oscillator operates with a 3.5795 MHz TV crystal giving 7.5 conversions per second. The device could work with a conversion rate of 30 samples per second. The IC also provides a reference voltage (pin 29) which is nominally 2.8V below VCC and has a typical temperature coefficient of ±80 ppm/°C. External high quality reference sources can be used when high-accuracy measurements are required.

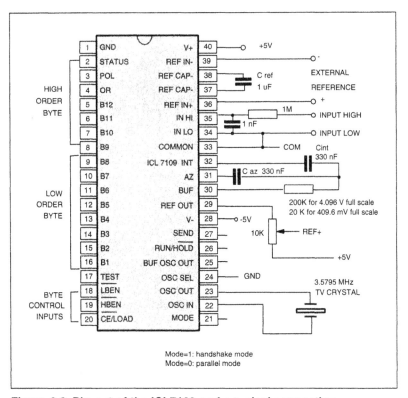

Figure 6.6 Pin-out of the ICL7109 and a typical connection

If RUN/-HOLD (pin 26) is unconnected (the pin is pulled to high state internally), the A/D converter performs conversions continuously. If it is low, the conversion is one shot. The conversion results appear at the 14 tri-state outputs B1 to B12, OR and POL. B1 through B12 give the conversion data, OR indicates whether the input signal is over range and POL indicates the polarity of the signal.

Data can be read from the A/D converter in one of the two modes: the direct mode and the handshake mode. Data transfer mode is configured using the Mode (pin 21) input, MODE=0 to select the direct mode and MODE=1 to select the handshake mode. In the direct mode, the 12-bit conversion data is accessible from the output pins under the control of -CE/LOAD, -LBEN and -HBEN. All the pins are active low. The chip enable -CE/LOAD is low to enable the IC. When -LBEN is low, B1 to B8 output the data. When -LBEN is high, B1 to B8 are in the high impedance state. -HBEN controls B9 to B12, OR and POL. During a conversion, the STATUS goes high. It goes low after the converted data is latched into the output latches. ICL7109 can be connected to a 6402 UART in the handshake mode. This is described in detail in the manufacturer's data sheet.

When the ICL7109 operates in the direct mode, it can be connected to a computer via an 8255 PPI or a 16-to-1 data selector circuit. An experimental circuit diagram using two 4051 analogue switches is shown in Figure 6.7. The circuit is connected to the Centronic experimental board. The software driver is written in TP6.

TP6 program list of 7109PARA.PAS

```
Program ICL7109_parallel_centronic;
(* Centronic ICL7109 test circuit *)
(* ICL7109 works in direct mode. Analogue switches are used for data transfer *)

uses
    dos,crt;

var
    dummy:real;


(* Include the TPLIB1.PAS files *)
{$I c:\ioexp\TPLIB1.pas}


Function Read_voltage:real;
(* get data from the 7109 and calculate the input voltage *)
var
    Low_byte, high_byte,i:byte;
    polarity:integer;

begin
    Low_byte:=0;
    high_byte:=0;

    for i:=1 to 8 do
```

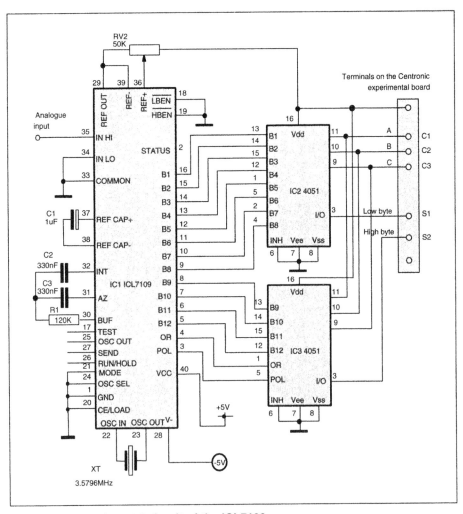

Figure 6.7 Experimental circuit of the ICL7109

```
begin

    Write_control_port(P_address,i-1); (* select a particular data output bit from the 7109 *)

    delay(1);

    low_byte:=low_byte+bit_weight(i)*(read_status_port(P_address) and 1);

    high_byte:=high_byte+bit_weight(i)*round((read_status_port(P_address) and 2)/2);

end;


if high_byte and 32 = 32 then polarity:=1 else polarity:=-1; (* find the polarity *)

high_byte:=high_byte and (1+2+4+8); (* this contains 4 upper bits of the A/D conversion data *)

Read_voltage:=(high_byte*256+low_byte)/2049*2*polarity;
```

```
        if (high_byte and 16)=16 then read_voltage:=999;
end;


(* Main Program *)
begin
        Centronic_address;
repeat
        gotoxy(20,10);
        write('Measured input voltage [V]  ',read_voltage:6:4);
        delay(9000);
until keypressed
end.
```

(d) ICL7135 digital voltmeter chips

The ICL7135CPI-2 (Maxim, RS427-483) is a precision A/D converter that combines dual-slope conversion reliability with ±1 count in 20,000 counts accuracy and is ideal for visual display digital voltmeters. It also features auto-zero and auto-polarity. It has multiplexed BCD outputs and requires LED display drivers to form a DVM. The outputs can be also interfaced to a computer. The pin-out is shown in Figure 6.8. The device requires ±5V power supplies. The supply currents to the positive and the negative power rail are 1.1 mA and 0.8 mA, respectively.

The analogue section of the ICL7135 requires four external components. They are the reference capacitor, C_{REF}, the auto-zero capacitor, C_{AZ}, the integrating capacitor C_{INT} and the integrating

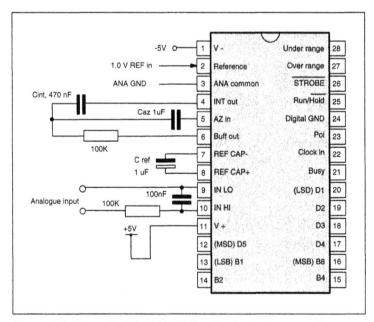

Figure 6.8 Pin-out of the ICL7135 and a typical connection

resistance R_{INT}. They have to be chosen to suit a particular application. The details are given in the manufacturer's data sheet.

The data output sequence is given in Figure 6.9. There are five digit drivers D5 to D1. It is a positive going signal and the scanning sequence is from D5, D4, D3, D2 and D1. The binary coded decimal bits appear at B8, B4, B2 and B1 pins in phase with the digit driver signals. -STROBE (pin 26) is a negative going output signal that can be used for transferring data to external circuits.

When RUN/-HOLD is high (or left open) the A/D converter will continuously run with equally spaced measurement cycles for every 40002 clock pulses. If it is low, the converter carries out the present measurement cycle and then holds the reading as long as the pin is held low. A short positive-going pulse on the pin (greater than 300 ns) will initiate a new measurement cycle.

BUZY (pin 21) goes high at the beginning of the signal integrate and stays high until the first clock pulse after the zero crossing. The line can be used for a single wire measurement. The number of clock cycles when the BUZY is high is measured. Then it is subtracted by 10001 to get the clock count during the reference de-integration. The input voltage can be calculated using the following equation:

$$V_{in} = \frac{10000}{\text{Clock count during reference deintegration}} V_{ref}$$

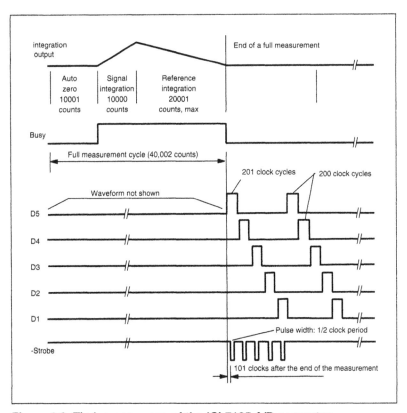

Figure 6.9 Timing sequence of the ICL7135 A/D converter

The first experiment shows how the ICL7135 is connected to a computer via only two wires and the Centronic experimental board is used. BUZY and the clock input to the 7135 are connected to S1 and S2 terminals on the experimental board. The ICL7135 is configured as a continuously running converter. A program is written to count the number of clock cycles when BUZY is high. In this experiment, the clock frequency is below 50 kHz.

TP6 program list of ICL7135S.PAS

```
Program ICL7135_single_wire;

uses
    dos,crt;

{$I c:\ioexp\TPLIB1.pas}

Function Count_clock:integer;
var
    Clock:integer;
    clock_status_old,value:byte;
begin
    clock:=0;
    clock_status_old:=16;
    repeat until port[P_address+1] and 8 = 0;
    repeat until port[P_address+1] and 8 = 8;
    repeat
            value:=port[P_address+1] and 16;
            if (clock_status_old=16) and (value = 0) then
                clock:=clock+1;
            clock_status_old:=value;
    until port[P_address+1] and 8 = 0;
    Count_clock:=clock-10001;
end;

(* Main Program *)
begin
    Centronic_address;
repeat
    writeln(Count_clock);
    delay(1000);
until keypressed
end.
```

The second experiment shows how the ICL7135 is connected to a computer via a 6402 UART. The circuit diagram is given in Figure 6.10. B4 to B1, POL, OVER, UNDER and D5 are connected to the

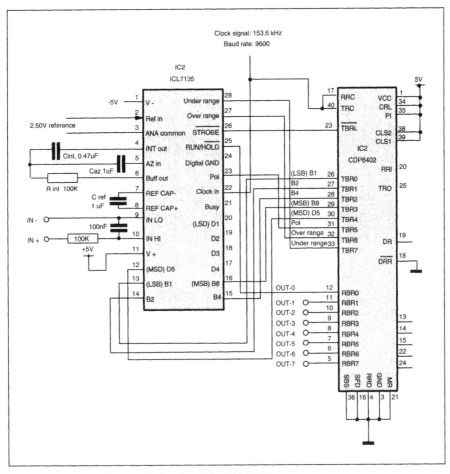

Figure 6.10 Experimental circuit of the ICL7135

transmit buffer register inputs (TBR0 to TBR7) of the 6402 UART. RUN/-HOLD on the 7135 is connected to DB0 of the receiver buffer register. In operation, serial data is transmitted from the computer to the 6402 UART to make DB0 of the receiver buffer register go from low to high and then low. At the positive going edge of the signal, the 7135 starts the A/D conversion. After the A/D conversion is completed, the five strobe signals from the -STROBE pin trigger the UART to transmit the data. The computer reads five times to get the conversion data. The clock to the converter is 153.6 kHz and is produced by the CD4060 crystal generator (see Chapter 2). The UART must transmit the data within 1.3 ms. If the UART operates at a 9600 baud rate with an 8-bit data length, one stop bit and no parity check, the transmitting time will be just over 1 ms. Therefore, such a UART configuration can be used. The software driver is written in VB3.

Visual Basic program list, 7135.FRM

```
'declare functions in DLL, WLIB1.DLL
'declared functions:    RS232(), Bit_weight(), Write_interrupt_enable()
'                          Read_interrupt_indentification()
'                          write_data_format(), write_transmit_buffer(), write_modem_status()
'                          write_receive_buffer(), read_modem_status()
Declare Function RS232 Lib "C:\Ioexp\Wlib1.dll" (ByVal X As Integer) As Integer
Declare Function Bit_weight Lib "C:\Ioexp\Wlib1.dll" (ByVal X As Integer) As Integer
Declare Function Write_interrupt_enable Lib "C:\Ioexp\Wlib1.dll" (ByVal address As Integer, ByVal datax As
Integer) As Integer
Declare Function Read_interrupt_identification Lib "C:\Ioexp\Wlib1.dll" (ByVal address As Integer) As Integer
Declare Function write_data_format Lib "c:\IOEXP\Wlib1.dll" (ByVal address As Integer, ByVal Baud As Integer,
ByVal parity As Integer, ByVal Data_byt As Integer, ByVal Stop_bit As Integer) As Integer
Declare Function Write_transmit_buffer Lib "C:\Ioexp\Wlib1.dll" (ByVal address As Integer, ByVal datax As Integer)
As Integer
Declare Function Write_modem_status Lib "C:\Ioexp\Wlib1.dll" (ByVal address As Integer, ByVal RTS As Integer,
ByVal DTR As Integer) As Integer
Declare Function Read_receive_buffer Lib "C:\Ioexp\Wlib1.dll" (ByVal address As Integer) As Integer
Declare Function Read_modem_status Lib "C:\Ioexp\Wlib1.dll" (ByVal address As Integer, ByVal X As Integer) As
Integer


Sub Command1_Click ()


DoEvents
    dummy = Read_receive_buffer(RS232_address)
    timedelay
    dummy = Write_transmit_buffer(RS232_address, 128)
    timedelay
    dummy = Write_transmit_buffer(RS232_address, 0)

    For i = 1 To 5
        Do While (Read_interrupt_identification(RS232_address) And 1) = 1
        Loop
        digit(6 - i) = Read_receive_buffer(RS232_address)
    Next i


    count_voltage = 0
    For i = 1 To 5
    count_voltage = count_voltage + 10 ^ (i - 1) * (digit(i) And 15)
    Next i
    Label3.Caption = count_voltage
End Sub
```

```
Sub Command1_MouseMove (Button As Integer, Shift As Integer, X As Single, Y As Single)
    label7.Caption = " Read data from 7135-UART"
End Sub


Sub Command3_Click ()
    'configure the selected RS232 port
    baud_rate = Val(text2(0).Text) 'assign baud rate
    parity = Val(text2(1).Text) 'assign parity
    data_bit_length = Val(text2(2).Text)'assign length of data bits
    stop_bit_length = Val(text2(3).Text) 'assign length of stop bits
    dummy = write_data_format(RS232_address, baud_rate, parity, data_bit_length, stop_bit_length)'write the
configuration to the seial data format register
End Sub


Sub Command3_MouseMove (Button As Integer, Shift As Integer, X As Single, Y As Single)
    label7.Caption = "Change the configuration of RS232 port"
End Sub


Sub Command4_Click ()
    End
End Sub


Sub Command4_MouseMove (Button As Integer, Shift As Integer, X As Single, Y As Single)
    label7.Caption = "Quit the program"
End Sub


Sub Command5_Click ()
    're-select the RS232 port
    dummy = MsgBox(Str(RS232(0)) & "  RS232 ports (COMs) are installed on your computer.  Their base addresses
are:  " & Format$(RS232(1), "###") & "     " & Format$(RS232(2), "###") & "     " & Format$(RS232(3), "###") & "
  " & Format$(RS232(4), "###") & "Decimal", 48, "RS232 ports (COM) on your computer") 'show RS232 information
    RS232_number = Val(InputBox$("Input 1, 2, 3 or 4 to select a RS232 port (COM) for the Mini-Lab Data Logger/
Controller", "Select COM ports")) 'select a RS232 port
    RS232_address = RS232(RS232_number) 'get the base address of the selected COM port
    Label2.Caption = "Selected  COM port :      " & Format(RS232_number) 'show information of the selected port
    Label4.Caption = "Base address of COM:   " & Format(RS232_address)
End Sub


Sub Command5_MouseMove (Button As Integer, Shift As Integer, X As Single, Y As Single)
    label7.Caption = "Change RS232 port number"
End Sub


Sub Form_Load ()
```

```
    For i = 0 To 11
        status(i) = 0
    Next i


    dummy = MsgBox(Str(RS232(0)) & "  RS232 ports (COMs) are installed on your computer.  Their base addresses
are:  " & Format$(RS232(1), "###") & "    " & Format$(RS232(2), "###") & "     " & Format$(RS232(3), "###") & "
  " & Format$(RS232(4), "###") & "Decimal", 48, "RS232 ports (COM) on your computer")
    RS232_number = Val(InputBox$("Input 1, 2, 3 or 4 to select a RS232 port (COM) for the RS232 Experimental
board", "Select COM ports"))

    RS232_address = RS232(RS232_number)
    Label2.Caption = "No of installed COMs:        " & Format(RS232_number)
    Label4.Caption = "Base address of COM:    " & Format(RS232_address)
    baud_rate = 96
    parity = 0
    data_bit_length = 8
    stop_bit_length = 1

    text2(0).Text = Format$(baud_rate)
    text2(1).Text = Format$(parity)
    text2(2).Text = Format$(data_bit_length)
    text2(3).Text = Format$(stop_bit_length)

    dummy = write_data_format(RS232_address, baud_rate, parity, data_bit_length, stop_bit_length)
    dummy = Write_interrupt_enable(RS232_address, 1) ' configure interrupt, received data ready interrupt

End Sub


Sub Label3_MouseMove (Button As Integer, Shift As Integer, X As Single, Y As Single)
    'show the received serial data
    label7.Caption = "Value of the serial input data"
End Sub


Sub Label6_MouseMove (index As Integer, Button As Integer, Shift As Integer, X As Single, Y As Single)
    Select Case index
    Case 0
    label7.Caption = "Baud rate = 115200, 19200, 9600, 2400, etc."
    Case 1
    label7.Caption = "0 = No Parity, 1 = Odd Parity, 3 = Even Parity"
    Case 2
    label7.Caption = "Input 5, 6,7 or 8 to select the data bit length"
    Case 3
    label7.Caption = "Input 1 or 2 to select Stop bit"
    End Select
End Sub
```

```
Sub Text2_Change (index As Integer)

    Select Case index

    Case 0:

    Case 1:

    Case 2:

    Case 3:

    End Select

End Sub


Sub timedelay ()

    For i = 1 To 100

    i = i

    Next i

End Sub
```

6.1.2 A/D converters with serial I/O interface

(a) TLC548 8-bit successive approximation A/D converter

The TLC548CP/TLC549CP (Texas Instruments, RS200-6757) is an 8-bit switched-capacitor successive-approximation A/D converter. It has an on-board sample-and-hold circuit, a 4 MHz system clock generator and a serial I/O interface. The TLC548 is able to sample 45,500 times per second and the TLC549 samples 40,000 times per second. It can be replaced by a TLC1540 converter, which has a 10-bit conversion accuracy and is hardware compatible to the former. The pin-out of the converter is shown in Figure 6.11. Pin 8 (VCC) and pin 4 (GND) are connected to the positive and negative rails of the power supply. The range of the power supply voltage is between 3 and 6V with a typical current assumption of 1.9 mA. Pins 1 and 3 (REF+ and REF−) are connected to an external band-gap voltage reference. REF- and GND are normally wired together.

The serial interface consists of two TTL-compatible input lines, the I/O Clock Input (I/O CK, pin 7) and Chip Select Input (-CS, pin 5) and one 3-state Data Output line (DATA OUT, pin 6). The system clock and the I/O clock are used independently. The operational sequence is explained below and is shown in Figure 6.12.

1 When -CS is high, the data output line is at high-impedance state. It also disables the clock input, I/O CLK. -CS goes low to start a read cycle. To reduce errors caused by noise at the -CS input, the internal circuitry waits for two rising edges and then a falling edge of the internal system clock after a high-to-low transition is detected on the -CS pin. Then it is accepted. The MSB of the previous conversion result (DB7) automatically appears on the DATA OUT pin.

2 The falling edges of the first four I/O CLKs shift out DB6, DB5, DB4 and DB3 of the previous conversion result on the DATA OUT pin. The on-chip sample-and-hold begins sampling an analogue input after the fourth falling edge of the I/O CLK.

3 Three more clock cycles are applied to the I/O CLK, DB2, DB1 and DB0 of the previous conversion result are shifted out on each falling edge of the I/O CLK.

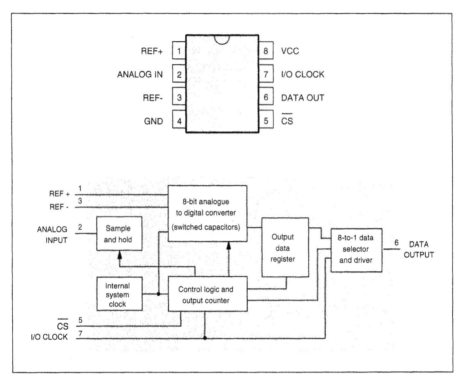

Figure 6.11 Pin-out of the TLC548 and its internal block diagram

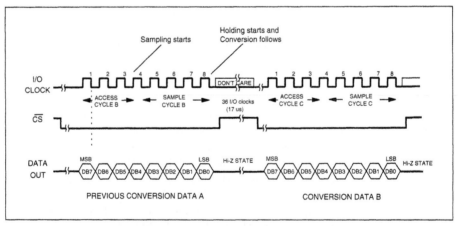

Figure 6.12 Operation sequence of the TLC548/549 serial A/D converter

4 The final (eighth) clock cycle is applied to the I/O CLK. The falling edge of this clock terminates the sample process and initiates the hold function. The hold function continues for the next four internal system clock cycles. After that the hold function terminates and A/D conversion is carried out during the next 32 system clock cycles. A complete A/D conversion takes 36 internal system clock cycles. During the conversion, -CS must go high or the I/O CLK remains low for at least 36 system clock cycles. -CS can be kept low during multiple conversion, however special care must be taken to prevent noise from getting into the I/O CLK, which otherwise causes the device and the external interface circuit to lose synchronization. If -CS is taken high, it must remain high until the end of the conversion. A valid falling edge of -CS will cause the device to reset and to abort the conversion in progress.

The experimental circuit in Figure 6.13 shows how it is connected to the Centronic experimental board. The reference voltage to the TLC548 is a 2.5V voltage supplied by a TLE2425 voltage reference. The I/O CLOCK and -CS of the device are connected to C1 and C2 terminals on the Centronic board. The DATA OUT is wired to the S1 on the board. The software driver is written in TP6 and is listed below.

TP6 program list of TLC548.PAS

```
Program TLC548;

(* driver for TLC548 serial I/O A/D converter. It is connected to the Centronic experimental board *)

(* CLOCK connected C1, -CS connected to C2, DATA OUT connected to S1 *)


uses

    Dos, Crt;
```

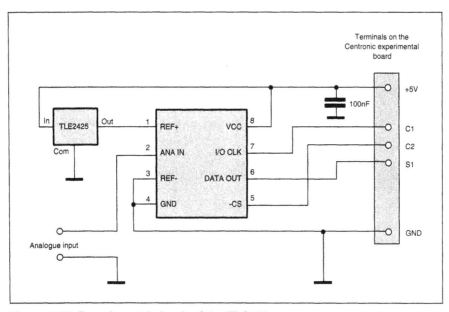

Figure 6.13 Experimental circuit of the TLC548

```
var
    i:integer;

{$I c:\ioexp\tplib1.pas }

Function AD_converter:real;
(* A/D conversion procedure *)
var
    data: array [1..8] of byte;
    ii,ij,addx:byte;
begin
(* two reads are performed to obtain the present A/D conversion result *)
 for ij:=1 to 2 do
    begin
        (* -CS is brought low to start A/D *)
        Write_data_port(P_address, 0+2); (* Clock=0, -CS=1 *)
        write_data_port(P_address, 0+0); (* Clock=0, -CS=0 *)

        for ii:=1 to 8 do begin        (* read the previous result *)
            data[ii]:=read_status_port(P_address) and 1; {read digit}
            write_data_port(P_address, 0+0); (* Clock=0, -CS=0 *)
            write_data_port(P_address, 1+0); (* Clock=1, -CS=0 *)
            write_data_port(P_address, 0+0); (* Clock=0, -CS=0 *)
                        end;
    end;
        (* calculate input voltage, reference voltage=2.5V *)
        AD_converter:=(128*data[1] + 64*data[2] + 32*data[3] + 16*data[4] +
                    8*data[5] + 4*data[6] + 2*data[7]+1*data[8])*2.5/256;
end;

(*  Main Program *)
begin
    Centronic_address;
    repeat
        gotoxy(25,10); write('Input voltage [V]: ',AD_converter:6:3);
        delay(2000);
    until keypressed;
end.
```

(b) TLC541 12-channel A/D converter

The TLC541IN/TLC540IN (Texas Instruments, RS649-289) is an 8-bit successive-approximation A/D converter. It has an on-board sample-and-hold circuit, a 12-channel analogue multiplexer and a serial I/O interface which enables it to perform simultaneous read and write operations. The TLC540 is able to sample 75,180 times per second and the TLC541 40,000 times per second. These converters can be replaced by TLC1540/TLC1541 converters, which have a 10-bit conversion accuracy and are fully compatible to the former. They are able to sample 32,258 times per second. The pin-out of the IC is shown Figure 6.14. Pin 20 (VCC) and pin 10 (GND) are connected to the positive and negative rails of the power supply. The range of the power supply voltage is between 4.75 to 6.5V with a typical power dissipation of 6 mW. Pins 14 and 13 (REF+ and REF–) are connected to an external band-gap voltage reference. REF- and Ground (pin 10) are normally wired together.

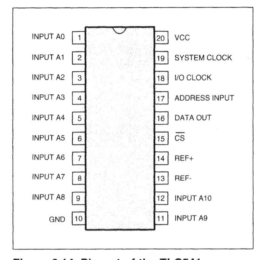

Figure 6.14 Pin-out of the TLC541

Amongst the 12 analogue multiplexers, the first 11 inputs could be accessed at pins 1 to 9, 11 and 12, corresponding to analogue inputs from 0 to 11. The twelfth input is connected internally to a 'self test' voltage reference. To select an analogue input, a 4-bit address should be written into the IC via the serial interface.

The serial interface consists of five TTL-compatible I/O lines: the System Clock input (SYS CK, pin 19), the I/O Clock input (I/O CK, pin 18), Chip Select input (-CS, pin 15), Address Input (ADD IN, pin 17) and Data Output (DATA OUT, pin 14). The SYS CK is the clock for A/D conversion operation. A maximum 4 MHz system clock can be applied for the TLC540 and 2.1 MHz for the TLC541, giving 75,180 and 40,000 samples per second respectively. For TLC1540/TLC1541 converters the maximum system clock is 2.1 MHz, giving 32,258 samples per second. The I/O CLK is used for synchronizing I/O operations. ADD IN is the serial address input for selecting the analogue multiplexers. DATA OUT is the serial data output. -CS is the chip enable. It must be at logic low to enable the IC. When -CS is high, the DATA OUT pin is three-state, The ADD IN and I/O CLK are all disabled. This allows several such devices to be used in a shared bus.

The SYS CLK and I/O CLK are used independently. The writing and reading sequences of the IC are explained as follows (see Figure 6.15).

1 -CS goes low to start read/write cycle. To minimize errors caused by noise at the -CS input, the internal circuitry waits for two rising edges and then a falling edge of the SYS CLK after the high-to-low transition is detected on the CS pin. Then it is accepted. The MSB of the previous conversion result (DB7) automatically appears on the DATA OUT pin.

2 A new multiplexer address (AD0, AD1, AD2 and AD3) is shifted into the IC on the first four rising edges of the I/O CLK. The MSB of the address (AD3) is shifted in first. The negative edges of the I/O CLK shift out DB6, DB5, DB4 and DB3 of the previous conversion result. The on-chip sample-and-hold begins sampling the newly addressed analogue input after the fourth falling edge of the I/O CLK.

3 Three clock cycles are further applied to the I/O CLK, DB2, DB1 and DB0 of the previous conversion result are shifted out on each negative edge of the I/O CLK.

4 The final (eighth) clock cycle is applied to the I/O CLK. The falling edge of the clock completes the sample process and initiates the hold function. Data conversion is then carried out during the next 36 SYS CLK cycles. After this I/O CLK, either -CS must go high or the I/O CLK remains low for at least 36 SYS CLK cycles to allow for the data conversion. -CS can be kept low during multiple conversions. However special care must be taken to prevent noise from getting into the I/O CLK, which otherwise will cause the device and the external interface circuit to lose synchronization. If -CS is taken high, it must remain high until the end of the conversion. A valid falling edge of -CS will cause the device to reset and to abort the conversion in progress.

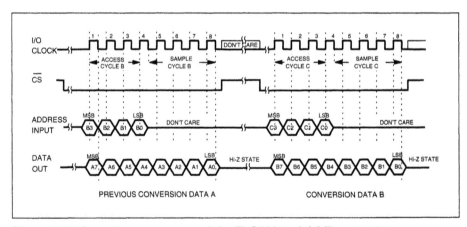

Figure 6.15 Operation sequences of the TLC541 serial A/D converter

The experimental circuit in Figure 6.16 shows how it is connected to the Centronic experimental board. The reference voltage to the device is 2.5V produced by a TLE2425 voltage reference. The clock signal can be generated by a circuit built around a 555 timer IC (see Chapter 2). The I/O CLOCK, -CS and DATA IN of the TLC541 are connected to D1, D2 and D3 terminals on the experimental board. The DATA OUT is wired to the S1 terminal on the board. The software driver is written in TP6 and is listed as follows:

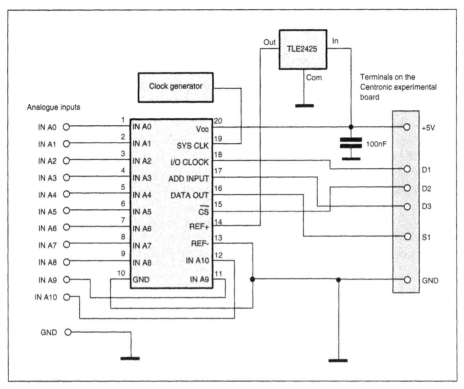

Figure 6.16 Experimental circuit of the TLC541

TP6 program list of TLC541.PAS

```
Program TLC541;
(* driver for TLC541 serial I/O A/D converter. It is connected to the Centronic experimental board *)
(* CLOCK connected D1, -CS connected to D2, ADD connected to D3
DATA OUT connected to S1 *)

uses
    Dos, Crt;

var
    i:integer;
    dummy:real;

{$I c:\ioexp\tplib1.pas }
```

```
Function AD_converter(address:byte):real;
(* A/D conversion procedure. Addresses: 0 to 11 *)
var
    add,data: array [1..8] of byte;
    ii,addx:byte;
 begin
    (* find the address bits *)
    for ii:=1 to 8 do add[ii]:=0;
    if address>=8 then begin add[1]:=1; address:=address-8 end;
    if address>=4 then begin add[2]:=1; address:=address-4 end;
    if address>=2 then begin add[3]:=1; address:=address-2 end;
    if address>=1 then begin add[4]:=1; end;


    (* -CS, bit 2, is brought low to start A/D *)
    write_data_port(P_address,4);
    write_data_port(P_address,0);
    delay(1);


    for ii:=1 to 8 do begin  (* read the previous result *)
        addx:=add[ii]*2;
        data[ii]:=read_status_port(P_address) and 1;       (* read digit *)
        write_data_port(P_address,addx);                 (* address bit loaded and I/O clock low *)
        write_data_port(P_address,1+addx);               (* I/O clock goes to  high *)
        write_data_port(P_address,addx);                 (* I/O clock goes to low again *)
        delay(1);
                        end;
    AD_converter:=(128*data[1] + 64*data[2] + 32*data[3] + 16*data[4] +
                    8*data[5] + 4*data[6] + 2*data[7]+1*data[8])*2.5/255;
 end;


(*  Main Program *)
begin
     Centronic_address;
     repeat
     for i:=0 to 11 do
       begin
            dummy:=AD_converter(i); (* run the A/D converter the first time *)
            delay(1);
            gotoxy(20,5+i); write('Input voltage [V] to Channel [',i:2,']: ',AD_converter(i):6:3);
                          (* AD_converter will read the previous A/D conversion results *)
       end;
     delay(2000);
     until keypressed;
end.
```

(c) LTC1288 12-bit serial I/O converters

The LTC1288CN8 (Linear Technology, RS197-1795) is a micropower successive approximation A/D converter with a 12-bit conversion accuracy. The pin-out and the internal block diagram of the IC are shown in Figure 6.17. It requires a power supply of 2.7 to 6V. Pin 8 and pin 4 are connected to the positive and negative rail of the power supply. Pin 8 also serves as the voltage reference input. The supply voltage must be free of noise and ripples. The typical supply current is 260 µA at a sampling rate 6.6 kHz and supply voltage of 2.7V. When the IC is in the standby mode, the supply current drops to several nA. It has two analogue inputs (pin 2 and pin 3) which can be configured in two modes. In the first mode, an input voltage can be applied to each input with respect to the ground (single-ended mode). In the other, an input voltage is applied across the two inputs (differential mode). The analogue input leakage current is typically 1 µA.

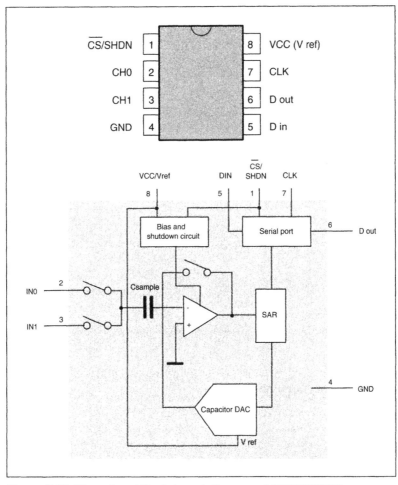

Figure 6.17 Pin-out and the internal diagram of LTC1288CN8

The LTC1288 communicates with other external circuitry through a 4-wire serial interface. -CS/SHDN (pin 1) selects the chip when it is held low. When it is at logic high, the IC is in the standby mode. CLK (pin 7) is the shift clock. It synchronizes the serial data transfer and determines the conversion speed. At the falling edge of the CLK, each bit of the A/D conversion result is transmitted. At the rising edge, data input to the IC is captured. Din (pin 5) is the digital data input which is used to shift in the address of the selected analogue input. Dout (pin 6) is the digital data output. The A/D conversion result is shifted out from this output.

The operating sequence of the LTC1288 is shown in Figure 6.18. Data transfer is initiated by a falling edge of the chip select (-CS/SHDN, pin 1). Then the IC looks for a start bit. A start bit is a logic 1 on Din (pin 5) and it is shift into the LTC1288 at the rising edge of CLK. Next, a 3-bit input word (bit 1, bit 2, bit 3) is shifted into the IC to configure the input mode and the serial data output format. At the falling edge of the fourth clock, an A/D conversion starts. Immediately after this falling edge, a null bit (logic 0) appears on the Dout (pin 6). At the next 12 falling edges of the clock input, the 12 bits of the A/D conversion result appear on Dout. Bits appearing on Din do not have any effects on the converter.

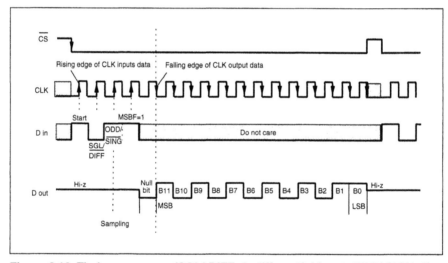

Figure 6.18 Timing sequence (SGL/-DIFF=0, differential input, ODD/-SIGN=1)

The bit function of the 3-bit input word is shown as follows. Bits 1 and 2 configure the analogue input mode. Bit 3 selects the output data format.

bit 1=1, bit 2=0   voltage between Channel 0 to GND (single-ended input)
bit 1=1, bit 2=1   voltage between Channel 1 to GND (single-ended input)
bit 1=0, bit 2=0   voltage between Channel 0 to 1 (differential input)
bit 1=0, bit 2=1   voltage between Channel 1 to 0 (differential input)
bit 3=1   bits of the converted result shift out from MSB to LSB (B11 to B0)
bit 3=0   bits of the converted result shift out from LSB to MSB (B0 to B11)

The experimental circuit using the Centronic experimental board is shown in Figure 6.19. CLOCK, -CS, DATA IN and DATA OUT are connected D1, D3, D2 and S1. The software driver is written in TP6 and is listed below.

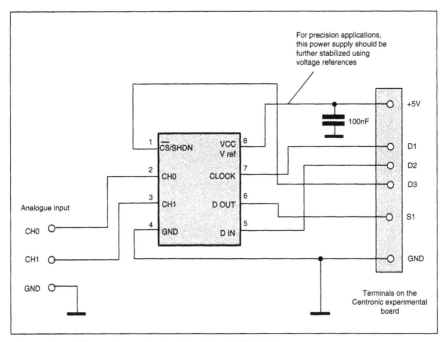

Figure 6.19 Experimental circuit of the LTC1288

TP6 program list of LTC1288.PAS

```
Program LTC1288;

(* driver for LTC1288 serial I/O A/D converter. It is connected to the Centronic experimental board *)

(* CLOCK connected D1, -CS connected to D3, DATA IN connected to D2, DATA OUT connected to S1 *)


uses

    Dos, Crt;


{$I c:\ioexp\tplib1.pas }


Function AD_converter(mode:integer):integer;

(* Mode 1, Single mode, Channel 0

    Mode 2, Single mode, Channel 1

    Mode 3, Differential mode, Channel 0 positive, Channel 1 negative

    mode 4, Differential mode, Channel 1 positive, Channel 0 negative *)
```

```
var
   ii, Single_differential, Odd_sign, dummy_byte:byte;
   IO_data: array[1..12] of byte;
   data:array[1..12] of integer;
   Digital_data:array[1..12] of byte;
   binary_weight, dummy:integer;


Procedure delay;
{A short delay}
var
      ij:integer;
begin
      for ij:=1 to 6 do ij:=ij;
end;


Procedure AD_control(datax:byte);
{output control bit to control A/D converter}
begin
          Write_data_port(P_address,0+2*datax); {CLK=0, Dout=datax, start bit=1}
       Write_data_port(P_address,1+2*datax); {CLK=1, Dout=datax, start bit is clocked into the A/D converter}
          delay;
          Write_data_port(P_address,0+2*datax); {CLK=0, Dout=datax}
          delay;
end;


Procedure Configure_mode;
{assign values for Odd_sign, Single_differential}
begin
      case mode of
          1:  begin Odd_sign:=0; Single_differential:=1; end;
          2:  begin Odd_sign:=1; Single_differential:=1; end;
          3:  begin Odd_sign:=0; Single_differential:=0; end;
          4:  begin Odd_sign:=1; Single_differential:=0; end;
        else  begin Odd_sign:=0; Single_differential:=1; end;
          end;
end;


begin
   configure_mode;      (* find the Single_differential and Odd_sign bits *)
   Binary_weight:=4096;
   Write_data_port(P_address,1+2+4); (* Clock=1, Data=1, -CS=1 *)
```

```
delay;
Write_data_port(P_address,1+2+0); (* Clock=1, Data=1, -CS=0, A/D conversion cycle initiated *)


(* output control bits to the A/D converter *)
AD_control(1);                  (* output start bit *)
AD_control(Single_differential);     (* output single_differential control bit *)
AD_control(Odd_sign);                 (* output channel selection bit *)
AD_control(1);                         (* output MSB first control bit *)


(* read serial data bits from B11 down to B0 *)
for ii:=1 to 12 do
begin
     Binary_weight:=binary_weight div 2;
     Write_data_port(P_address,1+2); (* Clock=1, Dout=1, -CS=0 *)
     delay;
     Write_data_port(P_address,0+2); (* Clock=0, Dout=1, -CS=0 *)
     delay;
     data[ii]:=(read_status_port(P_address) and 1) * binary_weight; (* read the serial data bit *)
end;


(* the 12 bits A/D conversion data all received *)
write_data_port(P_address,1+2+4);      (* after a complete A/D conversion, Clock=1, Data=1, -CS=1 *)


dummy:=0;
for ii:=1 to 12 do dummy:=dummy+data[ii];
AD_converter:=dummy;
end;


(*  Main Program *)
begin
     Centronic_address;
     repeat
          gotoxy(20,10); write('Input voltage [V] to Channel [0]: ',AD_converter(1)*5.06/4096:6:4);
          gotoxy(20,11); write('Input voltage [V] to Channel [1]: ',AD_converter(2)*5.06/4096:6:4);
                         (* reference voltage = power supply = 5.06V *)
     delay(2000);
     until keypressed;
end.
```

6.1.3 TSC500 A/D converter analogue processor

The TSC500ACPE (Telcom, RS656-697) contains all the analogue circuits needed to construct a dual-slope integrating A/D converter. It allows 16-bit A/D conversion to be performed. High conversion rates can be achieved for lower resolution. The converter uses time to quantize the analogue input signal. A software driver in the computer performs the digital function of 'counting clocks' for the dual-slope integrating converter process. Users can control the resolution and the conversion speed purely from the software. The pin-out of the TC500 is given in Figure 6.20. It has two digital inputs, A (pin 12) and B (pin 13), and one digital output, COMP OUT (pin 14). A and B select one of the four phases of the operation of the TC500.

A=0 B=0   zero integrator output phase
A=0 B=1   auto-zero phase
A=1 B=0   analogue signal integration phase
A=1 B=1   reference voltage deintegration phase

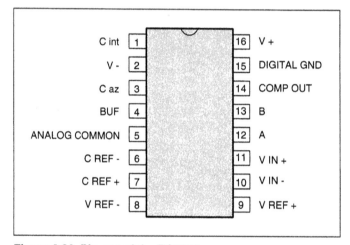

Figure 6.20 Pin-out of the TC500A

Pin 14 is the digital output of the TC500, which indicates a completion of a deintegration operation. The device requires several external components: a reference capacitor, an integration capacitor, an auto-zero capacitor, an integration resistor and an external voltage reference. A typical connection of components to the TC500 is given in Figure 6.22. The analogue voltage inputs are connected to Vin+ (pin 11) and Vin– (pin 10). The IC needs a dual power supply. For ±5 V operations, the digital inputs and output are TTL compatible and the supply current is 1 mA.

The operation phases are selected in the following order. The timing sequence is shown in Figure 6.21.

1. Auto-zero phase
2. Signal input voltage integration phase
3. Reference voltage deintegration phase
4. Integrator output zero phase

The auto-zero phase is used to compensate errors due to buffer, integrator and comparator offset voltages. After the auto-zero phase, the analogue input signal integration phase begins. This phase

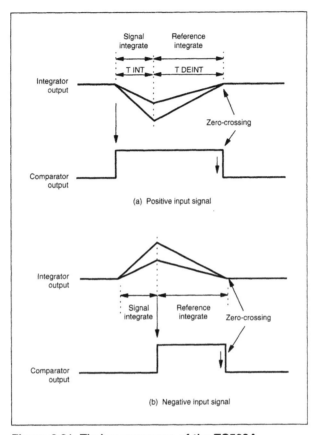

Figure 6.21 Timing sequence of the TC500A

integrates the differential voltage between the Vin+ and Vin– inputs. The integration capacitor is charged to a certain voltage. The polarity of the input signal can be indicated by the COMP OUTPUT (pin 14). If the input differential voltage is positive, the COMP OUTPUT becomes high immediately after the signal integration phase is entered. If the input voltage is negative, the COMP OUTPUT remains low until the reference voltage deintegration phase is entered. The integration period is T_{INT}. The reference voltage deintegration phase ramps the voltage of the output of the integrator back to zero by connecting the charged reference capacitor with the proper polarity. In this phase, the COMP OUT stays at logic high. When the zero-crossing of the output of the integrator occurs, the COMP OUT goes to logic low. The time period of the deintegration phase is measured. This period is T_{DEINT}. The input voltage can be calculated using the following equation:

$$\text{Input voltage} = V_{ref} \frac{T_{DEINT}}{T_{INT}}$$

The values of the external components should be chosen according to the manufacturer's data sheet.

Figure 6.22 shows an experimental circuit diagram of the TC500 using the Centronic experimental board. A and B are connected to the D1 and D2 terminals of the experimental board. COMP OUTPUT is connected to S1 terminal of the board. The computer first selects the auto-zero phase for a period of time (50 ms). Then it selects the input voltage integration phase and causes the TC500 to integrate the input signal for a period of 40 ms precisely. The computer does this using the on-board 8253 timer/counter which are available on every computer. The polarity of the input signal can be determined by polling the status of the COMP OUTPUT from S1. Next, the computer selects the reference voltage deintegration phase. As soon as the computer performs this action, it counts the time period until the COMP OUTPUT goes from high to low. This period, together with the 40 ms integration period, is used to find the input voltage. Values of the components are chosen according to the manufacturer's recommendation.

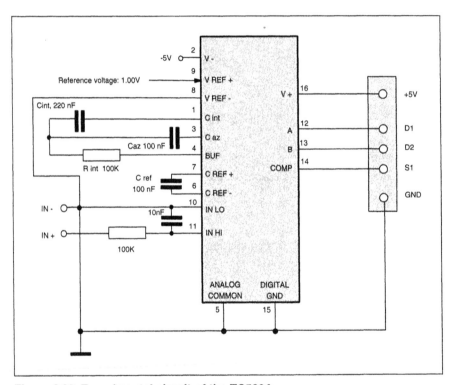

Figure 6.22 Experimental circuit of the TC500A

TP6 program list of TC500A.PAS

```
Program TC500A;
(* driver for TC500A integrating converter analogue processor.
++   It is connected to the Centronic experimental board
     A (pin 12) connected D1, B (pin 13) connected D2 *)
```

```
(* A connected to D1, B connected to D2, COMP OUTPUT connected to S1 *)

uses
    Dos, Crt;

var
    i,polarity:integer;
    dummy:real;

{$I c:\ioexp\tplib1.pas }

Procedure init_8253(low_count_byte, high_count_byte:byte);
(* load the low_byte and high_byte into the 3rd timer of 8253 *)
(* clock frequency to the 8253: 2 * 1,193,180 = 2386360 Hz clock period 1/f = 0.419 us *)
begin
(*  Control word= b6H = 10110111b
      10  = select counter 2
      11  = read/write low count byte first then high byte
      011 = mode 3
      0   = binary counting with 16-bit *)
    Port[$43]:=$b6; (* load control word to the control register of 8253 *)
    Port[$42]:=low_count_byte; (* load low count byte *)
    port[$42]:=high_count_byte; (* load high count byte *)
    port[$61]:=port[$61] or 1; (* disable speaker *)
    port[$43]:=$80; (* 80H is the counter latch command for counter 3 *)
end;


Procedure delay_8253(low_bytex, high_bytex:byte);
(* time delay using the 3rd timer of the 8253 *)
(* delay period is specified by low_bytex and high_bytex *)
var
    low_byte, high_byte:byte;
begin
    init_8253(low_bytex,high_bytex);
    repeat dummy:=port[$42] until (port[$42]=0) ;
    repeat low_byte:=port[$42]; high_byte:=port[$42]; until (low_byte<5);
end;


Function deintegration_counts:real;
(* find the deintegration period (number of counts of the 3rd timer of 8253 *)
var
    counts,low_byte, high_byte:byte;
    finished_flag:boolean;
begin
    counts:=0;
```

```
     repeat
       init_8253(255,255);    (* load 255 into the high and low counter registers of the 8253 *)
       repeat
              low_byte:=port[$42];
              high_byte:=port[$42];
              if port[P_address+1] and 8 = 0 then finished_flag:=true
                  else finished_flag:=false;
          until (low_byte<25) and (high_byte=0) or finished_flag;
          if not finished_flag then counts:=counts + 1;
     until finished_flag;
     deintegration_counts:=counts*(255*256+255) + (255.0-high_byte)*256 + (255-low_byte);
end;


Function Voltage:real;
(* find the input voltage *)
var
   add,data: array [1..8] of byte;
   ii,addx:byte;
begin

     write_data_port(P_address,0+2); (* zero the processor for 100 ms*)
     delay(500);

     write_data_port(P_address,1+0); (* signal integrating for 40 ms *)
     delay_8253(117,186);
     polarity:=read_status_port(P_address) and 1;
     delay_8253(117,186); (* delay 186*256+117 counts = 20 ms *)

     write_data_port(P_address,1+2); (* reference integrating *)
     dummy:=deintegration_counts;

     if polarity=0  then polarity:=-1;
     voltage:=polarity*dummy/(186*256+117)/2*1.5; (* reference voltage = 1.5V *)
     delay(100);

     write_data_port(P_address,0); (* integrator output zero for 5 ms *)
     delay(50);
end;

(*  Main Program *)
begin
     Centronic_address;
     write_data_port(P_address,0+2); (* zero the processor *)
     write('                        Press RETURN to start sampling');readln;
```

```
clrscr;
repeat
        gotoxy(20,10); write('Input voltage to the TC500: ',voltage:6:4);
        delay(1000);
    until keypressed;
end.
```

6.2 Voltage-to-frequency converters

A voltage-to-frequency converter is a device which converts a voltage into a pulse train with its frequency precisely proportional to the input voltage. The digital pulse train can be transmitted from the converter to a computer through various means such as opto-isolators, pulse transformers, radio links or fibre-optic links, etc.

6.2.1 Principles of V/F conversion

The principle of a voltage-to-frequency converter is shown in Figure 6.23. It consists of a switched current source, an input comparator and a one-shot timer. The voltage comparator compares a positive input voltage V1 to the voltage Vx. If V1 is greater than Vx, the comparator triggers the one-

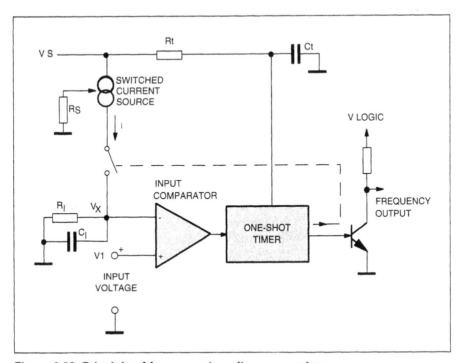

Figure 6.23 Principle of frequency-to-voltage converter

shot timer. The output of the timer turns on the frequency output transistor and the switched current source for a period of t = 1.1 Rt Ct. During this period, the current i flows out of the switched current source and provides a fixed amount of charge into the capacitor, Cl. This normally charges Vx up to a higher level than V1. At the end of the timing period, the current i turns off and the timer resets itself. Next, the capacitor Cl will gradually discharge via Rl until Vx falls to the level of V1. Then the comparator will trigger the timer and start another cycle.

6.2.2 LM331 V/F converter

The pin-out and a typical application of the LM331 (National Semiconductor, RS411-652) are given in Figure 6.24. The linearity between the output frequency and the input voltage is 0.01% of the full scale of frequency which ranges from 1 Hz to 100 kHz. The pulse train output is compatible with TTL and CMOS when it operates at the +5V power supply. It can drive three TTL loads. Pin 4 and pin 8 are connected to the negative and positive rails of the power supply. The power supply is in the

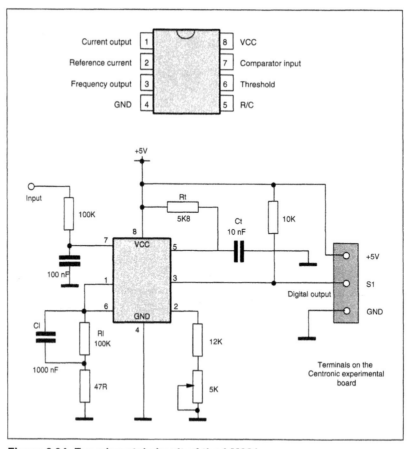

Figure 6.24 Experimental circuit of the LM331

range 4 to 40V. The supply current is typically 3 mA for a 5V power supply. Pin 2 is a 1.9V reference voltage. A current setting resistor Rs is connected between pin 2 and the ground. The reference current flowing through Rs is 1.9/Rs. This current flows out of pin 1 if the internal switch is switched to pin 1. Pin 5 is the R-C summing junction of the one-short timer. Pin 7 is the voltage signal input pin and pin 6 sets the threshold. Pin 3 is the open-collector output. The current flowing through the output driver is internally limited below 50 mA.

An experimental circuit is shown in Figure 6.24. The circuit is connected to the Centronic experimental board. The frequency output is connected to S1 terminal of the board. A software driver is used to measure the frequency of the output signal from the LM331. The sample program is written in TP6 and is listed below. The 8253 timer/counter chip inside the computer is used for measuring the frequency.

TP6 program list, LM331.PAS

```
Program LM331_Voltage_Frequency;
(* Software driver for LM331 V/F*)
uses
    graph,crt,dos;

var
   time_period:real;

(* to load three included library files *)
{$I c:\ioexp\tplib1.pas}

Procedure init_8253(low_count_byte, high_count_byte:byte);
(* load the low_byte and high_byte into the 3rd timer of 8253 *)
(* clock frequency to the 8253: 2 * 1,193,180 = 2386360 Hz clock period 1/f = 0.419 us *)
begin
(*   Control word= b6H = 10110111b
     10  = select counter 2
     11  = read/write low count byte first then high byte
     011 = mode 3
     0   = binary counting with 16-bit *)
     Port[$43]:=$b6; (* load control word to the control register of 8253 *)
     Port[$42]:=low_count_byte; (* load low count byte *)
     port[$42]:=high_count_byte; (* load high count byte *)
     port[$61]:=port[$61] or 1; (* disable speaker *)
     port[$43]:=$80; (* 80H is the counter latch command for counter 3 *)
end;

Function read_8253:integer;
(* read the two 8-bit counter registers *)
var
   low_byte, high_byte:byte;
```

```
begin
    low_byte:=port[$42];
    high_byte:=port[$42];
    read_8253:=low_byte + 256* high_byte;
end;


Function find_period(Address:integer; Bit_weight:integer):real;
(* find the period of an input digital signal.
   Input signal is specified by Input port address (Address) and bit.
   Bit 0, Bit_weight=1
   Bit 1, Bit_weight=2
   .....
   Bit 7, Bit_weight=128 *)
var
    count, Average_number,time1,time2:integer;
begin
        (* Testing the period of low state of a digital signal. This will be used
        for calculating Average_number *)
        repeat until port[Address] and Bit_weight=Bit_weight; (* signal state high *)
        repeat until port[Address] and Bit_weight=0;          (* signal state low *)
        time1:=read_8253;                                     (* read counts in 8253 first time*)
        repeat until port[Address] and Bit_weight=Bit_weight; (* signal state high again *)
        time2:=read_8253;                                     (* read counts in 8253 the second time *)
        Average_number:=round(100/(Time1-Time2));             (* find Average_number *)
        if Average_number=0 then Average_number:=1;
        repeat until port[Address] and Bit_weight=Bit_weight; (* signal state high *)
        repeat until port[Address] and Bit_weight=0;          (* signal state low *)
        time1:=read_8253;                                     (* read counts in 8253 first time *)
        for count:=1 to Average_number do                     (* find low going edge of a digital signal *)
        begin
        repeat until port[Address] and Bit_weight=Bit_weight;    (* signal state high *)
        repeat until port[Address] and Bit_weight=0;             (* signal state low *)
        end;
        Time2:=read_8253;                                     (* read counts in 8253 the second time *)
        Find_period:=((Time1-time2)*1/(2*1193180)*1e6/Average_number);
end;


(* Main program *)
begin
    Centronic_address;
    init_8253(255,255);  (* initialize 3rd timer of 8253 *)
    repeat
        time_period:=find_period(P_address+1, 8); (* P_address+1 is the address of the status port,
                                    8 is the bit weight of DB3 *)
```

```
       gotoxy(15,10); write('Time period of output signal [us]:   ', time_period:8:1);

       gotoxy(15,11);write('Frequency of the output signal [Hz]: ',1/time_period*1e6:8:1);

       delay(5000);

   until keypressed
end.
```

6.3 Digital sensors for measuring light intensity

6.3.1 TSL220 digital opto-sensor

Conventional opto-sensors convert light to a current, voltage or resistance signal. Amplification circuits are required to make the level of the signal high enough to be measured. If such a system is interfaced to a computer, an A/D converter is used. Light-to-frequency converters convert light intensity into a frequency signal and the signal can be fed into a computer.

The TSL220 (Texas Instruments, RS194-278) is a light-to-frequency converter. A 4 mm^2 silicon photodiode and a current-to-frequency converter are housed in one package. The output is a fixed-width pulse train signal with its frequency proportional to the light intensity falling on the photodiode. The pin-out and the internal block diagram of the IC are shown in Figure 6.25. The

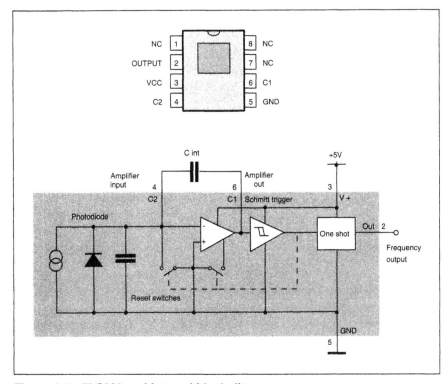

Figure 6.25 TLS220 and internal block diagram

current-to-frequency converter circuit consists of an op-amp integrator, transistor reset switches, a level detector and a one-shot pulse generator.

Since the output frequency of the TSL220 is determined by the current generated by the photodiode and the value of the external integration capacitor, the frequency range can be set to suit different applications by choosing different capacitors. A selection guide for the component values is provided in the manufacturer's data sheet. The capacitor is connected to the cathode of the photodiode (pin 4) and the op-amp output (pin 6). The output signal is 5V CMOS compatible. If it is connected to TTL logic circuits, an external 3.3 K pull-down resistor should be used. The device requires a supply voltage of 4 to 10V. At 5V supply voltage, the supply current is 7.5 mA.

An experimental circuit is shown in Figure 6.26. The circuit is connected to the Centronic experimental board. The output from the TSL220 is connected to S1 terminal of the board. A software driver is used to measure the frequency of the output signal. It is written in TP6 and utilizes the on-board 8253 timer/counter chip inside the PC.

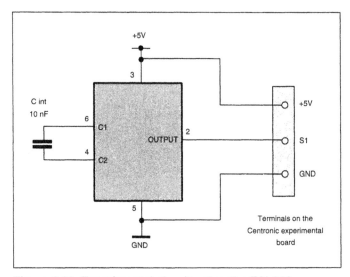

Figure 6.26 Experimental circuit using the TSL220

TP6 program list of TSL220

```
Program TSL220;

(* Software driver for TSL220 light-to-frequency converter*)

(* capacitor used for the TSL220: 10 nF, 1% *)

(* this software does not work if the light intensity is too low *)

(* output from the TSL220 is connected to S1 of the Centronic experimental board *)


uses

    graph,crt,dos;
```

```pascal
var
   time_period:real;


(* to load three included library files *)
{$I c:\ioexp\tplib1.pas}


Procedure init_8253(low_count_byte, high_count_byte:byte);
(* load the low_byte and high_byte into the 3rd timer of 8253 *)
(* clock frequency to the 8253: 2 * 1,193,180 = 2386360 Hz clock period 1/f = 0.419 us *)
begin
(*  Control word= b6H = 10110111b
     10  = select counter 2
     11  = read/write low count byte first then high byte
     011 = mode 3
     0   = binary counting with 16-bit *)
     Port[$43]:=$b6; (* load control word to the control register of 8253 *)
     Port[$42]:=low_count_byte; (* load low count byte *)
     port[$42]:=high_count_byte; (* load high count byte *)
     port[$61]:=port[$61] or 1; (* disable speaker *)
     port[$43]:=$80; (* 80H is the counter latch command for counter 3 *)
end;


Function read_8253:integer;
(* read the two 8-bit counter registers *)
var
   low_byte, high_byte:byte;
begin
     low_byte:=port[$42];
     high_byte:=port[$42];
     read_8253:=low_byte + 256* high_byte;
end;


Function find_period(Address:integer; Bit_weight:integer):real;
(* find the period of an input digital signal.
   Input signal is specified by Input port address (Address) and bit.
   Bit 0, Bit_weight=1
   Bit 1, Bit_weight=2
   .....
   Bit 7, Bit_weight=128 *)
var
   count, Average_number,time1,time2:integer;
begin
        (* Testing the period of low state of a digital signal. This will be used
        for calculating Average_number *)
```

```
    repeat until port[Address] and Bit_weight=Bit_weight; (* signal state high *)
    repeat until port[Address] and Bit_weight=0;          (* signal state low *)
    time1:=read_8253;                                     (* read counts in 8253 first time*)
    repeat until port[Address] and Bit_weight=Bit_weight; (* signal state high again *)
    time2:=read_8253;                                     (* read counts in 8253 the second time *)
    Average_number:=round(10/(Time1-Time2));         (* find Average_number *)
    if Average_number=0 then Average_number:=1;
    repeat until port[Address] and Bit_weight=Bit_weight; (* signal state high *)
    repeat until port[Address] and Bit_weight=0;          (* signal state low *)
    time1:=read_8253;                                     (* read counts in 8253 first time *)
    for count:=1 to Average_number do                (* find low going edge of a digital signal *)
    begin
        repeat until port[Address] and Bit_weight=Bit_weight;   (* signal state high *)
        repeat until port[Address] and Bit_weight=0;            (* signal state low *)
    end;
    Time2:=read_8253;                                    (* read counts in 8253 the second time *)
    Find_period:=((Time1-time2)*1/(2*1193180)*1e6/Average_number);
end;


(* Main program *)
begin
    Centronic_address;
    init_8253(255,255);  (* initialize 3rd timer of 8253 *)
    repeat
        time_period:=find_period(P_address+1, 8); (* P_address+1 is the address of the status port,
                                             8 is the bit weight of DB3 *)
        gotoxy(10,10); write('Time period of output signal from TSL220 [us]:    ', time_period:8:1);
        gotoxy(10,11);write('Frequency of the output signal [Hz]:            ',1/time_period*1e6:8:1);
        delay(2000);
    until keypressed
end.
```

6.3.2 TSL215 linear light detector array

The TSL215 (Texas Instruments) opto-sensor consists of two sections of 64 charge-mode pixels arranged in a 128 by 1 linear array. Each pixel is 120 µm by 70 µm with a 125 µm centre-to-centre spacing. The operation of the sensors involves two periods: an integration period and an output period. During the integration period, charge, which is induced by the incident light, is accumulated in each pixel. A pixel receiving a higher intensity of light results in a higher charge voltage. During the output period, the charge voltage from each pixel is clocked out from the analogue output. The voltage can be measured by A/D converters.

The pin-out of the TSL215 and its internal block diagram are shown in Figure 6.27. Pins 1 and 7 are V_{DD} and they are connected to +5V. Pins 5 and 12 are GND pins and connected to the ground.

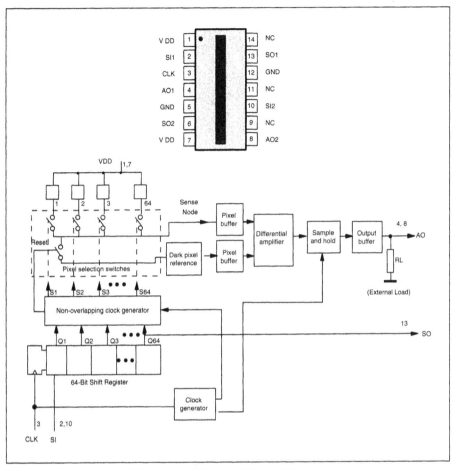

Figure 6.27 Pin-out of TSL215 and internal block diagram

AO1 (pin 4) and AO2 (pin 8) are analogue outputs for the first and second sections. CLK (pin 3) is the clock input. SI1 and SI2 (pins 2 and 10) are serial inputs for the two sections. They are used for controlling the integration period and the pixel output sequence. SO1 (pin 13) is the serial output of the first section and SO2 is the serial output of the second section.

The device has two output modes. One is the parallel mode and the other is the serial mode. In the parallel mode, the pixel voltages for the two sections are output from AO1 and AO2 under the control of CLK, SI1 and SI2 inputs. SI1 and SI2 are connected together. Two A/D conversion channels are required to read the two analogue signals. In the serial mode, AO1 and AO2 are connected together. The pixel voltages from the first section are output first and the voltages from the second section are output next. Only one A/D converter channel is required. The connection for the serial mode is shown in Figure 6.28. SO1 is connected to SI2. The external control signal is supplied to SI1. SI1 goes from low to high first. At the low-to-high transition of the clock input, the

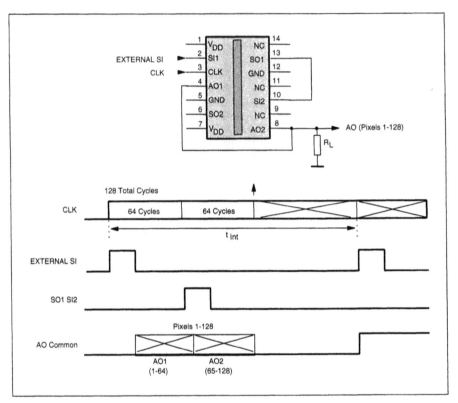

Figure 6.28 Timing sequence for the serial output mode

pixel integration period is terminated and the data output sequence is initiated. This also starts a new integration. Immediately after the clock transition, the voltage from the first pixel of the first section appears at AO1. Before the falling edge of the clock, SI should be set low. The next 63 clock cycles shift out all the pixel voltages of the first section. At the rising edge of the 64th clock cycle, SO1 goes from low to high which makes SI2 go from low to high. At the rising edge of the 65th clock, AO1 goes to a high impedance state. The integration period for the second section is terminated and the output sequence for the second section is initiated. The next 64 clock cycles shift out the pixel voltages of the second section. At the rising edge of the 129th clock cycle, SO2 goes high and AO2 goes to a high impedance state.

Figure 6.29 shows an experimental circuit in which a TSL 215 is configured in the serial output mode. The TSL215 is connected to the Centronic experimental board. CLK is connected to D1 and SI1 is connected to D2 terminals on the board. The pixel voltage output is fed to an oscilloscope which shows the pattern of the light intensity experienced by the sensor array. A TP6 program generates the CLK and SI1 signals. Some application ideas for the TSL215 sensor are shown in Figure 6.30.

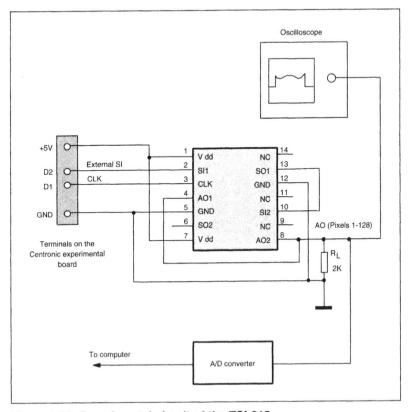

Figure 6.29 Experimental circuit of the TSL215

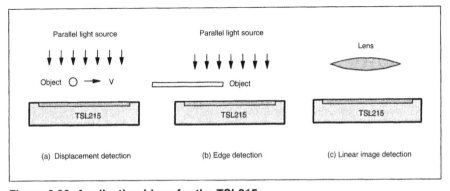

Figure 6.30 Application ideas for the TSL215

TP6 program list of TSL215.PAS

```
Program TSL215;
(* CLK connected to D1, SI connected to D2 *)

uses
    Dos, Crt;

var
    i,polarity:integer;
    dummy:real;


{$I c:\ioexp\tplib1.pas }


Procedure time_delay;
var
    ij:integer;
begin
    for ij:=1 to 1 do ij:=ij;
end;


Procedure Read_pixel;
begin
    write_data_port(P_address, 0+2);
    write_data_port(P_address, 1+2);

    for i:=1 to 128 do
    begin
        write_data_port(P_address,0+0);
        time_delay;
        write_data_port(P_address,1+0);
        time_delay;
    end;
end;


(* main program *)
begin
    Centronic_address;
    repeat
    read_pixel;
    delay(3);
    until keypressed
end.
```

6.3.3 Other digital opto-sensors

The IS1U60 (Sharp, RS577-897) is an infra-red receiver for remote controllers. It is housed in a 3-pin plastic package and incorporates a circuitry capable of receiving a modulated 38 kHz infra-red signal and converting it to a logic pulse train output. The pin-out and the internal block diagram of the IC are shown in Figure 6.31. The voltage supply is +5V and the current consumption is 3 mA. Digital signals which can be received reliably should have a high and low level pulse width less than 400 µs to 800 µs, respectively. The minimum operation distance is 5 metres and the receiving angle is ±30°.

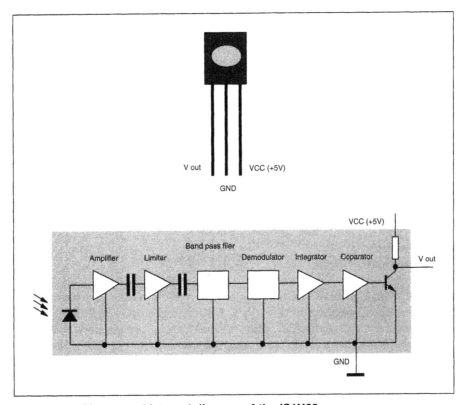

Figure 6.31 Pin-out and internal diagram of the IS1U60

The IS485/IS486 (Sharp, RS197-031) is an opto-Schmitt trigger detector housed in a side looking plastic package with an integral daylight cut-off filter. The device consists of a photodiode, an amplifier, a voltage regulator, a Schmitt trigger and a buffered output which is compatible with the TTL/LSTTL and CMOS logic. The pin-out and the internal block diagram of the IC are shown in Figure 6.32. It accepts a power supply from 4.5 to 17V. A load resistor (500 Ω to 50 kΩ) should be used at the output pin. When the load resistor is 1K, the rise time is 100 ns and the fall time is 50 ns. The receiving angle is ±20°.

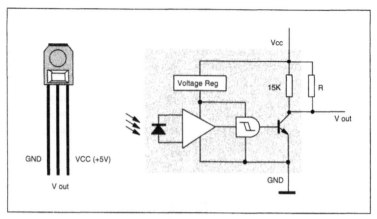

Figure 6.32 Pin-out and internal diagram of IS485/IS486

6.4 Digital sensors measuring temperatures

Reading temperature into a digital system requires a temperature sensor, a signal conditioning and A/D conversion circuits. Latest temperature sensors combine all these on a single chip.

6.4.1 DS1620 thermometer

The DS1620 (Dallas RS218–3810) digital thermometer and thermostat provides a 9-bit temperature reading to indicate the temperature of the device. It has three temperature alarm outputs which can be used for thermostat applications. The alarm setting can be programmed and stored in the on-board non-volatile RAM. It measures temperatures from –55°C to 125°C in 0.5°C increments. Conversion takes about one second.

The pin-out and the internal block diagram of the device are shown in Figure 6.33. Data is transferred between the device and external circuits via a three-wire serial bus: CLK/-CONV (pin 2), DQ (pin 1) and RESET (pin 3). These pins are TTL compatible. THIGH (pin 7) is the high temperature trigger. It goes high when the measured temperature exceeds the high temperature limit stored inside the chip. It remains high until the temperature is less than the stored value. TLOW (pin 6) is the low temperature trigger. It goes high when the temperature falls below the low temperature limit stored inside the chip. It remains high until the temperature is higher than the stored value. TCOM (pin 5) is a high/low combination trigger. It goes high when the measured temperature exceeds the high temperature limit and becomes low when the temperature falls below the low temperature limit. Pin 4 and pin 8 are connected to the ground and +5V rails of the power supply. The standby current is about 1 µA and the active supply current (when the device is performing the temperature measurement) is 1 mA.

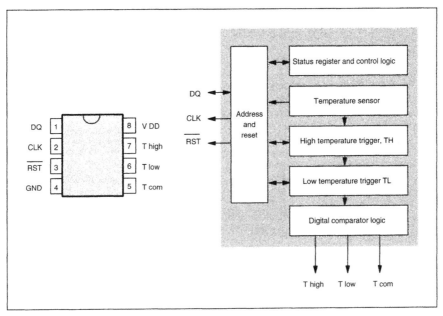

Figure 6.33 Pin-out and internal block diagram of the SD1640

The control sequence of the device has two stages. In the first stage, a control command is sent to the DS1620 serially via the bus. In the second stage, the temperature data (9 bits) is either read from the device or written to it via the bus. There are nine commands.

- **Read temp (AAh):** reads the register containing the last temperature conversion result. After executing the command, the 9-bit temperature data will be read from the device.
- **Start conversion T (EEh):** initializes temperature conversion. There is no further data transfer after this.
- **Stop convert T (22h):** stops a temperature conversion. There is no further data transfer after this.
- **Write TH (01h):** writes the high temperature limit into the TH register. After the command, the 9-bit temperature data is written to the device.
- **Write TL (02h):** writes the low temperature limit into the TL register. After the command, the 9-bit temperature data is written to the device.
- **Read TL (A1h):** reads the TH register. After the command, the device outputs the 9-bit temperature data.
- **Read TL (A2):** reads the TL register. After the command, the device outputs the 9-bit temperature data.
- **Write configuration (0Ch):** writes the configuration data to the configuration register. An 8-bit data should follow the command.
- **Read configuration (ACh):** reads the control data from the configuration register. After the command, the device outputs the 8-bit data.

The configuration word controls the operation mode of the DS1620. It is stored in the configuration register. The bit functions from bit 7 to bit 0 are shown below:

DONE   THF   TLF   XXX   CPU 1SHOT

X	don't care
DONE	1 = conversion completed, 0 = conversion in progress.
THF	Temperature high flag. The bit is set to 1 when the temperature is greater than or equal to the high temperature limit. It will remain 1 until reset by writing 0 into it or by removing power from the device.
TLF	Temperature low flag. The bit is set to 1 when the temperature is less than or equal to the low temperature limit. It remains 1 until reset by writing 0 into it or by removing the power from the device.
CPU	If CPU=0, the CLK/-CONV pin acts as a conversion start control. If CPU is 1, the DS1620 will be used with a CPU communicating to it over the 3-wire port.
1SHOT	One-shot mode, if 1SHOT is 1, the DS1620 will perform one temperature conversion upon the reception of the start conversion command. If 1SHOT is 0, the DS1620 will continuously perform temperature measurement.

Temperature readings have a 9-bit two's complement format. The relationship between temperature and the DS1620's data output is given below:

+125°C	0 11111010 (00FA)
+25°C	0 00110010 (0032)
1/2°C	0 00000001 (0001)
0°C	0 00000000 (0000)
−1/2°C	1 11111111 (01FF)
−25°C	1 11001110 (01CE)
−55°C	1 10010010 (0192)

The timing sequence for data transfer is given in Figure 6.34. A data transfer is initiated by supplying a high-to-low pulse to the -RESET (pin 3). Bringing pin 3 to the low state terminates the data transfer. Writing data to the device and reading data from the DS1640 are controlled by the clock input. A clock cycle is a sequence of a falling edge followed by a rising edge. When writing data into the device, data bits must be stable at the rising edge of the clock cycle. When reading data from the device, data bits are output from the device at the falling edge of the clock. The data bits remain valid until the rising edge of the clock. The DQ pin goes to the high-impedance state when the clock is high. Data bits are communicated via the bus with the LSB first. DQ pin outputs data and inputs data as well.

An experimental circuit using the Centronic experimental board is shown in Figure 6.35. As DQ is an input and an output, the interface between the IC and the experimental board must be able to cope with this. A transistor can be used for this purpose. The base of the transistor is connected to D1 terminal. When D1 is at the high state, the transistor conducts which brings DQ pin low. When D1 is at the low state, the transistor is switched off and DQ is pulled to +5V. The status of the DQ is controlled by the IC. DQ is connected to the S1 terminal of the Centronic experimental board and the status of DQ is then read into the computer. CLK/-CONV and -RST pins of the DS1620 are connected to C1 and C2 terminals of the experimental board. After -RST goes high from low, the DS1620 is set to receive the command bits. D1 will output the required data to the IC (note that the D1 is inverted due to the transistor circuit) under the control of the clock. If the DS1620 is to output data, after the command data bits are sent to the DS1620, D1 goes low. The serial data bits are then clocked out from the IC under the control of the clock. If the DS1620 is to receive data, the serial data will be clocked into the DS1620 under the control of the clock input. A TP6 program is used to perform various operations.

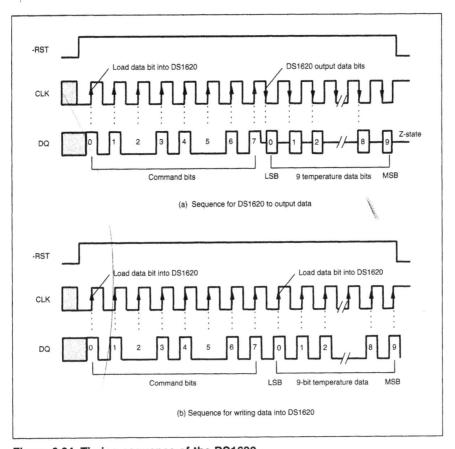

Figure 6.34 Timing sequence of the DS1620

TP6 program list of DS1620.PAS

```
Program DS1620_temperature_sensor;
(* software driver for the DS1620 temperature sensor *)
(* DQ data I/O connected to S1 (when read) and to D1 when write
   CLK/-CONV connected to C1
   -RST connected to C2 *)

uses
    crt, dos;

{$I c:\ioexp\tplib1.pas}

Procedure Write_protocol(datax:byte);
(* write protocol to DS1620 *)
```

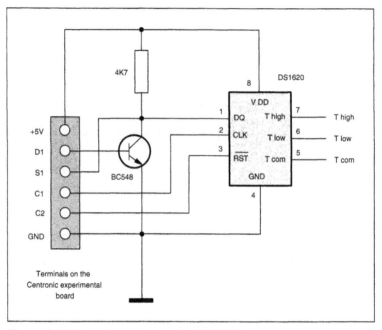

Figure 6.35 Experimental circuit of DS1620

```
var
      i:byte;
begin
      write_control_port(P_address,1+0); (* -RST at low, CLK at high *)
      delay(1);
      write_control_port(P_address,1+2); (* -RST brought high to start I/O cycle *)
                                  (* CLK at logic high *)
      delay(1);

      (* send protocol bits to the DS1620 *)
      for i:=1 to 8 do
          begin
              write_control_port(P_address,0+2);
              delay(1);
              write_data_port(P_address,1 - round((datax and bit_weight(i))/bit_weight(i)));
              (* output protocol bits to D1 terminal of the experimental board. the line is inverted *)
              delay(1);
              write_control_port(P_address,1+2);
              delay(60);
```

```
                end;
        delay(50);
end;


Procedure Write_temperature(temp:byte);
(* write temperature (temp) after protocol. temp = 0 - 250. -temp not supported *)
var
      i,datax:byte;
begin
      datax:=temp*2;
      (* send protocol bits to the DS1620 *)
      for i:=1 to 9 do
          begin
                write_control_port(P_address,0+2);
                delay(1);
                if i<=8 then write_data_port(P_address,1 - round((datax and bit_weight(i))/bit_weight(i)))
                    else write_data_port(P_address,0);
                (* output protocol bits to D1 terminal of the experimental board. the line is inverted *)
                delay(1);
                write_control_port(P_address,1+2);
                delay(60);
          end;
      delay(90);
end;


Function Temperature:real;
var
    i,tempx:integer;
    bitx:array[1..9] of byte;
begin
      write_data_port(P_address,0);

      for i:=1 to 9 do
      begin
          write_control_port(P_address,0+2);
          delay(1);
          bitx[i]:=read_status_port(P_address) and 1;
          write_control_port(P_address,1+2);
          delay(1);
      end;
      write_control_port(P_address,1+0);
      delay(10);
      tempx:=0;
      for i:=1 to 8 do tempx:=tempx + bit_weight(i)*bitx[i];
```

```
        Temperature:=(tempx + 0*bitx[9] * 256)/2;

end;


Procedure Example1;
(* An example shown how to set high and low temperature limit and read the
   set temperature back to the computer *)
begin
        writeln('Example 1, TH and TL are loaded with 35 and 25 deg C');
        writeln('Reading TH and TL temperature values from the DS1620 ');
        write_protocol(12);   (* 0Ch= Write configuration command*)
        write_protocol(0);    (* 00h= continuous configuration, not CPU mode  *)
        write_protocol(1);    (* 01h= Write high temp to TH command *)
        write_temperature(35);(* 85D= high temperature limit in deg C *)
        write_protocol(2);    (* 02h= write low temp to LH command *)
        write_temperature(25);(* 20D= low temperature limit in deg C *)
        write_protocol(161);  (* A1h= CPU read content in TH command *)
        writeln('High temperature limit: ',temperature:5:1,' °C');   (* read TH temperature from the DS1620 *)
        write_protocol(162);  (* A2h= CPU read content in TL command *)
        writeln('Low  temperature limit: ',temperature:5:1,' °C');   (* read TL temperature from the DS1620 *)

end;


Procedure Example2;
(* Testing other features *)
begin
        write_protocol(12);
        write_protocol(00); (* CPU mode and 1 shot mode *)
        write_protocol(34); (* 22h= stop the CPU *)
        writeln;
        repeat
              write_protocol(170); (* AAh= read temperature command *)
              gotoxy(8,10);
              write('DS1620 stopped, Old temperature measured by DS1620 [deg C]: ',temperature:5:1);
              (* As DS1620 stopped, one the old temperature is read *)
              delay(5000);
        until keypressed;
        readln;
        write_protocol(238); (* EEh= start temperature conversion *)
        repeat
              write_protocol(170); (* AAh= read temperature command *)
              gotoxy(5,12);
              write('DS1620 active, present temperature measured by DS1620 [deg C]: ',temperature:5:1);
              (* new temperature is continuously measured *)
              delay(5000);
```

```
        until keypressed;
end;


(* Main Program *)
begin
        Centronic_address;
        example1;
        example2;
end.
```

6.4.2 Single wire digital temperature sensor

The SMARTEC (LJK Technology) temperature sensor allows temperature to be measured digitally by a computer via a single wire. A 4 kHz TTL/CMOS compatible square wave with a modulated temperature-dependent duty cycle is output from the wire. By measuring the duty cycle of the square wave, the temperature can be measured. The sensor eliminates the use of A/D converters and utilizes one wire for I/O interfacing. The operating temperature range is from –45°C to 130°C. The total measurement accuracy is less than 2°C over the whole temperature range. It requires a power supply from 4.75 to 7V with a typical supply current of 200 µA.

The pin-out of the sensor is given in Figure 6.36. Pin 1 is the signal output; pin 2 and pin 3 are connected to the positive and ground rails of the power supply. The duty cycle of the output signal is linearly related to the temperature measured according to the equation:

$$\text{Duty cycle (\%)} = 0.320 + 0.00470 \times \text{Temperature (°C)}$$

The output pin is connected to one line of an input port of the computer. A computer program counts the time period when the output is high and the period when the output is low.

Figure 6.36 shows an experimental circuit using the sensor and the Centronic experimental board. The software driver is written in TP6.

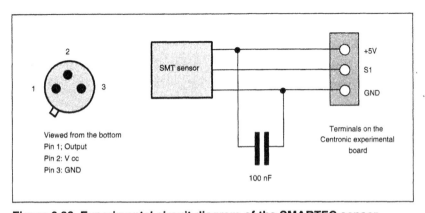

Figure 6.36 Experimental circuit diagram of the SMARTEC sensor

TP6 program list of SMT.PAS

```
Program Temperature_SMT_sensor;
(* Serial data load  (pin 1) connected to S1 *)


uses
    Crt, dos;


{$I c:\ioexp\TPLIB1.PAS }


Var
    C_or_F,i:byte;
    Datax:array[1..12] of byte;
    unitx:char;


Function temperature:real;
(* calculate duty cycles and then find the temperature *)


var
    lp,hp,i,total_scan:longint;
begin
    lp:=0; (* input low status counter reset  *)
    hp:=0; (* input high status counter reset *)
    total_scan:=300000; (* total scanning number *)

    for i:=1 to Total_scan do
    begin
        if port[P_address+1] and 8 =0 then lp:=lp+1;  (* if input = 0, low_count  +1 *)
        if port[P_address+1] and 8 =8 then hp:=hp+1;  (* if input = 1, high_count +1 *)
    end;
    temperature:=(hp/Total_scan-0.32)/ 0.0047
end;


(*   Main Program   *)
begin
    Centronic_address; (* select a Centronic interface *)
repeat
    gotoxy(10, 10);
    write('Temperature from the SMT temperature sensor: ',temperature:5:2,' °C');
until keypressed
end.
```

6.4.3 LCD thermometer modules

The temperature module (Maplin FE33L) has an on-board temperature sensor and a liquid crystal display. They are mounted on a small PCB board with a 16-way solder edge connection and the PCB is fixed to a small plastic bracket that houses a 1.5V battery. The module not only measures and displays the temperature, but also displays time. It draws 15 μA from the battery. This makes the battery life longer than a year. Some features of the module are summarized as follows:

Thermometer:	$3\frac{1}{2}$ digits display with °C or with °F indicator.
	Measurement from −20°C to +70°C with a resolution of 0.1°C.
	Accuracy: ±1°C from 0°C to 40°C and ±2°C for other ranges.
	Sampling rate: 10 or 1 second selectable.
	Alarm at highest and the lowest temperature.
	Serial BCD data output for temperature measurement.
Clock:	$3\frac{1}{2}$ digits display showing HOUR and MINUTE.
	Accuracy: 0.5 second per day.
Power supply:	One 1.5V battery with a life of over a year.

The pin-out and the typical connection are given in Figure 6.37. The module has a serial BCD data output, the format of which is shown in Figure 6.38. An experimental circuit is shown in Figure 6.37. Pins 10 and 9 are connected to S1 and S2 terminals of the Centronic experimental board via two transistor voltage translators. A Turbo Pascal 6 program reads the serial data and converts it into a temperature value.

TP6 program list of TMODULE.PAS

```
Program Temperature_LCD_module;
(* Serial data load  (pin 10) connected to S1. The line is inverted
   Serial data output (pin 9) connected to S2. The line is inverted *)
uses
    Crt, dos;


{$I c:\ioexp\TPLIB1.PAS }


Var
    C_or_F,i:byte;
    Datax:array[1..12] of byte;
    unitx:char;


Function Temperature:real;
(* read temperature reading from the LCD temperature module *)
begin
    write_data_port(P_address,1); (* power the two voltage translation transistors *)

    (* find the header. the header is an 1ms high pulse *)
    repeat
```

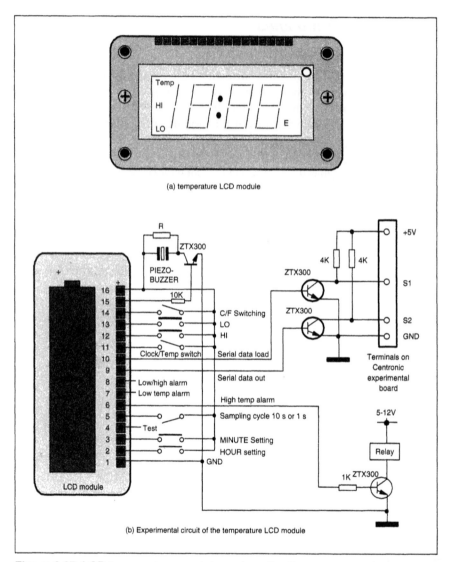

(a) temperature LCD module

(b) Experimental circuit of the temperature LCD module

Figure 6.37 LCD temperature module and application

```
repeat until read_status_port(P_address) and 1 = 1; (* find logic 0. the line inverted *)
repeat until read_status_port(P_address) and 1 = 0; (* find logic 1. the line inverted *)
delay(3);                                           (* delay 0.8 ms *)
C_or_F:=round(read_status_port(P_address) and 2/2); (* get deg C (=1) or deg F (=0) *)
if C_or_F=1 then unitx:='C' else unitx:='F';
until read_status_port(P_address) and 1 = 0;
```

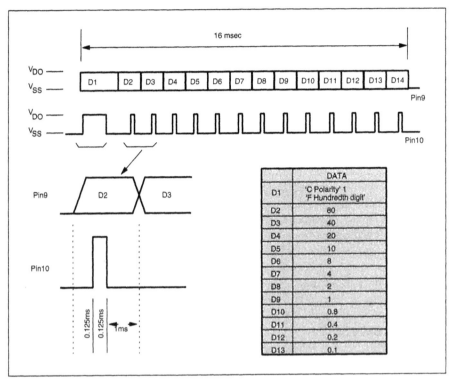

Figure 6.38 Format of the serial data output

```
(* read BCD data. read sequence: 80,40,20,10,8,4,2,1,08,04,02,01 *)

for i:=1 to 12 do

    begin

        repeat until read_status_port(P_address) and 1 = 1; (* find logic 0 *)

        repeat until read_status_port(P_address) and 1 = 0; (* find logic 1 *)

        repeat until read_status_port(P_address) and 1 = 1; (* find logic 0 *)

        datax[i]:=1-round(read_status_port(P_address) and 2/2); (* read data bit. bit inverted *)

    end;

(* generate temperature *)

Temperature:=10*( 8*datax[1] + 4*datax[2] + 2*datax[3] + 1*datax[4] ) +

            1*( 8*datax[5] + 4*datax[6] + 2*datax[7] + 1*datax[8] ) +

            0.1*( 8*datax[9] + 4*datax[10] + 2*datax[11] + 1*datax[12] );

end;


begin

    Centronic_address; (* select a Centronic interface *)

repeat
```

```
        gotoxy(20, 10);
        write('Temperature from the module: ',temperature:5:1,' °',unitx);
        delay(5000);
until keypressed
end.
```

6.5 Digital humidity sensors

The LCD humidity module (Maplin, ZA38R) has the same style as the temperature/clock module described above. The module and a typical application are shown in Figure 6.39. It measures the relative humidity (RH) in the range from 25% RH to 96% RH and records the minimum and maximum humidity levels measured at any time since the last reset. The humidity sensor is on the board. Normally, the LCD shows the present humidity value. But the minimum and maximum humidity can be displayed under the control of two push buttons which are identified by the MIN and MAX on the display. Both memories can be cleared by pressing down both buttons.

There are four pins to output the relative humidity values in a packed 4-bit BCD format. The format is shown in Figure 6.40. Each output line begins with a pair of sync pulses. It is followed by 4-bit data indicating the key press conditions. Then the two digits (MSB first) of the humidity are output.

An experimental circuit is shown in Figure 6.39. The module is connected to the Centronic experimental board and the four outputs are connected to S1 to S4 terminals of the experimental board via four transistor voltage translators. A TP6 program is used to read the data and to convert the data into the humidity reading.

TP6 program list of HMODULE.PAS

```
Program Humidity_LCD_module;
(* M1 (pin 4) connected to S1. The line is inverted
   M2 (pin 5) connected to S2. The line is inverted
   M3 (pin 6) connected to S3. The line is inverted
   M4 (pin 7) connected to S4. The line is inverted *)

uses
    Crt, dos;

{$I c:\ioexp\TPLIB1.PAS }

Var
    C_or_F,i:byte;
    Datax:array[1..12] of byte;
    unitx:char;

Function Input_data:byte;
```

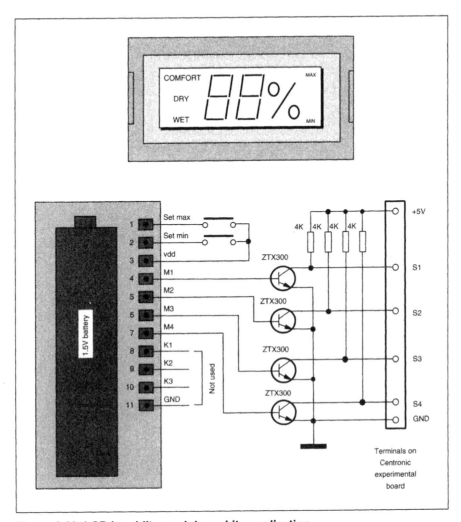

Figure 6.39 LCD humidity module and its application

```
(* All inputs to the status port are inverted *)
begin
     input_data:=15 - read_status_port(P_address);
end;


Function Humidity:real;
(* read humidity reading from the humidity module *)
var
    keypressed_data, digit_1st, digit_2nd:byte;
```

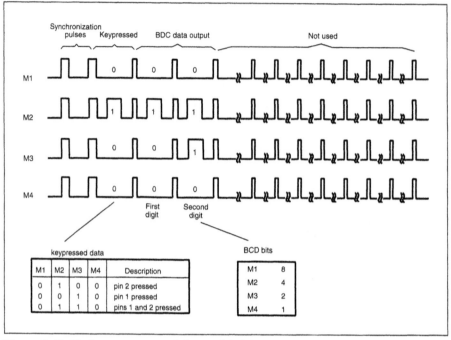

Figure 6.40 Timing sequence of the serial data output

```
begin
      (* find logic 0 before the header *)
      repeat until input_data = 15;     (* find logic 1 on all inputs *)
      delay(500);                       (* delay 50 ms *)
                                        (* after delay, it is the logic low *)
      (* skip the header, two high pulses *)
      repeat until input_data = 15; (* find logic 1 *)
      repeat until input_data = 0;  (* find logic 0 *)
      repeat until input_data = 15; (* find logic 1 *)
      repeat until input_data = 0;  (* find logic 0 *)


      (* read keypressed data *)
      repeat until input_data <> 0 ;        (* input the keypressed data *)
      Keypressed_data:=input_data;
      if keypressed_data < 15 then
         begin
      (* skip one sync. pulse *)
      repeat until input_data = 15; (* find logic 1 *)
      repeat until input_data = 0 ; (* find logic 0 *)
```

```
        end
        else repeat until input_data = 0;


    (* read the 1st digit *)
    repeat until input_data <> 0;          (* input the keypressed data *)
    digit_1st:=input_data;


    (* skip one sync. pluse *)
    repeat until input_data = 15;  (* find logic 1 *)
    repeat until input_data = 0 ;  (* find logic 0 *)


    (* read the 2nd digit *)
    repeat until input_data <> 0;          (* input the keypressed data *)
    digit_2nd:=input_data;
    if digit_2nd = 15 then digit_2nd := 0;


    (* generate humidity *)
    Humidity:=(digit_1st)*10 + (digit_2nd);
end;


begin
    Centronic_address; (* select a Centronic interface *)
repeat
    gotoxy(20, 10);
    write('Humidity from the module: ',humidity:5:1,' %');
    delay(5000);
until keypressed
end.
```

6.6 Digital sensors for fluid flow

The digital flow sensor (UCC International, RS185-9982) is a 3-terminal flow cell (Figure 6.41). It has a nylon rotor on a stainless steel shaft. The rotor is situated in the centre of the flow passage. When a fluid is flowing in the passage, the rotor spins. The rotation is detected by an infra-red emitter and a detector arrangement. When the rotor spins, it interrupts the infra-red light beam incident on the detector. The change in light intensity is converted to the change in voltage. After the signal is amplified and conditioned, a square wave signal is generated at the output terminals. All electronic circuits are housed inside the sensor. The frequency is proportional to the flow rate of fluids. For every litre of water passing through the sensor, approximately 752 pulses will be produced. It can measure a flow rate of water from 1 to 20 litres per minute.

Figure 6.41 also shows an experimental circuit in which the sensor is connected to the Centronic experimental board. The pulse train is fed into the S1 terminal of the board. A flow rate can be calculated by counting the number of pulses in a fixed period of time. This can be done easily in the

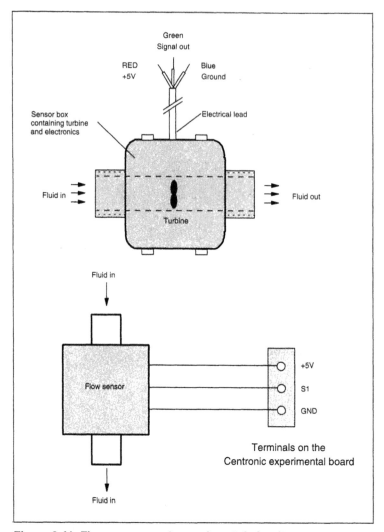

Figure 6.41 Flow sensor and experimental circuit

program. The program reads the start time first, then it counts the pulses from the sensor. After the count reaches a certain level, the program reads the time again. Finally, the program calculates the number of pulses per second and from this the flow rate of water can be calculated.

6.7 Digital sensors measuring magnetic field

6.7.1 FGM-3 digital magnetic field strength sensor

Reading the field strength of a magnetic field into a digital system requires a magnetic sensor, a signal conditioning circuit and an analogue-to-digital converter. The latest sensor developments combine all these on a single package. This significantly simplifies the process of reading the magnetic field into digital systems and improves the quality of the measurement.

The FGM-3 (Speake & Co.) is a three-terminal device. Two terminals are connected to the power supplies and the third terminal is the output. The pin-out is given in Figure 6.42. It is capable of measuring a magnetic field of 10 nT. The output is a digital signal with frequencies varying from 50 to 120 kHz. The period of the signal is proportional to the strength of the magnetic field experienced by the sensor. It also features a low temperature coefficient of 0.003% per °C. Due to its extreme sensitivity, the device can measure the strength of the earth's magnetic field. It can be used for detecting direction.

The device requires a power supply of +5V. The power supply can be generated using a 78L09 and a 78L05 in series. Such a supply provides a very stable voltage output. The measurement technique is to count the number of pulses for a fixed period of time to determine the frequency of the signal. The field strength can then be calculated. An experimental circuit is shown in Figure 6.42.

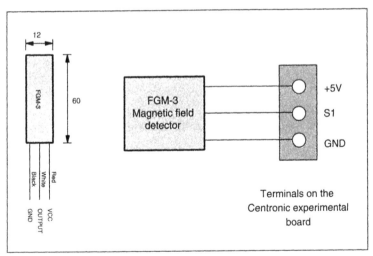

Figure 6.42 FGM-3 magnetic sensor and its experimental circuit

6.7.2 Digital magnetic field detector

The UCN3121 (Allegro, RS307-446) is an integrated Hall-effect open-collector switch. It contains a Hall-effect element, an amplifier, a Schmitt trigger, a voltage regulator and an open-collector follower. The pin-out and the internal block diagram are shown in Figure 6.43. It has a switch-on point of 350 G and a release point of 260 G. The output of the device is low when the magnetic field at the Hall sensor exceeds the threshold. When the strength is below the release point threshold, the output goes high. It requires a power supply of 4.5 to 24V with a typical supply current of 5 mA. The output stage is an open collector and can source 25 mA. To connect the output to a TTL/CMOS circuit, a 10K pull-up resistor should be connected across VCC and OUTPUT.

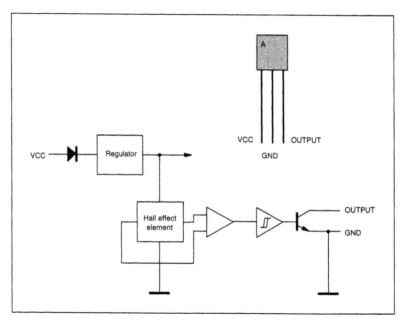

Figure 6.43 Pin-out and the internal block diagram of the UCN3121

6.8 Radio time bases

Radio time signal receivers allow access to a standard time which is accurate to a second in a million years. The radio signal is generated in Britain by the National Physics Laboratory. Every minute the NPL transmits a binary time code which contains the time, the date and the calendar day. NPL is part of an international network which allows world-wide clocks to agree to the nanosecond. MSF is the call sign of the NPL time code transmitter which is located in Rugby.

Every minute, the MSF transmitter broadcasts a data stream containing time information. The first second of every minute contains a fast code. The remaining 59 seconds contain a slow code which contains the time information. The format of the MSF time-code is shown in Table 6.1.

Table 6. 1 Time binary code of the MSF transmitter

Second	Description	BCD format	Description
0	Fast code		
1	DUT1 code		
2–16	–		
17	year (tens)	80	
18	year (tens)	40	
19	year (tens)	20	
20	year (tens)	10	give year 00 to 99
21	year (units)	8	
22	year (units)	4	
23	year (units)	2	
24	year (units)	1	
25	month (tens)	10	
26	month	8	
27	month	4	give month 01 to 12
28	month	2	
29	month	1	
30	day of month (tens)	20	
31	day of month (tens)	10	
32	day of month	8	
33	day of month	4	give day of month 01 to 30
34	day of month	2	
35	day of month	1	
36	day of week	4	
37	day of week	2	give day of week 1 to 7
38	day of week	1	
39	hour (tens)	20	
40	hour (tens)	10	
41	hour	8	
42	hour	4	give hour 01 to 24
43	hour	2	
44	hour	1	
45	minute (tens)	40	
46	minute (tens)	20	
47	minute (tens)	10	
48	minute	8	give minute 00–59
49	minute	4	
50	minute	2	
51	minute	1	
52	always "0"	0	
53–58	always "1"	1	
59	always "0"	0	

The MSF radio transmission signal is shown in Figure 6.44. The carrier frequency of the code is 60 kHz. It is transmitted at the beginning of each second for 100 ms and 200 ms. The 100 ms period corresponds to a zero and the 200 ms period corresponds to 1. Transmissions from 52 to 59 seconds are set permanently to 10000001. The sequence is unique and is used to synchronize the receiver.

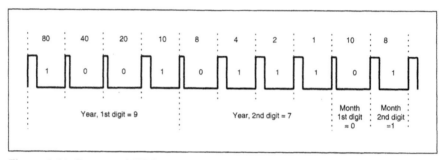

Figure 6.44 Format of MSF transmission data

The EM2 MSF receiver module (Maplin MK68Y) and the MSF antenna (Maplin MK72P) forms a complete time code receiver. It produces a serial digital output for external decoding. The EM2 contains a very sensitive radio receiver with a very tight bandwidth of 10 Hz. The module has a low-power standby mode and an active mode under the control of PON input. In the standby mode, maximum current consumption is 1 µA. In the active mode the current is 500 µA. The power supply voltage is a 1.5 to 3.5V single-rail supply. UB and GND are connected to the positive and ground rails of the supply. To reject the mains interference, a 1 kΩ resistor and a 10 µF electrolytic are used. The MSF data output is connected internally with an active low open collector npn transistor with a maximum current of 15 mA and a maximum collector voltage of 5.25V. An external 330 kΩ pull-up resistor is suitable for use with +3V and 470 kΩ at +5V. The MSF antenna is a pre-aligned LC tuned ferrite antenna which is specifically designed for the EM2 receiver module.

An experimental circuit using the Centronic experimental board is shown in Figure 6.45(a). The digital output from the MSF receiver is connected to the S1 terminal on the experimental board. The voltage level on the MSF receiver is converted to the TTL logic using a transistor voltage translator. A software decoder written in TP6 is shown below.

TP6 program list of MSF_RES.PAS

```
Program MSF_receiver;

(* MSF_receiver software driver, data connected to S1 of the Centronic experimental board *)


uses
```

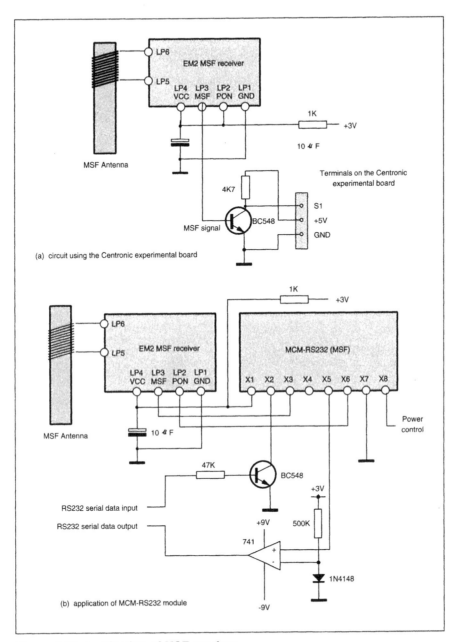

Figure 6.45 Application of MSF receiver

```
    crt, dos;
{$I c:\ioexp\tplib1.pas}


Function Period:byte;
(* find 1 or 0 for every second data transmission *)
begin
        repeat until read_status_port(P_address) and 1 = 1; (* find logic 1 *)
        delay(150*11);                                  (* delay 150 ms *)
        if read_status_port(P_address) and 1 = 1 then period:=1 else period:=0;
        (* if it is still logic high, the data transmission is 1
           if it is logic low, the data transmission must be 0 *)
        delay(700*11); (* delay 700 ms *)
end;


Procedure get_time_bit;
(* get time data *)
var
    count,i:byte;
    Year,Month,Day_of_month,Day_of_week,hour,minute:integer;
    Tbit: array [1..60] of real;
begin
        (* find the data transmitted from 3 to 16 seconds. all zero *)
        count:=0;
        repeat
                if period=0 then count:=count + 1 else count:=0;
        until Count>=14;

        (* get the first date transmitted *)
        repeat until period=1;
        TBit[1]:=1; (* Year data, bit 3 *)

        (* get the next 35 data *)
        for i:=2 to 36 do TBit[i]:=period;

        (* form the time information *)
        Year:= round((8*Tbit[1] + 4*Tbit[2] + 2*Tbit[3] + Tbit[4]) * 10 +
               (8*Tbit[5] + 4*Tbit[6] + 2*Tbit[7] + Tbit[8]));
        Month:=round(Tbit[9]*10 + (8*Tbit[10] + 4*Tbit[11] + 2*Tbit[12] + Tbit[13]));
        Day_of_Month:=round(10*(2*Tbit[14] + Tbit[15]) + (8*Tbit[16] + 4*Tbit[17] + 2*Tbit[18] + Tbit[19])));
        Day_of_week :=round(4*Tbit[20] + 2*Tbit[21] + Tbit[22]);
        hour        :=round(10*(2*Tbit[23] + Tbit[24]) + (8*Tbit[25] + 4*Tbit[26] + 2*Tbit[27] + Tbit[28])));
        Minute      :=round(10*(4*Tbit[29] + 2*Tbit[30] + Tbit[31]) + (8*Tbit[32] + 4*Tbit[33] + 2*Tbit[34] +
Tbit[35])));

        writeln('Year         : ',year);
```

```
        Writeln('Month       : ',Month);
        Writeln('Day of month: ',Day_of_month);
        writeln('Day_of_week : ',Day_of_week);
        writeln('Hour        : ',Hour);
        writeln('Minute      : ',minute);
end;


begin
        centronic_address;
        repeat
        clrscr;
        get_time_bit;
        until keypressed;
end.
```

The output of the MSF receiver can be fed into the MCM-RS232 microcontroller decoder module (Maplin MK73Q). The latter provides time information in a standard RS232 data format via a serial interface. External buffering to full RS232 level is required. The RS232 module provides the exact time information all the time. The host computer does not need to decode the data itself. The module also has a control output. The output can be connected to a suitable power switch for timed control applications. An application circuit is shown in Figure 6.45(b). A communication command set is

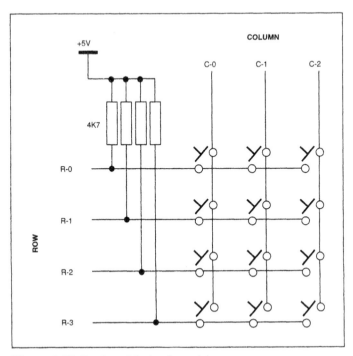

Figure 6.46 3 × 4 matrix keyboard

provided by the module for communications between the module and the computer. The details of the command are described in the manufacturer's data sheet.

6.9 Keys and keyboards

There are two ways of connecting a keyboard to a computer. One is the scanning keyboard type and the other is the encoded keyboard type.

The principle of a 12-key scanning keyboard is shown schematically in Figure 6.46. The keys are arranged in a 4 × 3 matrix. It has four rows and three columns. The three lines in the column are normally high and one of them is brought to low for a short period of time in turns. When one of the lines is in the low state, the status of the four rows lines are monitored. If there is no key pressed, these four lines will be high (note that four resistors are used for pulling up the row lines to +5V). If there is a key pressed and the column corresponding to the key is also at the low state, the row line is at the low state. Knowing the column and row numbers, the position of the pressed key is obtained.

The encoded keyboard involves a dedicated integrated IC or a circuit. The IC or the circuit detects the pressed keys and outputs a parallel encoded data. The computer reads the data and finds out what is the pressed key. An example of the keyboard detection IC is the MM74C922 (National Semiconductors).

Connecting other digital devices

7.1 Digital-to-analogue converters

A digital-to-analogue converter converts a binary code into an analogue voltage or current. It has wide applications in process control, speech/music synthesis and computer-controlled experiments.

7.1.1 A simple R-2R D/A converter

A simple D/A converter can be constructed using several resistors arranged in an R-2R ladder network as shown in Figure 7.1. This converter can only be used in less critical applications. Dedicated D/A converter ICs should be used to achieve high conversion quality.

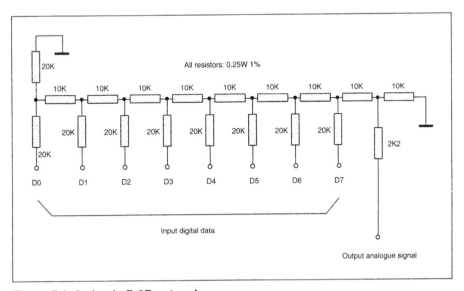

Figure 7.1 A simple R-2R network

7.1.2 Parallel I/O D/A converter, ZN428

The ZN428 (GEC-Plessey) is an 8-bit D/A converter with input data latches. It contains an R-2R ladder network and fast switches to give a conversion time of 800 ns. It provides a 2.5V voltage reference and requires a power supply of 5V with a quiescent current of 20 mA.

Figure 7.2 gives the pin-out and the internal block diagram of the device. Eight-bit data is placed on the data bus first. Then a high-to-low-then-high pulse is applied to the -ENABLE input (pin 4). The data is loaded into the registers and is converted to the analogue voltage.

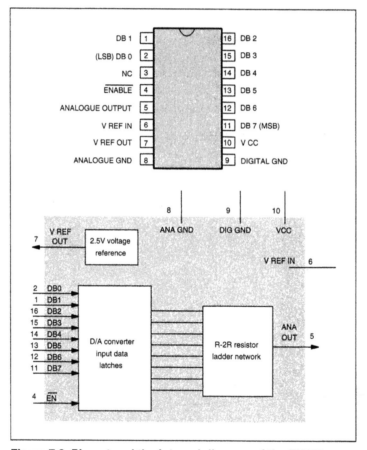

Figure 7.2 Pin-out and the internal diagram of the ZN428

The experimental circuit using the Centronic experimental board is given in Figure 7.3. The eight digital inputs are connected to D1 to D8 terminals of the board. -ENABLE is connected to C1 terminal. The waveform of the analogue output is monitored by an oscilloscope. The demonstration program is written in Turbo Pascal 6. The program sends 1 to 255 to the D/A converter continuously and the waveform of the output, therefore, is a saw-tooth wave.

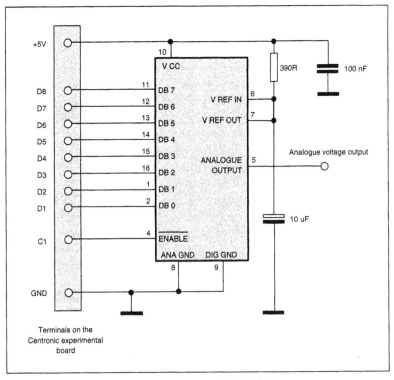

Figure 7.3 Experimental circuit of the ZN428 D/A converter

TP6 program list of ZN428.PAS

```
Program ZN428_DAC;
(* software driver for ZN428 D-A converter - signal generator *)
(* this driver shows how the ZN428 is used to produce a triangular wave *)

uses
    crt,dos;
var
    i:integer;


{$I c:\ioexp\tplib1.pas}


Procedure V_out(data:byte);
(* output a binary byte to change the voltage output*)
begin
    Write_data_port(P_address,data); (* put data on the data bus *)
```

```
        write_control_port(P_address,0); (* -Enabled pulled down to logic 0. data latched to ZN428 *)
        write_control_port(P_address,1); (* -Enabled logic high. data not latched to the ZN428 *)
end;


(* Main Program *)
begin
        Centronic_address;
        i:=0;
        repeat
                V_out(i); (* output 0,1,2,3...255 =  triangular wave output *)
                i:=i+1;   (* I increased by 1 *)
                if i=255 then i:=0;
        until keypressed
end.
```

7.1.3 Serial I/O D/A converter, DAC0854

The DAC0854BIN (National Semiconductor, RS853-315) is a quad 8-bit D/A converter with a serial I/O interface. The pin-out and the internal block diagram are given in Figure 7.4. It requires a +5V power supply with a typical supply current of 14 mA. Six digital I/O lines (-AU, CLK, -CS, -INT, DI and DO) control all operations of the converter. The DAC0854 contains four D/A converters, each having a reference voltage input (V_{REF}) and an analogue voltage output (V_{OUT}). The D/A section also has two bias voltage inputs (V_{BIAS1} and V_{BIAS2}) and a power supply input (AV_{CC}). A 2.65V internal voltage reference ($V_{REF\ OUT}$) is provided by the DAC0854.

The DAC0854 has two I/O operations: a write and read mode. In the write mode, 8-bit digital data is written to the D/A converter and is converted to an analogue voltage. In the read mode, the data that was written to the D/A converters is read back. Writing or reading can be performed with one D/A converter or with all D/A converters. The mode is set by a control word which is written to the control register. The control word is a stream of bits that is clocked into the DAC0854 from the Data Input. The bit functions of the word are given below.

bit 1   start bit = 1
bit 2   RD/-WR=0 for write operation, RD/-WR = 1 for read operation
bit 3   global operation: 1 = access all DACs, 0 = access to a single DAC
bit 4   update control: 1 = update the analogue output, 0 = no update
bit 5   address, A1 for selecting D/A channels
bit 6   address, A0 for selecting D/A channels

When accessing to a single DAC channel, A0 and A1 select one of the four channels. When the global operation is selected (bit 3 = 1), bit 5 and bit 6 are omitted (the control word only has four bits). When the update bit is 1, the input digital data is converted into an analogue voltage at the rising edge of -CS. -AU (asynchronous update) should be pulled high or left open. All operations are initiated by a low-going transition on -CS. Then the bits of the control word are placed on the DI pins. Each bit is clocked into the DAC at the rising edge of the clock. Figure 7.5 gives the timing sequence of the write operation.

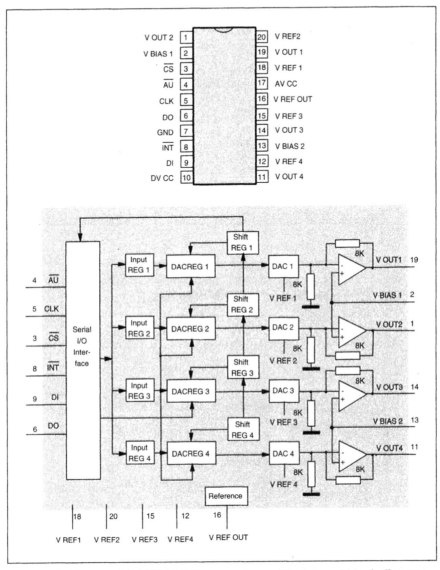

Figure 7.4 Pin-out of DAC0854 D/A converter and its internal block diagram

The range of the output voltage of the D/A converter can be varied. If the internal 2.65V reference is used as the voltage reference and a voltage divider network is used to provide a 1.4V voltage to the V_{BAIS}, the voltage range from 0.31 to 2.81V can be achieved. The relation between the output voltage (V_{OUT}) and the input digital data (DATA in decimal) is expressed by the following equation.

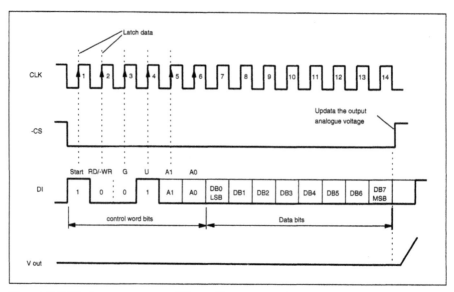

Figure 7.5 Timing sequence of the write command

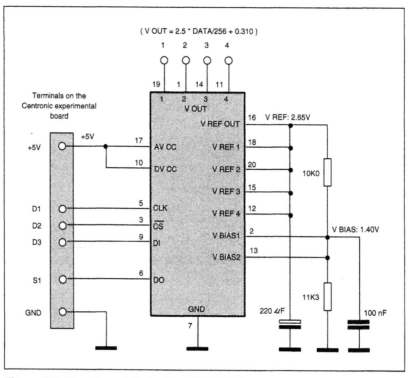

Figure 7.6 Experimental circuit of DAC0854

$$V_{OUT}(\text{volts}) = 2.500 \frac{\text{DATA}}{256} + 0.310$$

An experimental circuit using the Centronic experimental board is shown in Figure 7.6. D1, D2 and D3 on the board are connected to the CLK, -CS and DI. S1 terminal is connected to the DO. The software driver is written in Turbo Pascal 6. ALL_DAC (DATA:byte) writes DATA to all D/A converters. ONE_DAC(ADDRESS, DATA: byte) writes DATA to one D/A converter specified by the ADDRESS. The program causes the DAC0854 to generate a saw-tooth signal at the fourth D/A channel. The waveform can be observed using an oscilloscope.

TP6 program list of DAC0854.PAS

```
Program DAC0854_driver;

(* Software driver for DAC0854 4 channel D/A converter*)

(* Connection to the Centronic experimental board:

    -CS-chip select    D2

    C  -clock          D1

    DI -data in to ic   D3

    DO -data out       S1 *)


uses

    crt, dos;


{$I c:\ioexp\TPLIB1.pas}


var

    command,i:byte;

    D: array[1..130] of byte;


procedure Init;

(* initialize control lines *)

begin

    write_data_port(P_address,1+2+0); (* Clock = -CS = 1 *)

end;


Procedure load_data(data:byte);

(* load procedure, -CS: low, Data: stable, Clock: low to high *)

begin

    write_data_port(P_address,0+0+4*data);     (* output data *)

    write_data_port(P_address,1+0+4*data);     (* Clock from low to high to load data *)

    write_data_port(P_address,0+0+0);          (* clock low *)

end;
```

```
Procedure All_DAC(data:byte);
var
    i:integer;
begin
     load_data(1); (* load start bit *)
     load_data(0); (* load RD/-WR bit, 0, write operation *)
     load_data(1); (* load Global enable bit, 1, global enabled *)
     load_data(1); (* load Updating enable bit, 1, update when -CS changing from low to high *)
     (* load data *)
     for i:=1 to 8 do load_data(round (data and bit_weight(i) / bit_weight(i)));
     write_data_port(P_address, 0+2+0); (* -CS pin from low to high to update data *)
end;



Procedure One_DAC(address, data:byte);
var
    i:integer;
begin
     load_data(1); (* load start bit *)
     load_data(0); (* load RD/-WR bit, 0, write enable *)
     load_data(0); (* load Global enable bit, 0, singal DAC operation *)
     load_data(1); (* load updating enable bit, 1, update when -CS changing from low to high *)
     load_data(round(address and 2 / 2)); (* load address A1 *)
     load_data(address and 1);              (* load address A2 *)
     (* load data *)
     for i:=1 to 8 do load_data(round (data and bit_weight(i) / bit_weight(i)));
     write_data_port(P_address, 0+2+0); (* -CS pin from low to high to update *)
end;



(* main program *)
begin
     Centronic_address;
     init;
     repeat
     for i:=1 to 255 do one_DAC(3,i);
     until keypressed;
end.
```

7.2 Digital potentiometers

Digital potentiometers allow resistance to be changed digitally. Their applications include volume controls in digital audio equipment and in digitally-controlled variable gain amplifiers.

The X9C103 (Xicor) series is a CMOS non-volatile potentiometer. The series contains several devices: X9C103 (RS299-480), X9C503 (RS299-496) and X9C104 (RS299-503) which have a maximum resistance of 10 kΩ, 50 kΩ and 100 kΩ respectively. The resolution of the resistance is equal to the maximum resistance divided by 99. The power supply is +5V and the typical supply current is 1 mA in the active mode and 0.5 mA in the standby mode.

The pin-out and the internal block diagram of the IC are shown in Figure 7.7. The X9C series consists of an input control section, a counter and a decoder section, a non-volatile memory and a resistor array consisting of 99 resistors. Between each resistor and at both ends are tap points. Each point is connected to the wiper pin (Vw) via a transistor gate. The two ends of the resistor array Vh and Vl are equivalent to the fixed terminals of a mechanical potentiometer and can be connected to a voltage from –5V to +5V. Vw is the wiper terminal which is equivalent to the movable terminal of the potentiometer.

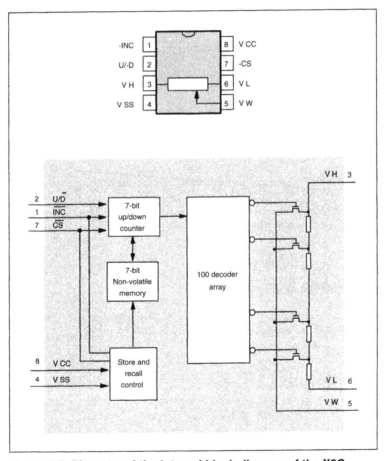

Figure 7.7 Pin-out and the internal block diagram of the X9C series

The position of the wiper is controlled by three control inputs: -CS (Chip select), U/-D (Up and down) and -INC (Increase). U/-D (1: Up, 0: Down) controls whether the counter is incremented or decremented. At the high-to-low transition of the -INC, the wiper position is moved up or down by one step. -CS is low to enable the device. The counter value is stored in the on-board non-volatile memory when -CS is high while the -INC input is high. After this, the IC is in the low power standby mode until the device is selected again.

An experimental circuit using the Centronic experimental board is shown in Figure 7.8. The -INC, U/-D and -CS pins are connected to D1, D2 and D3 terminals of the experimental board. The resistance value between the Vl and Vw is measured using a multimeter. The demonstration software is written in TP6.

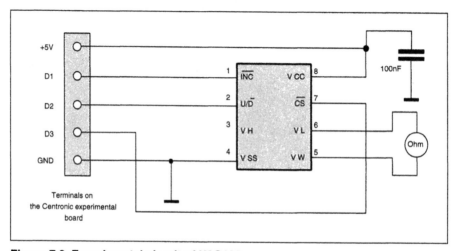

Figure 7.8 Experimental circuit of X9C103

TP6 program list of X9C104.PAS

```
Program X9C104;
(* software driver for X9C104 digital resistor network *)
(* connections to the Centronic experimental board:
    -INC (increase):    D1
    U/-D (up/down ):    D2
    -CS  (chip enable): D3 *)

uses
    crt,dos;

{$I c:\ioexp\tplib1.pas }
```

```
var
    up_down, step:byte;

Procedure INC_R(step,up_down:byte);
(* increase or decrease the resistance between Vl and Vw for steps *)
(* direction controlled by up_down *)
var
    i:byte;
begin
    for i:=1 to step do
    begin
        write_data_port(P_address, 1+2*(up_down)+0); (* Clock = 1 *)
        delay(100);
        write_data_port(P_address, 0+2*(up_down)+0); (* Clock = 0 *)
        delay(100);
        write_data_port(P_address, 1+2*(up_down)+0); (* Clock = 1 *)
        delay(100);
    end;
        write_data_port(P_address, 1+2*(up_down)+4); (* remember position *)
end;


Procedure test;
begin
    write('Increase [1] or decrease [0] resistance between Vl and Vw : ');
    readln(up_down);
    write('Input steps (1 to 100): ');
    readln(step);
    INC_R(step, up_down);
end;


(* main program *)
begin
    centronic_address;
    repeat
        clrscr;
        test;
        readln;
    until keypressed

end.
```

7.3 Memories

Memories are used to store digital data. RAMs are random access memories which allow data to be read or written at any time. When the power supply is switched off, the data is lost. ROMs are read-only memories which can only be read. Data can be programmed into the ROM. For PROMs, data can be programmed only once, while EPROMs can be programmed many times. EPROMs come in two types: the ultra-violet light erasable type (UVEPROMs) and the electrically erasable type (EEPROMs). The I/O interface of memories can be parallel or serial. A parallel I/O interface consists of eight bi-directional data I/O lines, several address lines and control lines. A serial I/O interface only requires three control lines and one data output line. Chips with an I^2C bus have two I/O lines. Memory chips with a MicroLan bus (Dallas Touch Memories) only have one I/O line.

7.3.1 ST93C56C serial I/O 2K EEPROM

The ST93C56C (SGS-Thomson) is a CMOS non-volatile, serial I/O 2048-bit EEPROM. The 2K bits of the memory can be organized in two configurations: the 128 register mode (16 bits per register) and the 256 register mode (8 bits per register). Each memory location can be written or erased up to 1,000,000 times.

The pin-out of the ST93C56C is given in Figure 7.9. VCC (pin 8) and VSS (pin 5) are connected to the +5V and GND rails of the power supply. The supply current is typically 2 mA in the active mode and 50 µA in the standby mode. Pin 1 is the chip select input; pin 3 is the Data input and pin 2 is the Clock input. There are seven instructions which control all operations of the ROM.

1. Read a byte or a word from the ROM, READ
2. Write a byte or a word to, WRITE
3. Erase and write enable, EWEN

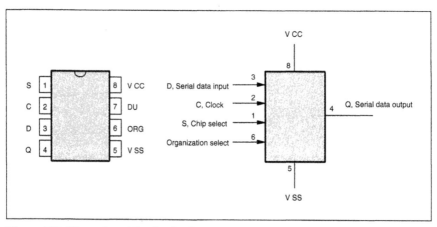

Figure 7.9 Pin-out and the logic diagram of the ST93C56

4. Erase and write disable, DWDS
5. Erase a byte or a word, ERASE
6. Erase all, ERAL
7. Write all, WRAL

The timing sequences consist of three or four steps and are shown in Figure 7.10. The first step is to tell the ROM to respond to an instruction by generating a start condition. This is followed by a 2-bit op-code which specifies an operation. The next step is to send address bits to the ROM and the final step is to transfer data. All instructions are initiated by a rising edge of S. Then a logic high on D is sampled at the rising edge of C. It is considered as the start condition (step 1). After this, the two op-code bits are clocked into the ROM at the rising edge of the clock (step 2). Next, the address bits are clocked into the ROM at the rising edge of the clock (step 3). If the ROM is configured to have a 16-bit register length, the number of the address bits is eight. These eight bits are clocked into the ROM with MSB bit first (step 3). Step 4 only exists for data read and write operations. The actual data bits (MSB bit first) are clocked into the ROM or out of the ROM at the rising edge of the clock. The instruction sets are summarized below:

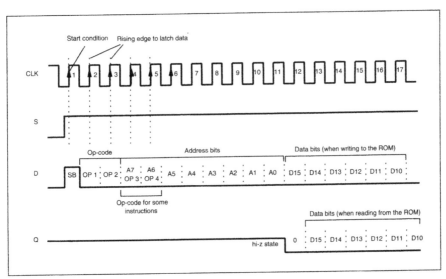

Figure 7.10 Timing sequence of the ST93C56C

READ	op-code=10	address=A7–A0	data=D15–D0
WRITE	op-code=01	address=A7–A0	data=D15–D0
EWEN	op-code=00	address=11XX XXXX	no data
EWDS	op-code=00	address=00XX XXXX	no data
ERASE	op-code=11	address=A7–A0	no data
ERAL	op-code=00	address=10XX XXXX	no data
WRAL	op-code=00	address=01XX XXXX	data=D15–D0

The EEPROM is connected to the Centronic experimental board as shown in Figure 7.11. D1, D2 and D3 terminals are connected to the S, C and D. S1 terminal is connected to Q. The ROM is configured in 16-bit register mode (ORG pin is left open). A TP6 software driver is listed below:

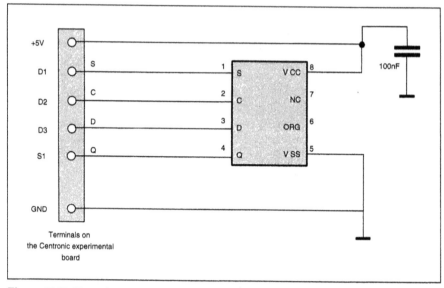

Figure 7.11 Experimental circuit of the ST93C56C

TP6 program list of 9356.PAS

```
Program EEPROM_93C56_driver;

(* Software driver for 93C56N 128 * 16 EEPROM *)

(* Connection to the Centronic experimental board:

   S-chip select    D2
   C-clock          D1
   D-data in to ic  D3
   Q-data out       S1 *)


uses

   crt, dos;


{$I c:\ioexp\TPLIB1.pas}



var

   command:byte;
   D: array[1..130] of byte;
```

```
procedure Init;
(* all control lines to the ic low *)
begin
     write_data_port(P_address,0+0+0);
end;


Procedure load_data(data:byte);
(* load procedure, Select: high, Data: stable, Clock: low to high *)
begin
     write_data_port(P_address,0+2+4*data); (* Select and Data = high *)
     delay(1);
     write_data_port(P_address,1+2+4*data); (* Clock from low to high to load data *)
     delay(1);
     write_data_port(P_address,0+2);          (* Select = high, Clock = Data = low *)
     delay(1);
end;


Procedure Start;
(* generate a start condition, Select high, Data high, Clock from low to high *)
begin
     write_data_port(P_address,0+0+0); delay(1); (* Select, Clock and Data = low *)
     write_data_port(P_address,0+2+4); delay(1); (* Select, Data = high; Clock = low *)
     write_data_port(P_address,1+2+4); delay(1); (* All inputs high *)
     write_data_port(P_address,0+2+0); delay(1); (* Select high; Data and Clock low *)
end;


Procedure Erase(enable_flag:boolean);
(* Erase enable and disable commands *)
var
   i:byte;
begin
     Start;               (* generate start condition *)
     load_data(0);        (* load first op-code 0 *)
     load_data(0);        (* load second op-code 0 *)
     if enable_flag then
     (* load 1 and 1, erase enable command *)
     begin
     load_data(1); load_data(1);
     end
     else
     (* load 0 and 0, erase disable command *);
```

```
    begin
        load_data(1); load_data(1);
    end;


    for i:=1 to 6 do load_data(0); (* load 6 dummy address bits *)
    delay(1);
    write_data_port(P_address,0);  (* all inputs low to terminate the command *)
    delay(10);
end;


Procedure Erase_all;
(* erase all memory locations, put 1 to all memory locations *)
var
    i:byte;
begin
    Start;              (* generate start condition *)
    load_data(0);       (* load first op-code 0 *)
    load_data(0);       (* load second op-code 0 *)
    load_data(1);       (* load 1 and 0 *)
    load_data(0);
    for i:=1 to 6 do load_data(0); (* load 6 dummy address bits *)

    write_data_port(P_address,0+0+0);  (* Select = low *)
    delay(1);
    write_data_port(P_address,0+2+0);  (* Select = high to check status *)
    delay(1);
    repeat until read_status_port(P_address) and 1 = 1; (* wait until ready state *)
    write_data_port(P_address,0+0+0);  (* Select = 0 to terminate the operation *)
end;


Procedure Write_all(byte_low, byte_high:byte);
(* write all memory locations with byte_high and byte_low *)
var
    i:byte;
begin
    Start;              (* generate start condition *)
    load_data(0);       (* load first op-code 0 *)
    load_data(0);       (* load second op-code 0 *)
    load_data(0);       (* load 0 and 1 *)
    load_data(1);
    for i:=1 to 6 do load_data(0); (* load dummy address bits *)

    (* load byte_high, MSB first *)
    for i:=8 downto 1 do load_data(round ( (byte_high and bit_weight(i)) / bit_weight(i)));
```

```
        (* load byte_low, MSB first *)
        for i:=8 downto 1 do load_data(round ( (byte_low and bit_weight(i)) / bit_weight(i)));
        write_data_port(P_address,0+0+0);
        write_data_port(P_address,0+2+0);
        repeat until read_status_port(P_address) and 1 = 1;
        write_data_port(P_address,0+0+0);
end;


Procedure WriteROM(address, byte_low, byte_high:byte);
(* write byte_high and byte_low to two 8-bit memory locations*)
var
    i:byte;
begin
        Start;                (* generate start condition *)
        load_data(0);         (* load first op-code 0 *)
        load_data(1);         (* load second op-code 1 *)

        (* load address *)
        for i:=8 downto 1 do
            begin
                load_data(round(address and bit_weight(i) / bit_weight(i)));
            end; (* load address 0 *);

        (* load byte_high, MSB first *)
        for i:=8 downto 1 do load_data(round ( (byte_high and bit_weight(i)) / bit_weight(i)));

        (* load byte_low, MSB first *)
        for i:=8 downto 1 do load_data(round ( (byte_low and bit_weight(i)) / bit_weight(i)));

        write_data_port(P_address,0+0+0);
        write_data_port(P_address,0+2+0);
        repeat until read_status_port(P_address) and 1 = 1;
        write_data_port(P_address,0+0+0);
end;


Function readROM(address,x:byte):byte;
(* read two 8-bit bytes in the 128 memory locations. x=0 to read low byte, x=1 to read high byte *)
var
    i,high_byte,low_byte,dummy:byte;
begin
        start;                (* Start *)
        load_data(1);         (* load opcode 1 *)
        load_data(0);         (* load opcode 0 *)
```

```
    (* load address *)
    for i:=8 downto 1 do
        begin
                load_data(round(address and bit_weight(i) / bit_weight(i)));
            end; (* load address 0 *);


    dummy:=0; (* start to read high byte *)
    for i:=8 downto 1 do
    begin
            write_data_port(P_address,0+2); delay(1); (* Clock low, Select high *)
            write_data_port(P_address,1+2); delay(1); (* Clock high, Select high *)
            dummy:=dummy + read_status_port(P_address) and 1 * bit_weight(i); (* read the data bit,
MSB first *)
            write_data_port(P_address,0+2);
    end;
    high_byte:=dummy;


    dummy:=0; (* start to read low byte *)
    for i:=8 downto 1 do
    begin
            write_data_port(P_address,0+2); delay(1);
            write_data_port(P_address,1+2); delay(1);
            dummy:=dummy + read_status_port(P_address) and 1 * bit_weight(i);
            write_data_port(P_address,0+2);
    end;
    low_byte:=dummy;


    (* assign the data *)
    if x=0 then readROM:=low_byte;
    if x=1 then readROM:=high_byte;
end;



Procedure Program_ROM;
(* a test program *)
var
    strx:string[250];
    i:byte;
begin
    writeln('This is the message originally stored in the EPROM');
    writeln;
    for i:=1 to 125 do
    begin
        write(chr(readROM(i,0)),chr(readROM(i,1)));
```

```
        end;

        writeln;

        write('Press RETURN to continue...'); readln;


        for i:=1 to 250 do strx[i]:=' ';

        writeln('Input the message which will be programmed into the EEPROM: ');

        readln(strx);

        for i:=1 to 125 do writeROM(i,ord(strx[2*i-1]),ord(strx[2*i]));

        writeln('The EEPROM has been programmed ');


        writeln('This is the message stored in the EPROM now');

        for i:=1 to 125 do

        begin

                write(chr(readROM(i,0)),chr(readROM(i,1)));

        end;

        readln;

end;


(* main program *)

begin

        Centronic_address;

        init;

        erase(true);

        program_rom;

end.
```

7.3.2 EEPROM with an I²C bus

The 24LC16B (Microchip, equivalent to X24C16P, Xicor, RS125-1401) is a 16K bit electrically erasable EEPROM with an I^2C bus. It operates as a slave device on the bus. The detailed description of the I^2C bus was given in Chapter 4. The memory is organized as 2k 8-bit memory locations. The erase and write cycles could be up to 1,000,000 times. It requires a power supply of 2.5 to 5V with typical current consumptions of about 1mA in active mode and 10 µA in the standby mode.

The pin-out and the internal block diagram of the chip are given in Figure 7.12. A0, A1 and A2 have no functions and can be left open. WP is the write protection (high active) and is normally tied to the ground to enable the write operation. SCL and SDA are the clock and data lines of the I^2C bus.

Data can be written to and read from the ROM via the I^2C bus. The write operation has two modes: the byte write mode and page write mode. The former writes a single byte to a memory location. The latter writes 256 bytes to a block in one go. The read operation has the current address read mode and the random read mode.

Following a start condition on the I^2C bus, an 8-bit slave address byte is clocked into the ROM from the master transmitter. The slave address from bit 7 to bit 0 is 1, 0, 1, 0, B2, B1, B0 and R/-W.

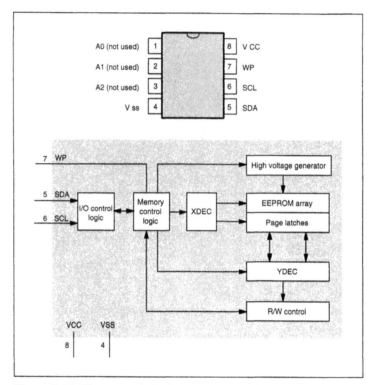

Figure 7.12 Pin-out and the internal block diagram of the 24LC16B

Bits 7 to 4 are the permanent address of the ROM. B2, B1 and B0 specify one of the four memory blocks. R/-W bit specifies whether the operation will be a read operation (R/-W = 1) or a write operation (R/-W =0). After the slave address bits are transferred, an address byte is transmitted to the ROM which specifies a memory location in the selected memory block. The address is written to the address pointer of the ROM and the value ranges from 0 to 255. If the operation is a write operation, the eight bits of the data are sent to the ROM next. In the random read mode, after writing to the address pointer, a start condition is generated again and it is followed by sending the slave address bits with the R/-W bit set to 1 (to read). Then data stored in the memory will be sent out bit by bit. The timing sequences for write and read operations are given in Figure 7.13.

A circuit diagram of the 24LC16B connected to the Centronic experimental board is given in Figure 7.14. D1 terminal controls the SDA lines. S1 reads data from the SDA line. C1 controls the SCL line. The demonstration software is written in Turbo Pascal 6 and is listed below.

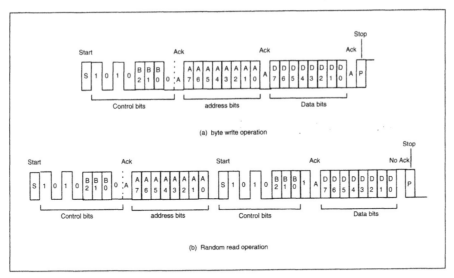

Figure 7.13 Timing sequences for write and read operations

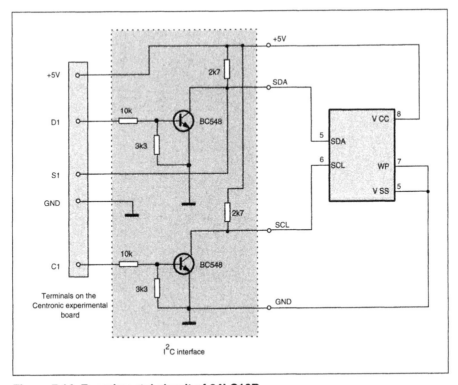

Figure 7.14 Experimental circuit of 24LC16B

TP6 program list of 2416.PAS

```
Program IIC_memory;
(* I squared C software driver resource *)
(* PC is the master receiver or transmitter. Other ICs or modules are slave receiver or transmitter *)
(* Connections to the Centronic experimental board:
               D1 = SDA, C1 = SCK, S1 = SDA. This can be altered *)


(* IIC bus conditions:
   SCL=1, SDA=1      : bus not busy
   SCL=1, SDA=1 to 0: start condition
   SCL=1, SDA=0 to 1: stop condition
   valid data : data stable when SCL=1.
   data change: when SCL=0*)


uses
   crt,dos;


{$I c:\ioexp\tplib1.pas}


var
   i,ij:integer;
   block,address,data: byte;



(* TP 6 IIC software library #1, BCD conversion *)
Function BCD(data:byte):byte;
(* convert a binary type data into binary BCD type data *)
begin
     BCD:= round((data div 10) * 16 + 10 * frac(data/10));
end;



(* TP 6 IIC software library #2, put data on SDA line *)
Procedure SDA(data:byte);
(* put data on SDA *)
begin
     write_data_port(P_address, 1-data);
end;



(* TP 6 IIC software library #3, SCL control *)
Procedure SCL(data:byte);
(* put data on SCL *)
```

```
begin
     write_control_port(P_address, 1-data);
end;


(* TP 6 IIC software library #4, Initialize IIC bus *)
Procedure INIT;
(* generate initial condition, SDA = SCL = 1 *)
begin
     SDA(1);
     SCL(1);
     delay(100);
end;


(* TP 6 IIC software library #5. Generating START condition *)
Procedure START;
(* generate START condition *)
begin
     SDA(1); SCL(1); SDA(0); SCL(0);
end;


(* TP6 IIC software library #6. Generating acknowledge related clock *)
Procedure ACK;
(* generate ACK, a acknowledge related clock *)
begin
     SCL(1); SCL(0);
end;


(* TP6 IIC software library #7. Transmit data on IIC bus *)
Procedure TRANSMIT(data:byte);
(* Transmit data via the bus *)
var
   i:byte;
begin
     for i:=8 downto 1 do
     begin
          SDA(round(data and bit_weight(i) / bit_weight(i)) );  (* put data on SDA while SCL low *)
          SCL(1);                                               (* SCL brought from low to high *)
          SCL(0);                                               (* SCL brought from high to low *)
     end;
     SDA(1); (* SDA is made logic high *)
     ACK;    (* generate a ACK related clock *)
end;
```

```
(* TP 6 IIC software library #8. Receive data from IIC bus *)
Function receive(stop_flag:boolean):byte;
(* receiver data via the bus *)
var
    i,dummy:byte;
begin
     dummy:=0;
     for i:=8 downto 1 do
     begin
          SCL(1); (* SCL brought high *)
          delay(1);
          dummy:=dummy + (read_status_port(P_address) and 1) * bit_weight(i);  (* read data from SDA *)
          delay(1);
          SCL(0); (* SCL brought from high to low *)
     end;
     if stop_flag then
     begin
          SDA(1);   (* if the received is the last, SDA has logic high *)
          ACK;
     end
     else
     begin
          SDA(0);                (* if the received is not the last, SDA has logic low to acknowledge *)
          ACK;                      (* generate a ACK related clock *)
          SDA(1);
     end;
     receive:=dummy;
end;


(* TP 6 IIC software library #9. Generating STOP condition *)
Procedure STOP;
(* generate STOP condition *)
begin
    SDA(0);  (* SDA line low *)
    SCL(1);  (* SCL line high *)
    SDA(1);  (* SDA line from low to high *)
end;



Procedure Write_ROM_byte(block,Address,data:byte);
(* program a rom byte, block and address specify a memory location *)
begin
    start;                   (* generate a start condition *)
```

```
        transmit(128+32+2*block);   (* transmit control bits and block address and RD/-WR (=0, configure into
write mode)*)
        transmit(address);          (* transmit memory address in a block *)
        transmit(data);             (* transmit data *)
        stop;                       (* generate stop bit *)
        delay(50);
end;


Function Read_ROM_byte(block,Address:byte):byte;
begin
        start;                      (* generate a start condition *)
        transmit(128+32+2*block);   (* transmit control bits and block address and RD/-WR (=0, configure into
write mode) *)
        transmit(address);          (* transmit memory address in a block *)
        start;                      (* generate a start condition *)
        transmit(128+32+2*block+1); (* transmit control bits and block address and RD/-WR (=1, configure into
read mode) *)
        Read_ROM_byte:=receive(true); (* receive data *)
        stop;                       (* generate stop condition *)
end;


Procedure test_write_read;
begin
        write('Select a memory block (0,1,2 and 3)    : '); readln(block);
        write('Select an address in the block (0-255): '); readln(address);
        write('Input the data to be written to ROM    : '); readln(data);
        write_ROM_byte(block,address,data);
        writeln;
        writeln('The data written to the ROM : ',read_ROM_byte(block,address));
        writeln('Press one RETURN to continue and two RETURN to stop');
        readln;
        delay(4000);
end;


(* Main Program *)
begin
        centronic_address;
        repeat
                clrscr;
                Test_write_read;
        until keypressed

end.
```

7.4 Real time clocks

Real time clock ICs enable microcontrollers to track time. The IC consists of a standalone clock/calendar circuit and an interfacing circuit. Traditional devices are connected to a microcontroller via a parallel bus which contains a bi-directional 8-bit data bus and several control lines. The HD146818 and MSM6242 are two examples. There are newer types which have an I^{2}C bus to reduce the number of I/O lines required in the hardware wiring. The MK41T56 and PCF8573 are two examples.

The MK41T56 (SGS-Thomson) is a low-power timekeeper which contains a 512-bit static CMOS RAM organized in 64 words by eight bits. The first eight bytes are used for storing time and date. It has an I^{2}C bus and operates as a slave device on the bus. The MK41T56 continually monitors Vcc. If Vcc falls below a certain value, the device terminates data transfer. This is to prevent erroneous data from being written to the device. The battery could be a 3V 30mAh lithium cell and the typical data retention period is in excess of 10 years.

The pin-out and the internal block diagram of the MK41T56 are shown in Figure 7.15. Pins 8 and 4 are connected to +5V and the ground rails of the power supply. It consumes 3 mA when the device

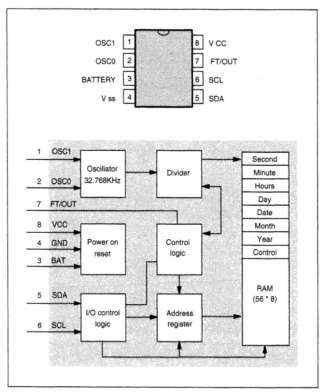

Figure 7.15 Pin-out and internal block diagram of the MK41T56

is active. The standby current (SDA and SCL are both high) is 1 mA. OSC0 and OSC1 are connected to a 32.768 MHz crystal. SCL is the clock line of the I^2C bus and SDA is the bi-directional data line. FT/OUT is the frequency test output. After writing a suitable control word to the internal control register of the MK41T56, the pin outputs a 512 Hz square wave signal. It can be used also as a software controlled output.

The functions of the 64 bytes memory locations are shown below:

address=0	seconds register (bits 0–6, 00–59, BCD format)
address=1	minutes register (bits 0–6, 00–59, BCD format)
address=2	hours register (bits 0–5, 00–23, BCD format)
address=3	day register (bits 0–2, 01–07, BCD format)
address=4	date register (bits 0–5, 01–31, BCD format)
address=5	month register (bits 0–4, 01–12, BCD format)
address=6	years register (bits 0–7, 00–99, BCD format)
address=7	control register (see later)
address=9–64	RAM

Bit functions of the control register from bits 7 to 0 are defined:

bit 7	output control, 0 or 1
bit 6	frequency test bit (bit 6=4, output test frequency)
bit 5	sign bit
bits 4–0	no functions

Data can be written to or read from the MK41T56 via the I^2C bus. Writing operation sets up the time and date. Read operation retrieves the time. Following a start condition on the I^2C bus, an 8-bit slave address is clocked into the ROM from the master transmitter. The slave address from bit 7 to bit 0 has the following format: 1, 1, 0, 1, 0, 0, 0, R/-W. Bit 7 to bit 1 are the permanent address of the timekeeper on the bus. R/-W bit specifies whether the present operation is a read operation (R/-W = 1) or a write operation (R/-W =0). After the slave address bits are transmitted, an 8-bit address byte is transmitted to the IC to specify a particular memory location. The address is written to the address pointer of the IC and the value ranges from 0 to 64. In the write operation, the eight bits of the data are transmitted to the MK41T56 next. In the read mode, after writing the address to the address pointer, a start condition is generated again and is followed by sending the slave address bits with the R/-W bit set to 1. Then the data stored in the memory is sent out. The timing sequences are given in Figure 7.16.

The circuit diagram of the MK41T56 connected to the Centronic experimental board is given in Figure 7.17. D1 controls the SDA lines. S1 reads data from the SDA line. C1 controls the SCL line. The demonstration software is written in TP6.

TP6 program list of 4156.PAS

```
Program IIC_timer;

(* I squared C software driver resource *)

(* PC is the master receiver or transmitter. Other ICs or modules are slave receiver or transmitter

*)

(* Connections to the Centronic experimental board:

          D1 = SDA, C1 = SCK, S1 = SDA. This can be altered *)
```

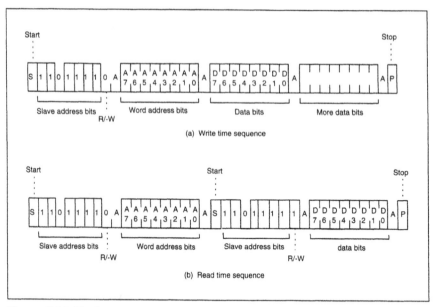

Figure 7.16 Timing sequences of the MK41T56

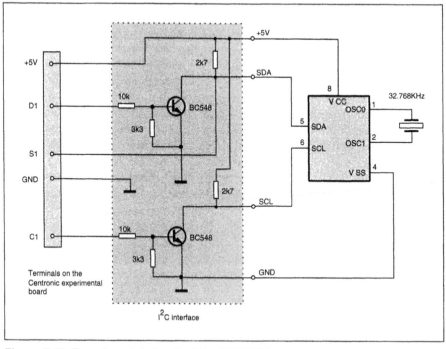

Figure 7.17 Experimental circuit of the MK41T56

```
(* IIC bus conditions:

    SCL=1, SDA=1        : bus not busy

    SCL=1, SDA=1 to 0: start condition

    SCL=1, SDA=0 to 1: stop condition

    valid data : data stable when SCL=1.

    data change: when SCL=0*)


uses

    crt,dos;


{$I c:\ioexp\tplib1.pas}


var

    i,ij:integer;

    second,minute,hour, day,date,month,year,control_word:byte;



(* TP 6 IIC software library #1, BCD conversion *)
Function BCD(data:byte):byte;
(* convert a binary type data into binary BCD type data *)
begin

     BCD:= round((data div 10) * 16 + 10 * frac(data/10));

end;


(* TP 6 IIC software library #2, put data on SDA line *)
Procedure SDA(data:byte);
(* put data on SDA *)
begin

     write_data_port(P_address, 1-data);

end;


(* TP 6 IIC software library #3, SCL control *)
Procedure SCL(data:byte);
(* put data on SCL *)
begin

     write_control_port(P_address, 1-data);

end;


(* TP 6 IIC software library #4, Initialize IIC bus *)
Procedure INIT;
(* generate initial condition, SDA = SCL = 1 *)
begin

     SDA(1);

     SCL(1);
```

```
        delay(100);
end;


(* TP 6 IIC software library #5. Generating START condition *)
Procedure START;
(* generate START condition *)
begin
        SDA(1); SCL(1); SDA(0); SCL(0);
end;


(* TP6 IIC software library #6. Generating acknowledge related clock *)
Procedure ACK;
(* generate ACK, a acknowledge related clock *)
begin
        SCL(1); SCL(0);
end;


(* TP6 IIC software library #7. Transmit data on IIC bus *)
Procedure TRANSMIT(data:byte);
(* Transmit data via the bus *)
var
    i:byte;
begin
        for i:=8 downto 1 do
        begin
            SDA(round(data and bit_weight(i) / bit_weight(i)) );  (* put data on SDA while SCL low *)
            SCL(1);                                               (* SCL brought from low to high *)
            SCL(0);                                               (* SCL brought from high to low *)
        end;
        SDA(1); (* SDA is made logic high *)
        ACK;    (* generate a ACK related clock *)
end;


(* TP 6 IIC software library #8. Receive data from IIC bus *)
Function receive(stop_flag:boolean):byte;
(* receiver data via the bus *)
var
    i,dummy:byte;
begin
        dummy:=0;
        for i:=8 downto 1 do
        begin
            SCL(1); (* SCL brought high *)
            delay(1);
```

```
          dummy:=dummy + (read_status_port(P_address) and 1) * bit_weight(i);  (* read data from
SDA *)
          delay(1);
          SCL(0); (* SCL brought from high to low *)
     end;
     if stop_flag then
     begin
          SDA(1);  (* if the received is the last, SDA has logic high *)
          ACK;
     end
     else
     begin
          SDA(0);                 (* if the received is not the last, SDA has logic low to acknowledge
*)
          ACK;                    (* generate a ACK related clock *)
          SDA(1);
     end;
     receive:=dummy;
end;


(* TP 6 IIC software library #9. Generating STOP condition *)
Procedure STOP;
(* generate STOP condition *)
begin
     SDA(0);  (* SDA line low *)
     SCL(1);  (* SCL line high *)
     SDA(1);  (* SDA line from low to high *)
end;


Procedure Init_time;
(* initialize time *)
begin
     write('Input initial second: ');   read(second);
     write('Input initial minute: ');   read(minute);
     write('Input initial hour  : ');   read(hour);
     write('Input initial day   : ');   read(day);
     write('Input initial date  : ');   read(date);
     write('Input initial month  : '); read(month);
     write('Input initial year  : ');  read(year);
     write('Input initial control word: '); read(control_word);
end;


Procedure init_41T56(second,minute,hour,day,date,month,year,control_word:byte);
(* set the timer's second, minute, hour, day, date, month and year *)
```

```
begin
     start;              (* generate Start condition *)
     transmit(208);      (* send slave address, R/-W = 0 *)
     transmit(0);        (* move pointer to address 9 *)
     transmit(BCD(second));  (* transmit second *)
     transmit(BCD(minute));  (* transmit minute *)
     transmit(BCD(hour));     (* ..... *)
     transmit(BCD(day));
     transmit(BCD(date));
     transmit(BCD(month));
     transmit(BCD(year));
     transmit(control_word);
     stop;
end;


Function MK41T56(x:byte):real;
var
    data:array[1..500] of byte;
begin
     Start;                 (* generate start condition *)
     transmit(208);         (* send slave address, R/-W = 0 *)
     transmit(0);           (* set the pointer address = 0 (second register) *)
     start;                 (* generate start condition again for reading *)
     transmit(208+1);       (* send slave address 208 + 1 D, R/-W = 1 *)
     for i:=1 to 6 do data[i]:=receive(false); (* read data with acknowledgement *)
     data[7]:=receive(true);               (* read data without acknowledgement *)
                                           (* when reading, register address automatically
added *)
     (* converter data into time format *)
     if x=1 then MK41T56:= data[1] and (64+32+16)/16*10 + data[1] and (8+4+2+1);
     if x=2 then MK41T56:= data[2] and (64+32+16)/16*10 + data[2] and (8+4+2+1);
     if x=3 then MK41T56:= data[3] and (32+16)/16*10 + data[3] and (8+4+2+1);
     if x=4 then MK41T56:= data[4] and (4+2+1);
     if x=5 then MK41T56:= data[5] and (32+16)/16*10 + data[5] and (8+4+2+1);
     if x=6 then MK41T56:= data[6] and (32+16)/16*10 + data[6] and (8+4+2+1);
     if x=7 then MK41T56:= data[7] and (128+64+32+16)/16*10 + data[7] and (8+4+2+1);
end;


Procedure show_time;
begin
     writeln('                          Inter IC bus 41T56 Timer');
     writeln;
     write('                 Input initial second : ');   writeln(MK41T56(1):5:0);
     write('                 Input initial minute : ');   writeln(MK41T56(2):5:0);
```

```
        write('                      Input initial hour   : ');    writeln(MK41T56(3):5:0);

        write('                      Input initial day    : ');    writeln(MK41T56(4):5:0);

        write('                      Input initial date   : ');    writeln(MK41T56(5):5:0);

        write('                      Input initial month  : ');    writeln(MK41T56(6):5:0);

        write('                      Input initial year   : ');    writeln(MK41T56(7):5:0);

end;


begin

        centronic_address;

        init_time;

        INIT;      (* intialize SCL and SDA lines *)

        init_41T56(second, minute, hour, day, date, month, year, control_word);


        repeat

            clrscr;

            show_time;

            delay(10000);

        until keypressed

end.
```

7.5 Digitally-controlled signal generators

Digitally-controlled signal generators allow digital or analogue signals to be generated with their frequencies controlled digitally. The 8253/8254 is a popular programmable timer/counter IC and is widely used for generating digital signals. The HSP45102 and the ML2036 are programmable sine wave generators.

7.5.1 8254 programmable timer/counter

The pin-out and the internal block diagram of the 8254 are shown in Figure 7.18. The device contains three 16-bit programmable counters. Each counter has three I/O lines: CLK, GATE and OUTPUT. The CLK is fed with a clock signal of a frequency from DC to 8 MHz. GATE controls the counter to start or stop counting. If GATE is high, the counter is enabled. The output signal from the counter appears at the OUTPUT. The IC is controlled via an 8-bit bi-directional data bus and five control lines (A0, A1, -WR, -RD and -CS). Data can be written into four internal registers: the control register and counter registers for counter 1, 2 and 3. Writing data to or reading data from a particular register is controlled by A0, A1, -WR and -RD. The relation between a register and its address bits is shown as follows:

A0=0, A1=0, to select the counter register 1
A0=1, A1=0, to select the counter register 2
A0=0, A1=1, to select the counter register 3
A0=1, A1=1, to select the control register

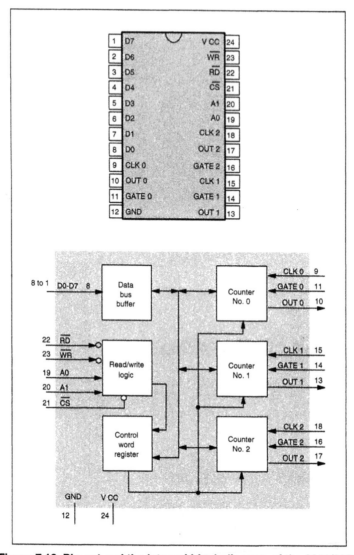

Figure 7.18 Pin-out and the internal block diagram of the 8253/8254

Before a counter can be used, it is configured first. This is achieved by writing a control word into the control word register. The bit functions of the control word are shown below. Bit 7 (SC1) and bit 6 (SC0) select the counter to be initialized.

bit 7=0	bit 6=0	to configure counter 0
bit 7=0	bit 6=1	to configure counter 1
bit 7=1	bit 6=0	to configure counter 2
bit 7=1	bit 6=1	to read-back command

Bit 5 (RW1) and bit 4 (RW0) control the format of the read and write for each counter register.

bit 5=0	bit 4=0	counter latch command
bit 5=0	bit 4=1	read/write least significant byte only
bit 5=1	bit 4=0	read/write most significant byte only
bit 5=1	bit 4=1	read/write least significant byte first, then the most significant byte.

Bit 3 (M2), bit 2 (M1) and bit 1 (M0) control the output modes. There are six output modes:

bit 3=0, bit 2=0, bit 1=0	Mode 0 – interrupt on terminal count
bit 3=0, bit 2=0, bit 1=1	Mode 1 – hardware one-shot
bit 3=x, bit 2=1, bit 1=0	Mode 2 – timed interrupt generator
bit 3=x, bit 2=1, bit 1=1	Mode 3 – square wave generator
bit 3=1, bit 2=0, bit 1=0	Mode 4 – software triggered strobe
bit 3=1, bit 2=0, bit 1=1	Mode 5 – hardware triggered strobe

Bit 0 configures the data format in the counter registers.

bit 0   0=16-bit binary counter, 1=4 decades BCD format

To write data to the 8254, firstly the 8-bit data A0 and A1 are present at the inputs to the 8254. Then a high-to-low-then-high pulse is supplied to the -WR. After this, the data is written into the selected register. -CS must be at low state to enable the IC during this operation.

Each counter of the 8254 has six output modes (see Figure 7.19). The *interrupt on terminal count mode* (Mode 0, Figure 7.19(a)) is used to generate an interrupt at the output after an interval of time has elapsed. After a control word (CW=10d) is written to the control register, the output pin of the counter 0 will go low. After the counter value (N) is written to the counter, the output will go high after N+1 clock pulses. The *hardware one-shot mode* (Mode 1, Figure 7.19(b)) is that when a pulse is applied to the trigger of a counter, its output goes low. After a fixed amount of time the output will automatically go high. The time period of the low state is determined by the frequency of the applied clock and a count number loaded into the counter. If a counter value N is loaded, the output will be low for N clocks. When a counter is configured in the *timed interrupt mode* (Mode 2, Figure 7.19(c)), the 8254 counter operates as a pulse generator the frequency of which is the clock frequency divided by N. N is the counter value loaded into the IC. If an 8254 counter is programmed in the Mode 3, the *square wave mode* (Figure 7.19(d)), and an even number is written to its counter register, the waveform of the output pin is a 50% duty cycle square wave. The frequency of the square wave equal to the frequency of the input clock divided by the number written to the counter register. If an odd number is written to a counter, the output waveform will be high for one more clock pulse than it is low.

Mode 4 is the *software triggered strobe* (Figure 7.19(e)). In this mode, the counter automatically begins to decrement upon loading with its initial counter value. It then decrements at a rate determined by the clock. When 0 count is reached, the counter generates a single low-going strobe pulse with a duration equal to one clock pulse at its output. Therefore, a counter produces a low-going strobe pulse of N+1 clock cycles after the counter value is written to the register.

The *hardware triggered strobe* (Mode 5, Figure 7.19(f)) is similar to Mode 4, except that counting is initiated by a high-going pulse at the Gate input. A rising edge of GATE starts the countdown process. When the trigger input is high, the counter value is transferred to the counter on the next clock pulse. The next clock pulse decrements the counter. When the counter reaches 0, OUT goes

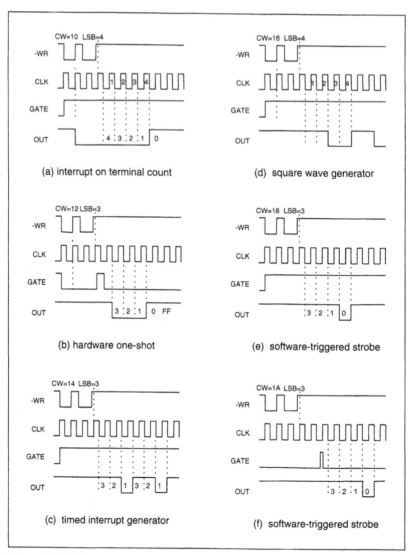

Figure 7.19 Output modes of the 8254

low for one clock pulse. Hence after the trigger input goes high, OUT goes low after N+1 clock pulses.

Figure 7.20 shows an experimental circuit of the 8254 using the Centronic experimental board. In this circuit, D1 and D2 terminals on the experimental board are used to load data serially into a 74LS164 shift register. The 8-bit parallel outputs of the 74LS164 supply data to the 8254. D5, D6, D7 and D8 are connected to -WR, A1, A0 and -CS inputs of the 8254. The counter 2 is used for

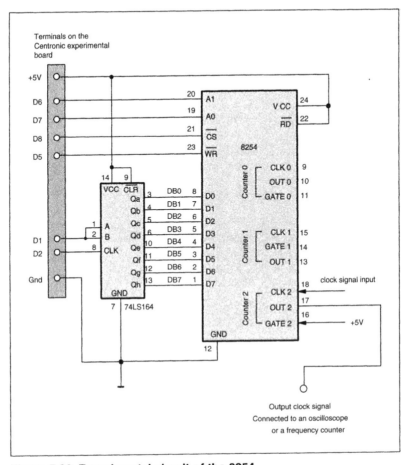

Figure 7.20 Experimental circuit of the 8254

experimenting, CLK2 is fed with a clock signal and GATE 2 is pulled to logic high to enable the counter. The software configures the counter 2 in the square wave generator mode. The frequency of the signal is controlled by the software.

TP6 program list of 8254.PAS

```
Program mini_sig_generator;
(* software driver for the 8254 timer/counter *)
(* Centronic data port connections:
     DB1=data, DB2=clock for 74LS164
     DB5=-WR, DB6=A1, DB7=A0 and DB8=-CS for 8253 *)
```

```
uses
    dos, crt;


{$I c:\ioexp\tplib1.pas }


Const
    base_frequency=2457600;
    (* The clock signal input to the 8254 *)


var
    command:byte;
    output_frequency:longint;


Procedure setbit(bitnumber,bitvalue:byte);
(* set the status of a particular bit of the command, bitnumber: 1-8;  bitvalue: 0 or 1 *)
begin
    if bitvalue=1 then command:=command or  bit_weight(bitnumber);
    if bitvalue=0 then command:=command and (255-bit_weight(bitnumber));
end;



Procedure initialization;
(* set all the lines to high status *)
begin
    command:=127;
    write_data_port(P_address,command); (* output command to the data port *)
    output_frequency:=1000;
end;



Procedure loaddata(address,data:byte);
(* load data to the shift register 74LS164 and write data to 8253
   address selecting Counter 0 to 2 and control register
   data being the data written to the registers

 During loading, (1) DB0 is loaded with the data sw[i],
                 (2) DB1 (CLOCK) goes low-to-high-then-low
                 (4) DB7 (-CS) must be low to enable the 8254
                 (5) DB6 and DB5 (A0 and A1) must be set to a proper address
                 (6) DB4 (-WR) goes from high-to-low-then-high after loading
                     DB4 should be high all other time *)
var
    d:array[1..8] of byte;
    i,A0,A1:byte;
```

```
begin
    if address=0 then begin A0:=0; A1:=0; end;
    if address=1 then begin A0:=1; A1:=0; end;
    if address=2 then begin A0:=0; A1:=1; end;
    if address=3 then begin A0:=1; A1:=1; end;


    (* find the serial data bits to be sent to the 74LS164 *)
    for i:=8 downto 1 do
        begin
            d[i]:=0;
            if data>=bit_weight(i) then begin
                                        data:=data-bit_weight(i);
                                        d[i]:=1;
                                  end;
        end;


    (* load data into the 74LS164 registers *)
    for i:=1 to 8 do
        begin
            setbit(1,d[i]);  write_data_port(P_address,command);
            setbit(2,0);     write_data_port(P_address,command);
            setbit(2,1);     write_data_port(P_address,command);
            setbit(2,0);     write_data_port(P_address,command);
        end;


    (* strobe the data to the 8253 IC *)
            setbit(7,A0);
            setbit(6,A1);    write_data_port(P_address,command);
            setbit(5,0);     write_data_port(P_address,command);
            setbit(5,1);     write_data_port(P_address,command);
end;



Procedure signal_generator(Base_frequency, frequency:longint);
(* Configure counter 2 in mode 3, signal generator *)
var
   divisor:longint;
   high_byte_0, low_byte_0:byte;
begin
    divisor:=round(base_frequency/frequency);
    high_byte_0:=divisor div 256;
    low_byte_0 :=divisor mod 256;
    if divisor>65000 then writeln('Error in delay time');
    loaddata(3,$b6);          (* load control word *)
```

```
        loaddata(2,low_byte_0); (* load low order 8-bit byte *)

        loaddata(2,high_byte_0);(* load high order 8-bit byte *)

end;


Procedure test_8253;

begin

        write('Input output frequency [Hz] (0 to quit); ');

        readln(output_frequency);

        signal_generator(base_frequency, output_frequency);

end;


{***********Main program**********}

begin

        Centronic_address;

        initialization;

        repeat

                if output_frequency>0 then test_8253

        until output_frequency=0;

end.
```

7.5.2 Numerically controlled oscillator HSP45102

The HSP45102 (Harris Semiconductor, RS284–977) is a numerically controlled oscillator which produces a 12-bit sine wave whose frequency and phase are controlled digitally. The frequency of the sine wave is determined by one of two pre-loaded 32-bit frequency words. A control pin selects which word is used to determine the output frequency. The phase of the sine wave is controlled by two inputs P0 and P1, which select a phase offset of 0, 90, 180 and 270°.

The pin-out and the internal block diagram are shown in Figure 7.21. VCC (pins 8 and 22) and GND (pins 7, 15 and 21) are connected to the positive and GND rail of the power supply. The supply voltage is 5V. The supply current is typically 99 mA in the active mode and the standby current is 500 µA. CLK (pin 16) is the clock input. The maximum frequency is 33 MHz.

SCLK (pin 14), SD (pin 13), MSB/-LSB (pin 11) and -SFTEN (pin 10) are control inputs for the frequency control section. SCLK and SD are clock and serial data inputs. Data bit present at SD is shifted into the internal registers at the rising edge of the SCLK input. -SFTEN is the shift enable inputs. This pin must be low to enable data shifting. When MSB/-LSB is high, the MSB bit is shifted first. When it is low, the LSB bit is shifted first.

$$\text{Output frequency (Hz)} = N * F_{CLK}/2^{32}$$

In which N is the value of the selected frequency word and F_{CLK} is the frequency of the clock signal.

-LOAD (pin 18), -TXFR (pin 17), -ENPHAC (pin 12) and SEL_L/M (pin 9) are control inputs for the phase accumulator. -ENPHAC enables the phase accumulator, SEL_L/- M selects the two frequency words. When it is high, it selects the least significant 32 bits of the 64-bit frequency register. When it is low, it selects the most significant register. When -TXFR is low, the frequency

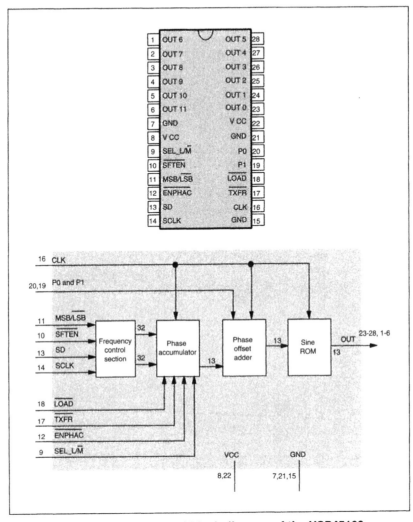

Figure 7.21 Pin-out and internal block diagram of the HSP45102

word selected by SEL_L/-M is transferred from the frequency register to the phase accumulator's input register. P0 (pin 20) and P1 (pin 19) are phase modulation inputs. A phase shift of 0, 90, 180 and 270° can be selected. The 12 outputs (pins 1–6 and pins 23–28) are the data outputs. The value ranges from 000h to FFFh, centred around 800h. D/A converters can be used to convert the 12-bit data into a sine signal.

An experimental circuit using the Centronic experimental board is shown in Figure 7.22. D1 and C1 on the board are connected to SD and SCLK of the HSP45102. The CLK (pin 16) is fed with a

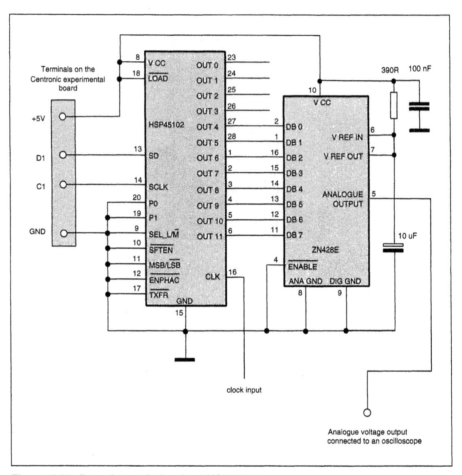

Figure 7.22 Experimental circuit of HSP45102

clock signal. The eight outputs (OUTPUT 11 to OUTPUT 4) are connected to an 8-bit D/A converter ZN428E. The other four outputs are not used. The control pins are either tied to the ground or +5V supply rail. The control software is written in Turbo Pascal 6. The output signal from the D/A converter is a sine wave which can be observed using an oscilloscope.

TP6 program list of 45102.PAS

```
Program HSP45102;
(* software driver for digitally control oscillator HSP4512 *)
(* Centronic experimental board connection:
    D1: SD, C1: SCLK *)
```

```
uses
    crt, dos;

{$I c:\ioexp\tplib1.pas}

var
    output_frequency:real;

Procedure load_frequency(frequency:real);
(* load frequency into the 45102 frequency register *)
(* frequency measured in Hz *)
var
    i,j,k:byte;
    bytex:array[1..4] of byte;
    n:longint;
begin
    n:=round(frequency * 256*256*256*256 / 2.4576e6);

    (* convert number n into four 8-bit byte bytex[1] to bytex[4] *)
    bytex[4]:=round(n/256/256/256);
    n:=n - bytex[4] * 256 * 256 * 256;
    bytex[3]:=round(n/256/256);
    n:=n - bytex[3] * 256 * 256;
    bytex[2]:=round(n/256);
    n:=n - bytex[2] * 256;
    bytex[1]:=round(n);

    (* load first 32 bits of data *)
    for i:=1 to 4 do
    begin
        for j:=1 to 8 do begin
        write_data_port(P_address,round((bytex[i] and bit_weight(j))/bit_weight(j)));
        write_control_port(P_address,0);
        write_control_port(P_address,1);
        write_control_port(P_address,0);
                        end;
    end;

    (* load second 32 bits of data *)
    for i:=1 to 4 do
    begin
        for j:=1 to 8 do begin
        write_data_port(P_address,round((bytex[i] and bit_weight(j))/bit_weight(j)));
        write_control_port(P_address,0);
```

```
            write_control_port(P_address,1);
            write_control_port(P_address,0);
                                end;
        end;
end;



Procedure test_45102;
begin
        write('Input output frequency [Hz] (0 to quit); ');
        readln(output_frequency);
        load_frequency(output_frequency);
end;



begin
        Centronic_address;
        repeat
                Test_45102;
        until output_frequency=0;
end.
```

7.5.3 ML2036 programmable sine wave generator

The ML2036 (Micro Linear) is a sine wave generator capable of producing a sine wave signal with a frequency from DC to 50 kHz and it only needs a few components. Data can be input serially in phase with the positive-going clock. After 16 data bits are loaded, a rising edge on the latch pin loads the data into a 512 point sine wave look-up table. The values obtained are then fed to an 8-bit D/A converter and then into a low pass filter to smooth the output to achieve a pure sine wave signal. The signal is buffered on chip and has an amplitude of $\pm V_{ref}$ or ± 0.5 V_{ref} depending on pin configuration. If a 4.1943 MHz crystal is used, an output frequency from 0.5 Hz to 32.768 kHz is yielded. The output frequency is calculated by using the following equation:

$$\text{Output frequency (Hz)} = \text{Crystal frequency} * N/8388680$$

in which N is the counter number sent to the ML2036.

Computer remote control and network applications

8.1 Telecommunication ICs

The PCD3311C (Philips Semiconductors, RS273-545) produces dual-tone multi-frequency (DTMF) and modem frequencies. It requires a 5V power supply and the operating current is 0.9 mA. The standby current is only 3 μA. The pin-out and the internal block diagram of the IC are shown in Figure 8.1. The timebase for the IC is an on-board crystal controlled oscillator which requires an external 3.58 MHz crystal connected between OSC1 and OSC0. It interfaces to a computer via a parallel I/O port or an I^2C bus. When the MODE input is connected to the logic high state, parallel data loading is selected. When it is left open or connected to the logic low, the I^2C bus operation is selected. The signal output from the TONE output is filtered by an on-chip switched-capacitor filter followed by an active RC low-pass filter. An on-chip reference voltage ensures that the output signal has an rms value from 150 to 190 mV.

In the parallel data loading mode, the operation of the PCD3311 is controlled by a control word which is written into the chip from D0 to D5. The data must be stable before the positive-going edge of the STROBE pulse. The input data is latched into the device at the negative-going edge of the STROBE pulse and the output signal is produced at the TONE output. The output signal remains unchanged until the next negative-going edge of the STROBE pulse is received. The timing sequence is shown in Figure 8.2.

D5 and D4 of the control word select operation modes. D3 to D0 select frequency combinations of DTMF or frequencies of modern tones. The details can be found in the manufacturer's data sheet.

The PCD3311C can be connected to the Centronic experimental board to form a PC-based telephone dialling system. D0 to D5 are connected to the D1 to D6 terminals. STROBE is connected to the C1 terminal.

8.2 Modem IC

The TCM3105 (Texas Instruments) is a frequency shift keyed (FSK) voiceband modem. It contains a transmitter and receiver channel which can work in the same time. The transmitter is a programmable frequency synthesizer which produces two frequencies at the output representing the

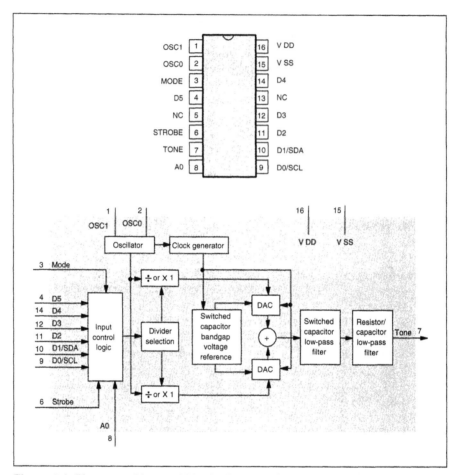

Figure 8.1 Pin-out and internal block diagram of the PCD3311C

logic status 0 or 1. The receiver demodulates the input analogue signal and outputs either logic 0 or logic 1 depending on the frequency of the signal.

The pin-out and the internal diagram of the IC are shown in Figure 8.3. The supply voltage is 5V and the supply current is 5.5 mA. A 4.4336 MHz crystal is connected to OSC1 and OSC2. TXR1 and TXR2 select the baud rate and TRS selects a telecommunication standard. TXD and TXA are digital input and analogue output of the transmitter channel. RXA and RXD are analogue input and digital output of the receiver channel. CDT is the carrier detect output. A low level on this pin indicates that the receiver fails to receive the analogue signal. The carrier detect threshold can be adjusted by CDL input.

The transmitter consists of an FSK modulator which is a programmable frequency synthesizer which derives the output frequencies by a variable division of the 4.4336 MHz clock frequency. The

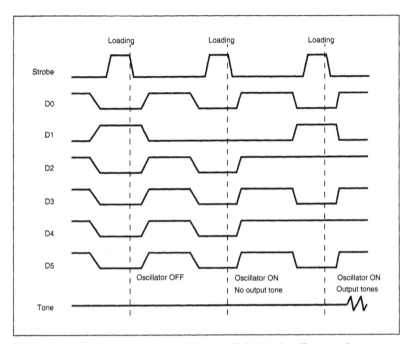

Figure 8.2 Timing sequence of the parallel data loading mode

division ratio is set by TRS, TXR1 and TXR2. If TRS = TXR1 = TXR2 = 0, the output frequency is 1300 Hz for logic high. It is 2100 Hz if the input is at logic low. The receiver section performs demodulation of the input analogue signal.

The IC can be connected to the RS232 experimental board to form an RS232 modem. The transmitter and receiver can be linked by various means such as radio, infra-red or sound.

8.3 Radio links

8.3.1 TMX/SILRX FM radio links

These are 418 or 433 MHz surface acoustic wave controlled FM radio transmitters and receivers and are specially designed for radio telemetry and telecommand applications. They are type-approved to the Radio Communications Authority in the UK. This implies that if the customized circuits complie to the RA requirements, there is no need to submit the final product for further type approval.

(a) TMX transmitter

The pin-out and the internal block diagram of the TMX transmitter (Radiometrix, RS740-290) are given in Figure 8.4. The transmitter requires a power supply at pin 3. Pins 1 and 4 are connected

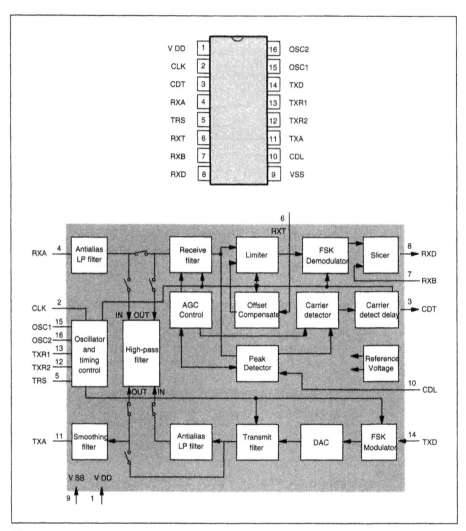

Figure 8.3 Pin-out and internal block diagram of the TCM3105

together internally and form the ground. The transmitter operates over a wide voltage range from 6 to 12V DC with a typical current sink of 6 mA at 6V. Available frequencies are 418 MHz and 433 MHz. Pin 5 is the data modulation input which requires a CMOS logic level at the same supply voltage. An antenna is connected to pin 2. The serial digital data is fed into the DATA IN pin. It first passes through an R/C low-pass filter, which restricts the bandwidth of the modulation signal below 10 kHz. It is then fed into a wideband frequency modulator. The modulator drives a varicap diode, the changing capacitance of which modifies the frequency of the next stage, a radio frequency oscillator. The central frequency of the oscillator is precisely set by a surface acoustic wave resonator

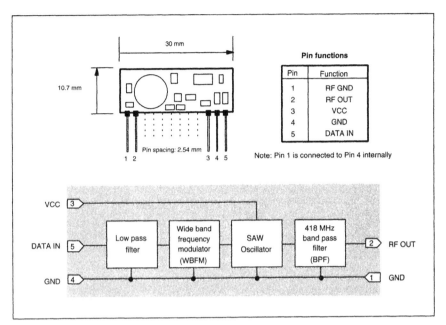

Figure 8.4 Pin-out and internal diagram of the TXM-418-A

in the 418 MHz band (417.90 to 418 MHz). The final filtered RF output appears on pin 2 and is connected to an antenna.

The antenna for the transmitter have three versions, the helical type, the loop type and the whip type (see Figure 8.6). The helical antenna is small (17 mm length and 2.5 mm diameter). It has a high 'Q' factor and therefore needs to be optimized for the exact wavelength in use. The loop antenna consists of a loop of PCB track, which is tuned by a variable capacitor. The whip-type antenna is a wire, rod, PCB track or a combination of these. The optimum total length should be 16.5 cm.

The radio transmitter module is type-proved to the RA MPT1340 for licence exempt use within the UK for telemetry, telecommand and in-building security, provided the following requirements are met.

1. The transmitting antenna must be one of the three variants given above.
2. The transmitter module must be directly and permanently connected to the transmitting antenna without the use of an external feed. Increasing the rf power level by any means is not permitted.
3. The module must not be modified nor used outside its specification limits.
4. The module may only be used to send digital data. Speech or music is not permitted.
5. The equipment in which the module is used must carry an inspection mark located on the outside of the equipment and clearly visible; the minimum dimensions of the inspection mark shall be 10 × 15 mm and the letter and figure height must be not less than 2 mm. The wording shall read: 'MPT 1340 W.T. LICENCE EXEMPT'.
6. The trimmer control on the module must not be easily accessible to the end user. This control is factory set and must never be adjusted.

(b) SILRX receiver

The pin-out and the internal block diagram of the SILRX receiver (Radiometrix, RS740-304) are shown in Figure 8.5. The receiver requires a power supply at pin 5. The radio signal input is at pin 1. Pins 2 and 4 are the ground. The module operates over a voltage range from 4.5 to 9V DC with a typical current of about 13 mA. Available frequencies are 418 MHz and 433 MHz. The incoming radio frequency signal, picked up by the antenna, goes to a 418 MHz band pass filter via a capacitor. A radio frequency pre-amplifier boosts the signal before it enters the first mixer stage. The first local oscillator runs at a frequency of 433.92 MHz, which is produced by a surface acoustic wave resonator. The signal is mixed with the received 418 MHz signal to produce the first intermediate frequency signal at 15.92 MHz, This is then fed to the second mixer, where a second local oscillator running at 16 MHz produces the final intermediate frequency at a frequency of 80 kHz. Then it is amplified and demodulated to produce an audio frequency signal. A carrier detect signal is also produced. To improve the signal-to-noise performance, the audio signal is processed by a third order lower pass filter. The signal is finally converted into a digital signal and is output from pin 7. The signal has a CMOS logic level. Any types of the antenna described above can be used.

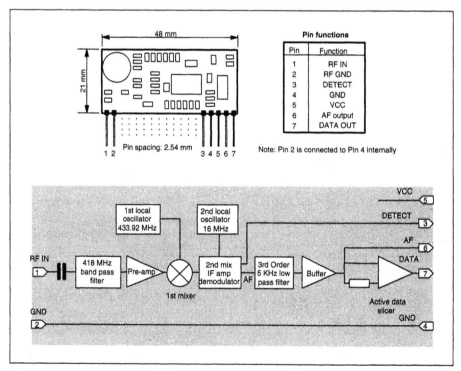

Figure 8.5 Pin-out and internal diagram of the SILRX-418

8.3.2 AM-TX1/AM HHR3 AM radio link pairs

The AM-TX1 (RF Solutions) is a miniature hybrid RF transmitter providing on-off modulation. It can be used to transmit data from any standard CMOS/TTL source with a baud rate of 1200. The pin-out and the application circuit are given in Figure 8.7. It is also very simple to operate, requiring only two connections. The module is very efficient, using only 2.3 mA. The output is connected to an antenna which could be a tuned loop or a whip antenna. The transmitting range is up to 100 metres. Available frequencies are 418 MHz and 433 MHz. It is type approved to MPT1340 for use in telemetry and telecommunications products when the antenna shown in Figure 8.6 is used.

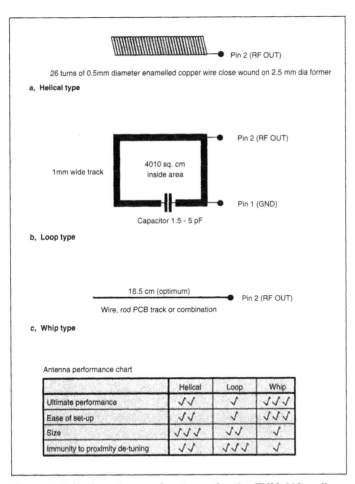

Antenna performance chart	Helical	Loop	Whip
Ultimate performance	√√	√	√√√
Ease of set-up	√√	√	√√√
Size	√√√	√√	√
Immunity to proximity de-tuning	√√	√√√	√

Figure 8.6 Various types of antenna for the TXM-418 radio transmitter

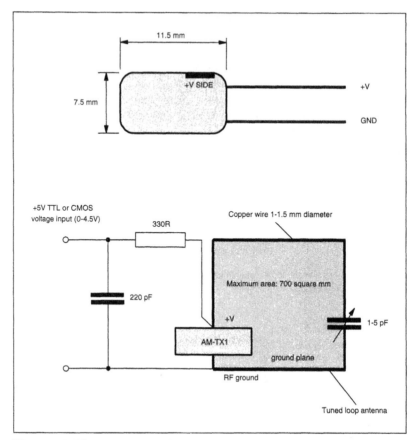

Figure 8.7 Pin-out and a typical application of the AM-TX1

The AM HHR3 (RF Solutions) is a compact modular RF receiver, which can be used to capture data transmitted from the AM transmitter. The pin-out is shown in Figure 8.8. The output is TTL/CMOS compatible. It requires a supply voltage of 5V and consumes 2.5 mA.

8.3.3 Experimenting with the radio link

Figure 8.9 shows a circuit which converts 12 parallel bits into a serial data format. The serial data can then be transmitted using the TXM-418 or the AM-TX1 transmitter module. The HT-12E is used as the parallel-to-serial data converter. The 12 bits of data can be supplied by the Centronic experimental board. The address bits A0 to A6 are connected to D1 to D7 of the board and the data

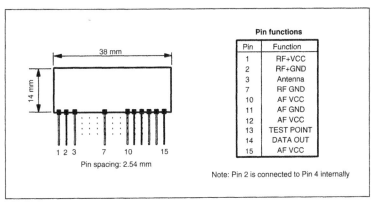

Pin functions

Pin	Function
1	RF+VCC
2	RF+GND
3	Antenna
7	RF GND
10	AF VCC
11	AF GND
12	AF VCC
13	TEST POINT
14	DATA OUT
15	AF VCC

Note: Pin 2 is connected to Pin 4 internally

Figure 8.8 Pin-out of the AM-HRR3

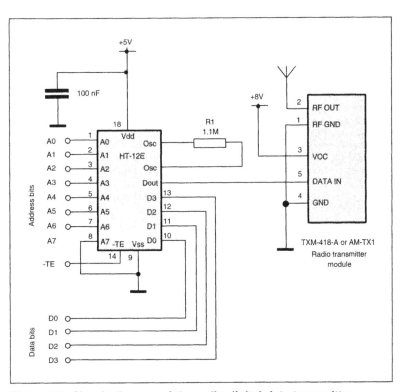

Figure 8.9 Circuit diagram of the radio digital data transmitter

bits D0 to D3 are connected to C1 to C4 of the board. -TE is connected to D8 of the Centronic experimental board. A7 is pulled down to the ground permanently.

Figure 8.10 shows a circuit which receives the radio digital data and decodes the serial data into a parallel data. The SILRX-418 or the AM-HRR3 receiver module and the HT-12D are used.

Such a system allows one transmitter connected to the Centronic port to transmit 4-bit data to any one of 127 receivers. It has a potential application in radio remote control. The radio transmitter and receiver pairs can be also used for non-contact data reading applications. Serial I/O A/D converters can also be used to form such a system.

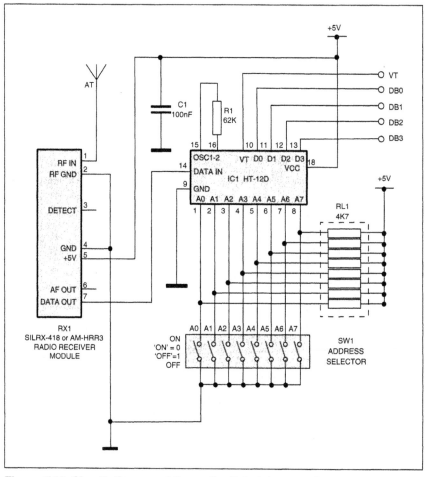

Figure 8.10 Circuit diagram of the radio digital data receiver

8.4 Radio transceiver modules

8.4.1 BiM-418-F radio transceiver

The BiM-418-F radio transceiver module has two versions, BiM-418-F and BiM-433-F (Radiometrix). The first one operates at 418 MHz frequency band and is type-approved to the Radio Communication Authority in the UK (MPT1340). The latter is for European uses in the 433.92 MHz frequency band. They allow a bi-directional half-duplex data transmission at a speed up to 40 kbyte/s over a distance of 30 metres inside buildings and 120 metres in the open field.

The pin-out is of the BIM-418-F (Radiometrix) shown in Figure 8.11. The working principle of the transmitter and the receiver part of the transceiver are similar to the TMX series radio transmitter and SILRX series receiver modules as described above. Pins 9, 10 and 18 are the ground pins (0 Volts) which are connected to the negative rail of the power supply. Pin 17 is the positive supply pin (Vcc). A DC supply voltage between 4.5 and 5.5V should be connected. When the module is in transmit and receive modes, the current assumption is about 12 mA. When it is in the standby mode, the current reduces to 1 µA. Pin 14 is the transmit data input pin (TXD). It can be driven directly by CMOS logic running on the same supply voltage as the module. Analogue signals generated by modems or DTMF encoders can be also fed into this pin. Pin 12 is the output of the received data. It can be connected directly to CMOS logic. Pin 13 is the output of the analogue signals. It can be used with modems or DTMF decoders. Pin 11 (-CD) is the carrier detect. When the module is in the receive mode, a low state indicates a signal above the detection threshold is being received. Pins 15 (-TX) and 16 (-RX) are used for selecting operation modes of the module.

Pin 15=1	Pin 16=1	standby mode
Pin 15=1	Pin 16=0	receive mode
Pin 15=0	Pin 16=1	transmit mode
Pin 15=0	Pin 16=0	self loop test mode

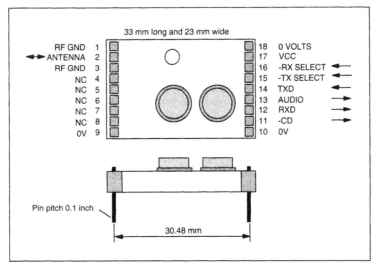

Figure 8.11 Pin-out of the BiM transceiver

Pins 1 and 3 are the RF ground. They are internally connected to pins 9, 10 and 18 and should be connected to the ground plane of the user's PCB board against which the antenna radiates. Pin 2 is connected to the antenna. Three types of integral antenna are recommended and approved for use with these modules. The configuration of the antenna and selection chart are given in Figure 8.6.

8.4.2 Requirement for serial data to be transmitted

The data path through a pair of BiMs is AC coupled. Several constraints are placed for a successful data transfer. The pulse with time (i.e. the time between any two consecutive transitions) in the serial code must be within 25 μs and 2 ms. The receiver BiMs require at least 3 ms of 10101010 preamble to be transmitted before the actual data is transferred. The receiver is optimized for data waveforms with 50:50 mark-to-space averaged over any 4 ms period. It will work reliably for sustained asymmetry up to 30/70 either way, but this will result in pulse width distortion and a decreased noise tolerance.

The radio transceiver modules can be used for transmitting RS232 signals between two computers. The experimental circuit is given in Figure 8.12. The RS232 serial data can be transmitted at 4.8 to

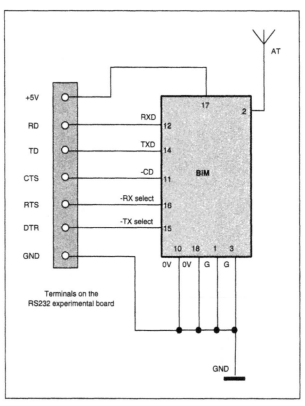

Figure 8.12 Experimental circuit diagram of an RS232 radio modem

38.3 kb/s baud rate between a pair of BiMs. In order to send an RS232 serial data through the BiMs, the data should be packetized in order to meet the requirements by the BiMs. The packetized data includes the following parts: (1) 3 ms of preamble data (55H or AAH) to allow the receiver BiM to settle; (2) 1 or 2 byte of FFH; (3) 1 byte of 01H to show the start of data; (4) data bytes and (5) check bits. In practice, the format of the packetized data may vary according to users' situations.

There are three methods to improve the mark-space ratio of the serial data to be transmitted. The first method is to divide each byte into two. The first half is the bit to be sent and the second half is its compliment. Each byte has a guaranteed mark-to-space ratio of 50:50. Amongst the 256 possible 8-bit codes, 70 codes contain 4 zeros and 4 ones which have a 50:50 mark-to-space ratio. For example, 17H, 1BH, 27H, E8H, etc. They can be transferred between two RS232 ports using an RS232 format of one start bit and one stop bit with no parity check bit. The actual data to be sent will be translated to these codes. This is the second method. For the third method, each byte is sent twice. The first one is the true data and the other is its compliment. This will give 50:50 mark-to-space ratio.

8.5 Mains line modem LM1893

The LM1893 (National Semiconductors) Bi-line Carrier Current Transceiver is specially designed for transferring a serial data amongst remote locations utilizing the mains lines. The pin-out of the IC is shown in Figure 8.13. The typical application is shown in Figure 8.14. The IC requires a power supply of 14–30V. V+ (pin 15) and GND (pin 14) are connected to the positive and negative rails of the power supply. The transmitting (Tx) and receiving (Rx) modes are selected by Tx/Rx input (pin 5). When the Tx/Rx pin is held high the chip is in the transmitting mode (Tx). The input digital data up to 5 kHz is fed into the DATA IN input (pin 17) to generate a switched 0.9871/1.0221 control current to drive a current-controlled oscillator (ICO). The central modulation frequency is between 50 to 300 kHz and is determined by R3, VR1 and C8. The signal passes through a sine-wave shaper which delivers a current sinusoid through an automatic level control (ALC) circuit to a current output amplifier. The ALC circuit is used to provide a stable output signal with changing mains impedance. C4 and R2 control the

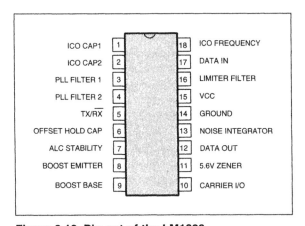

Figure 8.13 Pin-out of the LM1893

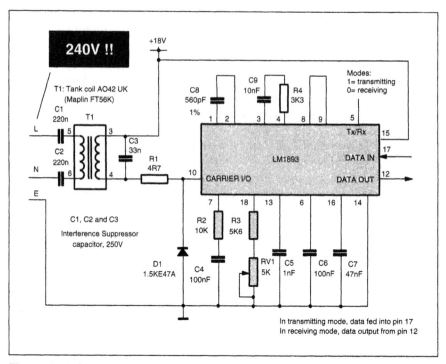

Figure 8.14 Circuit diagram of LM1893 used as a receiver and a transmitter

dynamic characteristics of the ALC circuit. Drive current from the carrier I/O (pin 10 which is an output when the IC is in the transmitting mode and is input when in the receiving mode) develops a voltage swing on the resonant tank coil T1. This voltage then passes through T1 and coupling capacitors C1 and C2 onto the mains lines. The tank coil serves as a further isolation and matches the impedance of the power line so as to produce the maximum carrier signals on the mains. C3 is chosen so that the tank resonant frequency is equal to the internal modulation frequency. R1 and D1 are used for protecting the IC during the transient voltage surges which are frequently present on the power lines.

When Tx/Rx (Pin 5) is low, the chip is configured as a receiver. The transmitting section is disabled. The signal picked up by the receiver is the sum of various signals present on the mains lines. The signal is fed into the receiver's input high pass filter consisting of C1, C2 the tank coil T1 and the band pass filter made up of C3 and T1. These filters allow the carrier signal to pass and attenuate heavily on the 240V AC and transient spike. The signal is fed into the carrier I/O receiver input (pin 10). The amplifier removes DC offsets, attenuates line frequency, acts as a band pass filter, and limits the signal to drive the phase lock loop (PLL) phase detector. The output signal from the phase detector containing AC and DC data signals, noise, system DC offset, and other frequency components passes through an RC low pass filter and finally passes through a noise filter to produce serial data at the open collector output data out (pin 12). C7, C6 and C5 are the components determining the characteristics of the receiving circuit.

8.6 RS485 interface

The RS485 interface is an improved version of RS232 interface. It is widely used in implementing control systems and data distribution. It uses a twisted pair link to reduce noise and to improve the performance of data transfer. The maximum data rate on the bus is 10 Mb per second and the maximum transmitting distance is 1200 m.

The RS485 interface uses the differential inputs on the receiver. The signals on the two wires are always in anti-phase. Noise induced in the two wires is always in phase. Therefore the noise is automatically cancelled at the receiver's differential inputs. Data transmission over the RS485 interface is best protected by ensuring that the cable is terminated with the characteristic impedance. In practice, this impedance is the same as the output impedance of the transmitter.

A device which could implement an RS485 easily is the SN75176B (Texas Instruments, RS 630-904). The pin-out and the internal diagram of the IC are shown in Figure 8.15. A single RS485 driver can drive 32 receivers. All transmitters and receivers are connected to the two wires. This means that the bus is only suitable for half-duplex connections. Only one transmitter can talk at a time. Others are either in the high-impedance state or in the listening mode. Figure 8.11 shows a simple RS485 local network. It uses the RS232 experimental board.

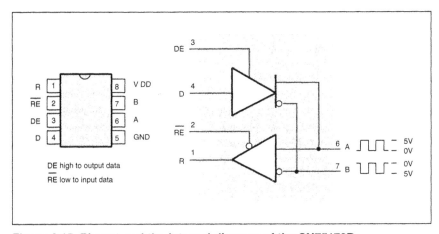

Figure 8.15 Pin-out and the internal diagram of the SN75176B

8.7 The infra-red data link – IrDA standard

IrDA stands for Infra-Red Data Association. The association united the forces of several manufacturers involved in optical data transmission technology. The aim is to set a standard for data exchanges via infra-red light. The data exchange scheme is particularly suitable for data exchanges between laptop/desktop PCs and printers, telephone sets and fax machines. The biggest advantage is the total absence of cable connections.

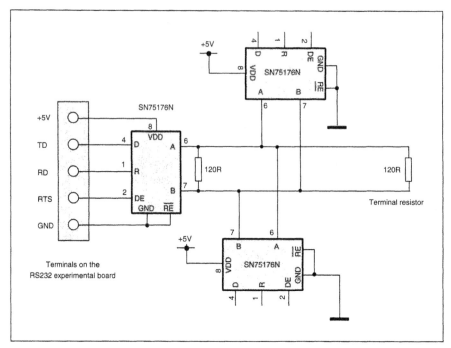

Figure 8.16 Circuit for converting an RS232 port into an RS485 port

The IrDA specifies a relatively short communication range of 1 metre to ensure a low current consumption and to prevent interference between different IrDA devices. The point angle is 30°. The IR diodes transmit in the spectrum range 850 to 900 nm. IrDA-1 specifies a data exchange rate of 115.2 kb/s in half-duplex mode. Since then, a standard with 4 Mb/s has been issued.

The IrDA link extends the RS232 interface (or UARTs). A light emitting diode is connected to the serial output of the RS232 via an infra-red emitter interface. A photodiode is connected to the receiver via an infra-red receiver interface. The emitter interface reduces the length of pulses from the RS232 interface to a maximum of $\frac{3}{16}$ of the original bit length. This is to reduce the driving power to the LEDs. At the receiver side, the infra-red receiver interface restores the pulses to their original length, allowing them to be processed in the normal way by an RS232 interface.

Modules are available for IrDA applications. They consist of a light emitting diode and a driver, a photodiode and an amplifier, etc. The HDSL-1000-101 (Hewlett Packard, RS 193-4780) is an example. The pin-out, the internal diagram and a typical application of the device are given in Figure 8.17. The input of the module is driven by the shortened serial pulses. They are converted into infra-red light pulses by the light emitting diode. The infra-red light pulses, which are detected by the photodiode, are converted into TTL pulses at the output. The infra-red emitter and receiver interfaces for the pulse length shaping are not included in the module. To implement the IrDA link

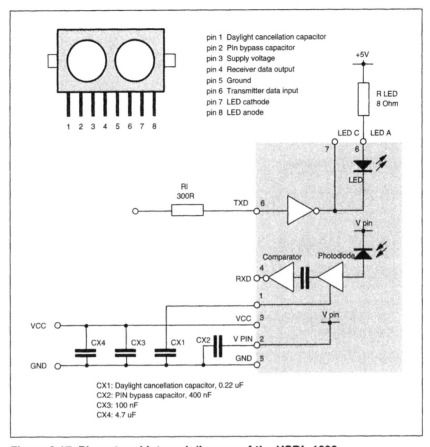

pin 1 Daylight cancellation capacitor
pin 2 PIn bypass capacitor
pin 3 Supply voltage
pin 4 Receiver data output
pin 5 Ground
pin 6 Transmitter data input
pin 7 LED cathode
pin 8 LED anode

CX1: Daylight cancellation capacitor, 0.22 uF
CX2: PIN bypass capacitor, 400 nF
CX3: 100 nF
CX4: 4.7 uF

Figure 8.17 Pin-out and internal diagram of the HSDL-1000

to an existing RS232 interface, an HSDL-7000 (Hewlett Packard RS233–2242) infra-red emitter and receiver interface can be used. Figure 8.18 shows the circuit.

The CS8130 (Crystal Semiconductor RS207–2473) is an infra-red transceiver integrated circuit. The receive channel includes on-chip high gain PIN diode amplifier, IrDA, HPSIR, 500 kHz ASK and 38 kHz TV remote compatible decoder and data pulse stretcher. The transmitter channel includes IrDA, HPSIR, ASK and TV remote compatible encoder and LED driver. It accepts data from UART with a baud rate from 1200 to 115200. External PIN diode and LED are required. The supply voltages to the IC are from 2.7 to 5.5V. The IC draws a 2.5 mA current.

The pin-out and a typical application of the IC are shown in Figure 8.19. It provides four infra-red transmission modes: IrDA/HPSIR, 500 kHz ASK, 38 kHz TV remote control and direct access mode. In the IrDA/HPSIR mode, a pulse of infra-red energy indicates a logic 0. No IR energy

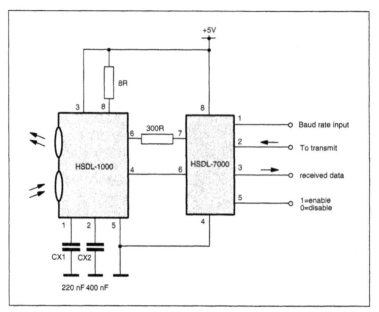

Figure 8.18 Experimental circuit for RS232 serial data transmission

indicates a logic 1. The pulse width can be from 1.6 μs (for 115200 baud rate) to 78 μs (1200 baud rate). The width of the pulse may be fixed at 1.6 μs for all baud rates. The initial baud rate for IrDA is 9600 and this can be set to baud rates from 1200 to 115200. In the ASK mode, when a carrier wave of 500 kHz is present, it indicates a logic 0. The absence of a carrier is treated as a logic 1. The baud rates are 9600, 19200 and 38400. The TV remote control is similar to the ASK mode, except that the carrier frequency is 38 kHz. The baud rate is 2400. In the direct access mode, the IR transmitter tracks what is present on the TXD pin. Logic 1 means that the LED is off. Logic 0 means that the LED is on. For the receiver, a logic 1 at the output (RXD) means that no infra-red energy is detected. Logic 0 indicates that infra-red energy is detected.

To transmit data, the data is written to the CS8130 via the TXD pin first. The selected modulation scheme is then applied to the data to be transmitted. The transmission modes are selected by writing a control word into an appropriate internal control register. There are various control registers in the CS8130 to control the operation modes. The receiver modes can be also selected by writing the control word into the CS8130 registers. Data is written into the control registers by taking D/-C low. The details of the functions of the registers are described in the manufacturer's data sheet.

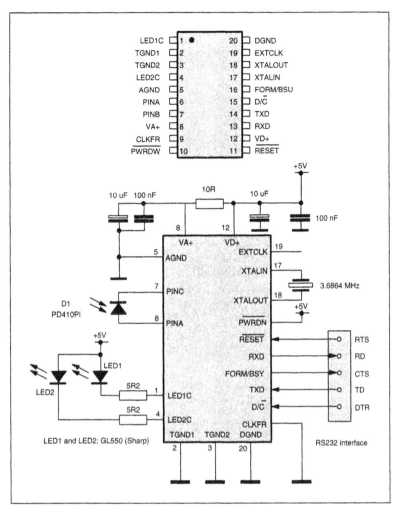

Figure 8.19 Pin-out and a typical application of the CS8130

Further reading

Owen Bishop (1983) *Easy Add-on Projects for Spectrum, ZX81 and Ace*, ISBN 0859340996, Bernard Babani Publishing Ltd.

Roger G. Gilbertson (1994) *Muscle Wires Project Book*, ISBN 1-879896133, Mondo-tronics, Inc.

Hans-Peter Messmer (1993) *The Indispensable PC Hardware Book*, ISBN 0201624249, Addison-Wesley.

Mustafa A. Mustafa (1994) *Microcomputer Interfacing and Applications*, Second edition, ISBN 0750617527, Butterworth-Heinemann.

Que Corporation (1995) *Using Visual Basic 3*, ISBN 156529763X.

Michael Tooley (1990) *Electronic Circuits Handbook*, ISBN 0434919683, Butterworth-Heinemann.

Data sheets for components from various manufacturers.

Index